THE
GNOSTIC PYNCHON

THE
GNOSTIC PYNCHON

Dwight Eddins

INDIANA UNIVERSITY PRESS
Bloomington and Indianapolis

The paper used in this publication meets the minimum requirements of
American National Standard for Information Sciences—Permanence of
Paper for Printed Library Materials, ANSI Z39.48-1984.

⊗™

Manufactured in the United States of America

Library of Congress Cataloging-in-Publication Data

Eddins, Dwight
The gnostic pynchon / Dwight Eddins.
p.   cm.
Includes bibliographical references.
ISBN 0-253-31907-2 (alk. paper)
1. Pynchon, Thomas—Criticism and interpretation.   2. Gnosticism
in literature.   I. Title.
PS3566.Y55Z64   1990

813'.54—dc20   89-45998

CIP

1 2 3 4 5 94 93 92 91 90

Contents

Preface

It has become more or less *de rigueur* to open (or close) acts of Pynchon criticism with acts of contrition for imposing integrating structures—however tentative—on what would appear to be God's own plenty of ethical chaos, narrative disruption, and psychic incoherence. Thoroughly Postmodern Pynchon—the image graven by the prevailing interpretation—is a jealous god, fixing the bawds of totalizing order with a Baal-ful eye, and consigning them to the ineluctable démodality of the risible. Whether or not this deity enjoys omnipotence, the orthodoxy of the unorthodox based upon it is supported by some fairly intimidating scripture—indeterminacies, discontinuities, and paradoxes culled directly from the master's fiction—and by some extremely cogent and articulate exegetes.

Even so, apostasy seems to be spreading, side by side with heresy. The first takes the form of readings that propagate what we might call corrective ideas of order with regard to the cosmos of Pynchon's fiction, the second the form of revising the very tenets of postmodernism in the direction of tentative value structures. The effect of both, as I shall argue, is to reveal a persistent *modernist* nostalgia for vanished axiological foundations in the midst of vividly experienced anomie. In Pynchon's case, this nostalgia certainly does not produce any miraculous stabilization of the carefully engineered instabilities that have been labeled "postmodern," but it forces us to view them *thematically* as a corrupt deviation from a normalizing, i.e., humanizing, structure rather than as a liberating refutation of that structure in the name of *jeu*.

Two of the recent readings that abet this revised perspective are Thomas Moore's *The Style of Connectedness* and Kathryn Hume's *Pynchon's Mythography,* both concerned almost exclusively with *Gravity's Rainbow*.[1] Moore opts unabashedly for a comprehensive "connectedness" based on C. G. Jung's principle of *synchronicity*—"the hypothesized principle of an acausal but meaningful ordering of events within a 'psychic relativity of space and time' " (p. 277). Convinced that the book offers a paradigm by which inner/outer dichotomies can be resolved in an act of psychic integration, he deigns to take only "incidental issue with readers and critics who have found *Gravity's Rainbow* to be essentially nihilistic, ultimately downbeat in its view of the nature of human experience" (p. 2). Cagier, perhaps more wary of the poststructuralist Eumenides, Hume distinguishes between what she believes to be unresolvable embodiments of instability, incoherence, and contradiction in the text, and three "devices" that "stand out as managing to escape the deconstruction applied to other unifying features: a principle of multiplicity, a group of psychoanalytical theories, and one kind of mythology" (p. 9). She devotes her primary attention to an elaborate mapping and analysis of the "mythology," which her structuralist grid reveals as an ordering principle systematic and pervasive enough to suggest T. S. Eliot's modernist conception of how myth functions in Joyce's modernist *Ulysses*: "It [myth] is simply a way of controlling, of ordering, of giving a shape to the immense panorama of futility and anarchy which is contemporary history."[2]

What Hume finally ends up with is a carefully calibrated equilibrium in which structuralist and poststructuralist readings of *Gravity's Rainbow* complement each other in a sort of symbiotic binarity. An equable synthesis of this sort usually has, however, as Hegel's basic paradigm suggests, an ancestry of violent dialectic. In any area of art, radical stylistic experiments represent in themselves a polemical antithesis to the prevailing conventions—an antithesis that tends to be seized upon by partisans and opponents alike as evidence of an equally radical revaluing of perceived reality. What the reactors often fail to see is that the style/substance equation may be inexact, that there may exist an unaccounted-for remainder—in the words of a well-known French revaluer, a *supplement*—wherein traditional values and modes of ordering existence operate in new guises and with a newer and more timely significance.

Some such machinery as this may explain the parallel between the critical histories of *Gravity's Rainbow* and Joyce's *Ulysses*—those rival encyclopedias that are frequently said to be incommensurable, and just as frequently used to measure each other.[3] Kathryn Hume notes this commonality, pointing out that "when *Ulysses* first appeared, critics reacted most strongly to its dissonant and disturbing elements and stressed its negative effects. Only gradually did Joyce's positive elements also gain recognition" (p. 32). Positive, indeed. Today, sixty-five years after the initial storms of reaction (both pro and con) over the depiction of a day in the life of Dublin, the *Weltanschauung* of this exemplary High Modern seems much closer to the model of civilized, humane balance presented in a study such as S. L. Goldberg's *The Classical Temper* than it does to the generalized iconoclasm and nihilism that the earlier reactors projected from the novel's formal innovations.

The revisionism that affects our understanding and categorizing of Pynchon's fiction is proceeding not only in specific studies of his fiction but—as I indicated earlier—in our perception of the categories themselves. Recent developments in value theory, especially, have tended to blur certain distinctions between modernism and postmodernism, with results that bear directly upon where we locate Pynchon's own axiology in the spectrum between a value-free nihilism and a value-positive traditionalism. In the introduction to *Life after Postmodernism*, an extremely useful collection of essays he edited, John Fekete outlines the development from a "pre-modern" condition in which the "validity or significance of values was . . . a metaphysical given" to a modern "secularized onto-epistemological paradigm" in which value has lost its ontological ground, i.e., its immediate relation to the "realm of fact (being)" (p. iii), but is under constant pressure to "reconnect" itself with this realm; and thence to the postmodern abandonment of this paradigm in favor of an "anti-episte-mological" neopragmatism which insists that "there is no fixed nature of things and no truth of correspondence, no linguistic picture and no literary imitation for any inquiry to discover or decode" (p. xii), and which has tended to relegate value questions to a position of irrelevance (p. xii).[4]

It is not hard to see how such an episteme (or antiepisteme) is construed as a "skeptical or nihilistic construction" of existence, especially when it is preoccupied with what it is not, i.e., with the denial of all ultimate foundations for knowledge and being (p. xiv). Nor is it hard to see how the spirit if not the letter of this particular postmodern negativity has provided a useful context for those critics who find Pynchon's larger project to be one of decentering and destabilizing the foundations of knowledge and our sense of being.

Fekete feels, however, along with a number of his essayists, that the time is ripe to locate a new positivity, i.e., a new rationale for value judgments, in the poststructuralist discourse. His name for this relatively affirmative perspective is "pragmatism plus," a label inevitably suggestive of a new, improved detergent that not only cleans away metaphysical residue but adds a value-sheen to the philosophical crockery (p. xiv). He postulates that "we can identify as postmodern *a certain value-rational opening to the human world . . . as home,* though a home whose plan we do not have and which we have never quite (and will never quite) finish building and fitting to ourselves, just as we who build it and for whom it is to be fit change with every alteration of it, with every bit of construction and deconstruction" (p. xi).

It is at this point that Fekete makes an admission crucial to my own project of recontextualizing Pynchon: "I put it this way to acknowledge that the postmodern ethos has a certain continuity with the projects and horizons of secularizing and historicising modernity, but also to suggest its difference from the ethos of modernism." This "difference" is intended to be reflected in the tentative, piecemeal, open-ended nature of the "home-building," but it is certainly possible to locate these qualities in the quests of the great modernists for a suitable cosmic habitat—Eliot wondering whether he should "at least set" his "lands in order" and deciding to shelter in "fragments . . . shored up against" his "ruins"; Pound elaborating from his temporary cage-house *The Pisan Cantos,* an always unfinished architecture of such fragments; Joyce founding his provisional mythic framework for human existence upon a world that is itself "founded . . . macro and microcosm, upon the void."[5]

The "home" metaphor itself is inescapably linked (and this is Fekete's point) to something in humanity that will not let go, despite what seems to be the philosophical case of things, the yearning for the sense of metaphysical belonging that preceded modernist alienation. Identity threatens to overshadow difference in this instance, as it does when Fekete locates a distinguishing hallmark of modernism in "the stigma of the wound left by the amputation of the Standard." He finds the "modernist structure of feeling" to be articulated by the "antinomic polarities" of a "delusional euphoria and an obsessional depression, settling into the culture from a persisting phantom Standard effect," and believes that "postmodernism may at last be ready . . . unneurotically, to get on . . . without any capitalised standards."

But truly persistent phantoms are not so easily exorcised, and the neurotically repressed has a way of continuing to return. The "continuity" between modern and postmodern value projects provides the dark passage down which the ghosts of Platonic and Judaeo-Christian metaphysics glide in a serial haunting that perpetually raises the question of what values define the "human" and of what force these values have if they are not perceived as somehow grounded in the very structure of being. Pynchon, I argue, does not escape these questions, which inform his novels even at (and especially at) their most flamboyant moments of discontinuity and instability, and ultimately lend his black comedies their aura of a tragic falling away. As Fekete himself observes, the "tragic mask" of literary modernism is constituted by the "secular abyss, the interval of uncertainty, the absence of transcendental guarantees" opened by the failure of an ontological basis for value (pp. iii–iv).

Even Fekete's own projected escape from a realm of values underwritten by absolute "warranties" and "inherited guarantees" ends up haunted—and ultimately subverted—by the magisterial shadow of that realm (p. xi). He imagines a postmodern value project that would lead us into a "livelier, more colorful, more alert . . . more tolerant culture that draws enjoyment from the dappled relations between meaning and value" and that would be generally characterized by "upbeat possibilities." I have no intention of mocking Fekete's scrupulous and intelligent inquiry, but there is no escaping the dilettantish epicureanism of the subtext here. The implied values are perceived in a relentlessly aesthetic valuation, as a variety of diverting dappled things for which even Gerard Manley Hopkins would have difficulty glorifying God. As for "upbeat," the very word is like a bell tolling the inexorable onslaught of a *truly* postmodern ethos that recycles the most serious and disturbing phenomena of human existence as grist for a ubiquitous but oddly unexhilarated hedonism.

It seems a long way from Fekete's judicious, humane argument to the anarchic "postmodern scene" described in the apocalyptic prose of Arthur Kroker (one of whose essays is included in Fekete's collection), but the premises of the former open into the realities of the latter, which portrays a society dedicated to uncommitted, indiscriminate dabbling:

We don't have to wonder; we know just for the "fun of it." We write just for the fun of it, just as we think, make love, parody, and praise. . . . we are having a nice day, maybe a thousand nice days. The postmodern scene is a panic

site, just for the fun of it. And beneath the forgetting, there is only the scrib-
bling of another Bataille, another vomiting of flavourless blood, another het-
erogeneity of excess to mark the upturned orb of the pineal eye. The solar
anus is parodic of postmodernism, but again, just for the fun of it.[6]

Here, we are recognizably in Pynchon's world of "Mindless Pleasures"
(as *Gravity's Rainbow* was originally to be titled), with its violent comic
excess and its anarchical parody—but with a crucial difference. Whereas
the denizens of Kroker's postmodern scene transmute even the great axiological structures of the past (and present) into mere voyeuristic *frissons*,
these structures survive (I argue) in Pynchon as implicit "phantom Standards" to frame and invalidate a mode of existence that has lost its humanizing core of values. Pynchon *is* comically postmodernist in the sense
that the "parody, kitsch, and burnout" of contemporary life are embedded
in his work, but tragically modernist in the pervasive, poignant sense of
massive axiological catastrophe that provides the normative context for
this lived caricature of life.[7]

My own study undertakes to formulate a sort of "unified field theory"
that will account for both modern and postmodern Pynchon—the Pynchon whose world-view is suffused by acute nostalgia for vanished foundations and values, and the Pynchon whose field of vision seems occupied
with discontinuities and absurdities that threaten our sense of a comprehensible, mappable, even affirmable existence. Where Moore finds Pynchon's unity in an all-subsuming mystical positivity and Hume in the
equilibrium of parallel but ultimately incompatible discourses, I locate it
in a comprehensive grid of religious responses to epistemological and
ontological crisis. The grid itself is organized around the concept of *gnosticism* as that concept is expanded from ancient to modern applications
by Hans Jonas and Eric Voegelin—an expansion I discuss in my intro-
ductory chapter.

It is important to make clear at this early point that I am not claiming
any direct influence from these writers on Pynchon. I have no evidence
that he ever read them as he certainly read (and was influenced by) Henry
Adams, Norbert Wiener, Max Weber, Norman O. Brown, and others. The
crucial commonality is a sort of philosophical force field that finds its
origin in the Judaeo-Christian Gnostics of antiquity (with whom Pynchon
is demonstrably familiar) and spreads into modern (and very Pynchonian)
concerns with such issues as existentialist vacuity and the cabalistic manipulation of history. It is also a field that generates specific and quite
useful mechanisms for dealing with the central tensions and cruxes of
Pynchon's fiction as a whole. As for Voegelin in particular, those already
familiar with his political philosophy—a philosophy with admittedly reactionary implications—will probably be shocked to hear his ideas linked
to those of a novelist whose outlook seems to derive in so many ways
from the anarchist currents of the 1960s; but it is part of my revisionist

mission to demonstrate a selectively reactionary streak in Pynchon and to show how it colors the vision of humanity at the heart of his norm.

The only other critics to develop the notion of gnostic strains in Pynchon's work—so far as I know—are Harold Bloom and Charles Hohmann. Bloom's brief but highly suggestive comments are located in his introduction to the anthology of Pynchon essays in the Chelsea House series, and center on the view that "Pynchon's is a Gnosis without transcendence."[8] I find the matters of gnosis *and* of transcendence in Pynchon more problematic than does Bloom, and will return to this issue in the course of my discussion. Hohmann's treatment of gnosticism in his recent book *Thomas Pynchon's "Gravity's Rainbow"* is rather more extended.[9] He concentrates, in the section of his third chapter that he devotes to the subject, on parallels between the ancient Gnostic religions and the structures suggested by "paranoia" in Pynchon's novel, with occasional references to Jonas's extrapolations of these religions into the modern *Zeitgeist*. He does not note my earlier article on the subject, one that covers at least some of the same basic ground—a fact I remark only to absolve myself of the responsibility for footnoting territory already homesteaded.[10]

Finally, however, our focuses are significantly different. Hohmann examines, in the main, traditionally defined gnosticism as one aspect of one novel, whereas I undertake to elaborate gnostic structures and attitudes (and, correspondingly, antignostic structures and attitudes) into a schema that will comprehend not only the dialectics and indeterminacies of Pynchon's various fictions, but also the dynamic of development from his first story, "The Small Rain," to *Gravity's Rainbow*. Mine is, considering the critical times, a rashly centripetal project, and as such stands in significant contradistinction to Hohmann's erudite, elaborately argued de-centering. Although I can agree with Hohmann, from my very different perspective, that Pynchon is neither "Realist, Modernist, [n]or post-Modernist," I see him delineating a much more sharply resolved vision than that of an author who is "riding an 'interface' between literary modes leaving his readers in an aesthetic limbo where they can experience neither heaven nor hell" (TPGR, p. 378). With this cosmic disposition of affairs, it is time for both of our books to enter what Harold Bloom might call the Roman arena of strong readings, and utter—along with previous interpretations—their own stoical *morituri: t*hose about to be judged salute you.

I owe special thanks to Ward Allen for introducing me to the philosophy of Eric Voegelin. Gratitude is also due Bill McMinn and Phil Beidler for their insightful comments on portions of my manuscript, to Jilana Enteen and Ed Malles for their help in indexing, and to Eleanor Tubbs and Angie Bramlett for indispensable clerical aid.

THE
GNOSTIC PYNCHON

Introduction

The Gnostic Matrix

About a third of the way through *Gravity's Rainbow* there suddenly looms, in all its recondite glory, a partial differential equation. Even in the bizarre fleamarket of the encyclopedic novel, this constitutes a singular event, and it would be no surprise if it caused a number of the already faltering to experience *Brennschluss*—in this case, a premature cut-off of their reading-rockets. A longer look at this apparition, however, transforms it into a paradigm of Pynchon's enterprise and of the criticism that enterprise has engendered. The equation, in Pynchon's own words, describes "motion under the aspect of yaw control," and was used to design the feedback system that kept the V-2 rocket from veering off course.[1] In context, however, the symbols open into ominous possibilities of a much more comprehensive "Discipline of Control." Pynchon capitalizes the term *control* here, as he does many other terms in the novel, to suggest an elaborate conspiracy so potent and pervasive that it acquires a quasi-transcendental status—a status that is the result (I shall argue) of a religious valuation.

In the passage under consideration, the conspiracy is suspected of modulating the radical mood changes of entire societies, and even extremes of weather, to a nonthreatening blandness. As for the mathematical symbols, they are esoteric signifiers—completely incomprehensible to the unscientific masses who will become their victims, but easily glossed by the scientific elite who have achieved some degree of gnosis—in this case, the secret knowledge of Control. This arcane text of rocket stability, however, may represent only the "bourgeois" reduction of an even more arcane "Text" that outlines a plan of absolute domination. The basic apparatus of Pynchon's paranoid vision—the world-historical conspiracy with its conspirators, its victims, its secret encodings, and its infinite regress of layers—is all here, together with the dramatically subversive possibility that the vision is *mere* paranoia. The author veers back and forth between the hypotheses of absolute connectedness and absolute nonconnectedness, setting up various dialectics of order and chaos.

It is this veering that has led most of Pynchon's recent critics to assert their own form of yaw control in the proposition that he carefully refuses validation to either extreme. Molly Hite states it succinctly when she says of V. in particular that "the two poles of cosmic 'plot' and total randomness leave room for any number of 'middles.' "[2] This principle, which we might label "epistemological indeterminacy," becomes for Hite and a number of other important critics the key to Pynchon's conceptual universe, the category that subsumes all others. Thomas Schaub asserts that "Pynchon's books . . . establish for the reader an intentional and strict uncertainty, for they repeat in our relation to them the conditional relation to the world which [Henry] Adams's either/or logic so clearly expresses."[3] Similarly, for Peter Cooper, these books represent "a plethora of intricately woven hieroglyphic patterns, patterns that phase at some uncertain latitude into random congeries of things and events, patterns that promise but never quite yield the final answer. In place of revelation, Pynchon gives the Ellipses of Uncertainty."[4] David Seed goes even further, discovering in *Gravity's Rainbow* a novel that ends with a radical questioning of its own "early procedures" as Pynchon "turns against his own fiction" in a "deconstruction" that "denies the text any formal stability" by dissolving it into its originary "technologies and media."[5]

Once the possibility of a determinative perspective is discredited, the way is open to apply Einstein's relativity, Heisenberg's indeterminacy, Gödel's Theorem, and other rationales of the irrational, and to analyze the fiction as an elaborate web of carefully structured ambiguities, paradoxes, and discontinuities. The result has been to locate Pynchon's dramatic center in a sense of unremitting epistemological crisis—failed quests for certainty, mysterious causal nexuses, revelations tainted by paranoia, garbled messages, satiric subversions of the serious—and to validate this sense by reference to the self-critiques of science and the paradigms of contemporary philosophy.

But is this drama, which undeniably gives Pynchon's works their characteristic flavor, the ultimate, enveloping drama of his fiction? The answer to this question is complicated by the nexal relation between epistemology and ontology, as Brian McHale makes clear in a cogent analysis that in turn takes us back to the modern/postmodern dialectic in Pynchon:

> Intractable epistemological uncertainty becomes at a certain point ontological plurality or instability: push epistemological questions far enough and they "tip over" into ontological questions. By the same token, push ontological questions far enough and they tip over into epistemological questions—the sequence is not linear and unidirectional, but bidirectional and reversible.[6]

For McHale, the distinguishing mark of a modernist text is that it "foregrounds" epistemological questions such as "how can I interpret this world of which I am a part?" and "backgrounds" the ontological questions—such as "which world is this?"—to which they lead, while postmodernist texts are distinguished by the reversal of this sequence (pp. 9–

10). His paradigm modernist text is Faulkner's *Absalom, Absalom,* which "foregrounds such epistemological themes as the accessibility and circulation of knowledge, the different structuring imposed on the 'same' knowledge by different minds, and the problem of 'unknowability' or the limits of knowledge." Even so, as McHale points out, this paradigm gives way to its postmodern converse at the point that Quentin and Shreve pass beyond "reconstruction" into "pure speculation" and abandon "the intractable problems of attaining to reliable knowledge of our world" in order to "improvise a *possible* world," to "*fictionalize.*"

More apropos of our present inquiry, McHale locates this paradigmatic rupture in Pynchon's first two novels, both of which he classifies as modernist in their emphasis upon a problematic perspectivism. The rupture, or "hemorrhage," occurs in *V.* in the epilogue, when the "fantastic alternative reality" that Herbert Stencil has constructed and that—in McHale's view—has been heretofore "kept safely within the frame of Stencil's unreliable information" suddenly seems confirmed by an "authoritative" viewpoint and "threatens to break through into a postmodernist version of the fantastic" (p. 22). Similarly, in *The Crying of Lot 49,* Oedipa Maas's finely maintained epistemological dilemma concerning Tristero's existence is constantly threatened by the ontological possibility that she may be witnessing the machinations of "other orders of being . . . 'another world's intrusion into this one' " (p. 24). In *Gravity's Rainbow,* however, Pynchon transcends the "dead-ending of epistemology in solipsism" by an explicit shift to "a postmodernist poetics of ontology" that involves "the unconstrained projection of worlds in the plural" (p. 25).

McHale's analysis here within the terms that he sets himself is trenchant and discriminating, but the onto-epistemological model applicable to *Absalom, Absalom* (or, for that matter, to *Lord Jim, Ulysses, To the Lighthouse,* and other modernist classics) may not be equally applicable to Pynchon's novels. For one thing, the wild dance of varying perspectives and possibilities that engages Quentin, Marlow, Stephen, Bloom, and Mrs. Ramsay among others is always (Joyce's "Nighttown" episode is an exception) around a realistically conceived, ontologically homogeneous world in which no alien orders of being supervene to change the ground rules of historical process. "I do not like that other world," writes Leopold Bloom's epistolary *amoreuse,* leading him to reflect (during a cemetery visit), "No more do I."[7]

But Pynchon does, at least in the sense that he likes to keep the possible usurpation of *our* world by this "other" constantly before us. And it is precisely because this threat is so constant and its menacing otherness so palpable that the ontological drama in his first two novels refuses to yield contextual priority to the epistemological drama. The two enter into a unique dialectic in this author's work, producing a synthesis in which the terror of uncertainty is not really separable from, or prior to, the terror of an alien dispensation. The same dialectic operates in *Gravity's Rain-*

bow, where the admittedly more cavalier and unheralded projection of "worlds in the plural" nonetheless must share equal thematic billing with the characters' anxiety over how real these projections are. If we choose to look back at the earlier fiction in *this* perspective, we sense a much less radical disjuncture than that depicted by McHale's paradigm shift.

The notion that Pynchon's prevailing epistemological drama is really an *onto*-epistemological drama is one that has significant consequences for the determined secularity of most Pynchon criticism. It is natural enough to set up problems of certainty and perspective within the confines of an analytical monism, but the problematic of various modalities of existence—if taken seriously—raises the banished specter of metaphysics, and in turn that of religion. It seems possible that the *enveloping* drama of Pynchon's fiction—the one that subsumes the onto-epistemological drama—is a *religious* one, in a sense that I will shortly explain.

It is true, of course, that epistemology can just as easily, on a purely conceptual level, subsume religion; so can science. One of the reasons literary criticism resembles a Darwinian struggle is that its organizing categories lead a cannibalistic existence; even space and time, in Schopenhauer's dialectic, finally fall upon each other with intent to devour. The laying of a new conceptual template over Pynchon's fiction can be justified only if the resulting analysis better accounts for the complex relations among his themes, for the multifarious sources of dramatic suspense in his tangled plots, for his welter of ambiguities and paradoxes, and for the atmosphere that pervades and encompasses his peculiar cosmos. This book is an attempt to demonstrate that a religious construction of existence, with its inherent dialectics, is such a template.

Definitions of religion are usually ranged on a spectrum anchored at one end by convictions about supernatural influence on our existence and at the other by ardent and absolute devotion to any cause, principle, or doctrinal system. Most of these senses are apropos at one point or another in Pynchon's works, but we can arrive at a useful composite sense by thinking of a religion as a totalizing commitment to a particular construct of ultimate reality, including the nature of humanity, the significance of history, and the governance of the cosmos; and not ruling out the existence of spiritual forces both malign and benevolent. If we accept this definition, even the briefest survey of the fiction reveals it as a sequence of religious conflicts and tensions.

In the beginning, for Pynchon, was the malaise, and in the early stories its matrix is a *Weltanschauung* shaped by existentialist premises: mankind alone and alienated in an indifferent cosmos, vulnerable to entropy and nihilistic despair. This sense of a sterile, enveloping neutrality is challenged almost at once, however, by a paranoia of religious dimensions—the increasing suspicion, suggestive of ancient Gnosticism, that humanity is trapped in a history increasingly manipulated by antihuman forces. It is this dialectic between the concepts of cosmic indifference and of quasi-demonic conspiracy that generates the larger significations of the novel *V.*, and—in a different form—of *The Crying of Lot 49*. The latter unfolds as an explicit analogue of Pentecostal revelation, with the difference that what is to be revealed is tinged with the moral ambiguities of the animating conspiracy. Finally, in *Gravity's Rainbow*, this conspiracy draws a substantial portion of its strength from scientism, in effect the worship of scientific method and its attendant axia of control (or Control) through technology. Pynchon makes it clear that scientism is descended from Puritanism, which postulated a divine mandate for the exploitation of earth; and that both find a desirable antithesis in religions such as that of the African Hereros, who consecrated the natural order and the symbiotic notion of cyclical return. It is from this consecration, augmented ironically by scientific sophistication, that Pynchon draws the normative construct I call *Orphic naturalism*, a counterreligion to the worship of mechanism, power, and—ultimately—death.

Both the existential *fait accompli* of Pynchon's early work and the shadow of world-historical conspiracy that infringes upon it have their origins in late nineteenth-century nihilism. The strains represented by Henry Adams, who directly influenced Pynchon, and Friedrich Nietzsche, who—so far as we know—did not, are the most clearly apropos. Both the American man of affairs and the German solitary stared out on the same bleak vistas of shifting power configurations and crumbling value structures, but what they saw registered in very different lights. When the author and subject of *The Education of Henry Adams* projected himself into the place of a "child born in 1900," he was overwhelmed by "the new multiverse," a "world which would not be a unity but a multiple." It is a prophetic vision of a future in which order is viewed as "an accidental relation obnoxious to nature . . . against which every free energy of the universe revolted; and which, being merely occasional, resolved itself back into anarchy at last"; but this vision is perpetually colored by nostalgia for an earlier, humanized "Universe" created "after the image" of the Virgin's "own fecundity"—a universe in which "God was a father and nature a mother, and all was for the best."[8] The "multiverse," on the contrary, is imaged by the dynamo—a cold, impersonal pseudodeity that represents, in the words of Melvin Lyon, "a final great effort of man to give order to multiplicity," but ironically emerges as the very "symbol of multiplicity."[9] The courageous, clear-eyed prognosis that sees the neutralization of nature, that sees energy triumphant over order and entropy triumphant over energy, is also an implicit lament for the harmonizing constructs that made the universe a home.

This nostalgia—which is, finally, the modernist nostalgia for ontologically grounded values—enters Pynchon's perspective on modernity along with more familiar Adamsian influences such as the obsession with entropy and the metaphor of the Virgin become dynamo. It is worth remembering in the case of the latter (in her predynamo manifestation) that

Pynchon was—if we may trust the scholarly integrity of *Playboy*—raised as a Catholic and still attending mass while at Cornell.[10] At any rate, nostalgia is most consistently present in his work as a sort of normative weighting, a backward drag against the dehumanizing plunge of the twentieth century.

We locate it, in this form, by using Pynchon's unsettling evidence of abnormality to project a life-affirming norm: what the Virgin was, or might have been, as opposed to the exaggerated horror of what she has become in the Bad Priest of *V.*; what the America of *The Crying of Lot 49* might have been, or might still be, outside the stultifying restrictions of Control. But it is also present, more explicitly, in the Adams-like ruminations of both Stencils and in Oedipa Maas's imaginings of the virgin continent before defilement. By the time of *Gravity's Rainbow* Pynchon is an unabashed cultivator of nostalgia as a potential mode of moral illumination: "At least one moment of passage, one it will hurt to lose, ought to be found for every street now indifferently gray with commerce, with war, with repression ... finding it, learning to cherish what was lost, mightn't we find some way back?" (p. 693).

A "moment of passage" here is a moment of intensely realized maturation, an epiphany in which the very meaning of the human is revealed by a sudden awareness of the rich initiations it entails—all of this in contradistinction to Control and its cancerous mechanization of existence. It seems odd to speak of Pynchon and Adams as reactionaries; but it is certainly true that both base their norms on earlier equilibria, cultural configurations that made certain communal values effective, and do so in strong reaction to those growing tendencies that threaten the very possibility of equilibrium. Pynchon, in fact, demonstrates a more radical (and activist) nostalgia than Adams in daring to broach the possibility of "some way back" from the prospect of slowly metastasizing apocalypse.

That a reactionary stance is not incompatible with radical activism is one of Pynchon's themes in the essay "Is It O.K. to Be a Luddite?" which brings his Adamsian nostalgia into the realm of modern socio-political realities. Using the machinery-smashing Luddites of the Industrial Revolution as his "Badass" heroes, Pynchon extends the iconic and iconoclastic power of their appellation to all of those—King Kong, Dwight Eisenhower, and other opponents of the military-industrial complex—who "insist on the miraculous" and undertake to "deny to the machine at least some of its claims on us, to assert the limited wish that living things, earthly and otherwise, may on occasion become Bad and Big enough to take part in transcendent doings."[11] Even in the glib, quasicomic context that Pynchon establishes here, the references to "miraculous" and "transcendent" carry overtones of yearning for the lost metaphysic that claimed to enable such phenomena, as well as the hope that some form of it may return to underwrite the higher potentialities of "living things." It is in nonfiction passages such as this that we can see most clearly how the macrocosmic dimension of the fiction—the growing ascendancy of the artificial over the natural, mitigated by a gradually evolving dream of Orphic unity—translates into Pynchon's more immediate political concerns.

If Adams really was, as he once styled himself, the "child of the seventeenth and eighteenth centuries," Nietzsche was the *enfant terrible* of the nineteenth (EHA, p. 723). Deprived of Adams's socializing access to the machinery of public decision, Nietzsche reacted with a pure, Dionysian fierceness to the spectacle of approaching nihilism. A self-described connoisseur of "world-historical irony,"[12] he sardonically chronicled the decadence and death struggles of Judaeo-Christian theism and prophesied with some exuberance a future of vicious power struggles among ideologies, each intent upon colonizing the moral void with its own "Revaluation of All Values."[13] This celebration of the will to power in the name of a war against transcendental principles has an apocalyptic corollary, as René Girard explains in *Violence and the Sacred*:

> As soon as the essential quality of transcendence—religious, humanistic, or whatever—is lost, there are no longer any terms by which to define the legitimate form of violence [i.e., the kind that prevents other kinds] and to recognize it among the multitude of illicit forms. The definition of legitimate and illegitimate forms then becomes a matter of mere opinion, with each man free to reach his own decision. . . . demystification leads to constantly increasing violence, a violence perhaps less "hypocritical" than the violence it seeks to expose, but more energetic, more virulent, and the harbinger of something far worse—a violence that knows no bounds.[14]

There is a relative passivity about Henry Adams's prophecies, a melancholy sense of cosmic victimization, that leaves us unprepared for the Faustian élan of Nietzsche's, couched as the latter are in a prose edged with satirical knowingness and mischievous, unpredictable subversions. Pynchon, the twentieth century's child, does not need Nietzsche as intermediary in order to understand this joyous acquiescence in apocalypse; he intuits it, absorbs it by osmosis, and lets it enter his fiction in the demonic energies and presumptions of the world-historical conspiracies that he creates there, as well as in his own ironic humor. It is a peculiar sensitivity to the *Zeitgeist* that links these two writers, and the link extends even to artistic stratagems. When Nietzsche menacingly images the advent of nihilism as "this weirdest of all guests" that "stands before the door," he is engaging in the same dramatics of paranoia that Pynchon will so deftly exploit.[15]

We have, then, with Adams and Nietzsche, a common prognosis of a nihilistic future, and two diverging reactions that may be roughly characterized as Apollonian rejection and Dionysian embrace. Both reactions are incorporated into Pynchon's work, where they correspond roughly to a humanity-centered norm without effective defenders and to the dehumanizing forces and/or conspiracies that besiege it. Yet another antithesis that correlates with these reactions is that between the scenario of an existential wasteland that is prey only to a growing spiritual emptiness and entropy's indifferent ravagings, and the scenario of a world in the grip of fanatical cabals that seek control of historical process. It would not be an unfair summation of Pynchon's development to say that he moves from basic acceptance of the first scenario in the early short stories to the most urgent consideration of the second in *Gravity's Rainbow*. In between, the two possibilities form, in various mixtures and guises, the onto-epistemological cruxes that have fascinated critics.

These considerations constitute the parameters that generate the complex religious dialectic of Pynchon's fiction: a fluctuating tension between nostalgia for cosmic harmony and commitment to amoral power worship, superimposed upon the fluctuating tension between the notion of a neutral, structureless universe and that of a universe infiltrated by insidious structures of Control. This imposition might seem to create an unchartable melange of shifting vectors; but its particular points—which are the particular significations of Pynchon's fiction—can be located and interpreted in a religio-historical grid that is determined to a striking extent by the same parameters. I have in mind a composite of the conceptual frameworks developed by Hans Jonas and Eric Voegelin to link the Gnostic religion of antiquity to such seemingly diverse modern ideologies as existentialism, Marxism, and fascism—a framework that includes the humanizing norms transgressed by gnosticism in its various guises.

Pynchon's own frame of reference provides support for this linkage of ancient and modern cosmologies under the single rubric of gnosticism (I will use a small g for the general term and a capital for the earlier Judaeo-Christian heresy). He not only gives us sinister twentieth-century conspiracies that fit—as we shall see—the gnostic patterns described by Jonas and Voegelin, but he constantly alludes to ancient Gnostic lore—especially in *Gravity's Rainbow*—in order to lend a certain historical and religious resonance to these conspiracies. When he invokes the Kabbalah, for instance, by referring to contemporary organic chemists as "coal-tar Kabbalists" (GR, p. 590), he invests modern scientism with the spirituality of an ancient Jewish tradition that Gershom Scholem has described as embracing "an esotericism closely akin to the spirit of Gnosticism, one which was not restricted to instruction in the mystical path but also included ideas on cosmology, angelology, and magic."[16] One particular sect within the kabbalistic tradition centered upon a phenomenon known as Merkabah mysticism, which concerned itself with the Chariot (*merkabah*) of God and the possibility of mystical ascents therein. Pynchon draws explicitly on the doctrines and imagery of this sect, as we shall see, in order to lend a mystical mystique to the ascent of Gottfried in the 00000 Rocket. Since Scholem specifically identifies the Merkabah lore as "an inner Jewish concomitant to Gnosis . . . [which] may be termed 'Jewish and rabbinical Gnosticism' " (K, p. 13), we are presented with a second explicit linkage of ancient gnostic cabals and their modern technological successors.

Another variant of the Kabbalah, of particular importance in Pynchon's fiction, is that authored by the sixteenth-century mystic Isaac Luria Ashkenazi. The central event of Lurianic Kabbalism, as it is called, is the *shevirah*, the "breaking of the vessels." As Scholem describes this myth, the vessels designed to receive the creative light of God—vessels themselves consisting of "lower mixtures of light"—are shattered under the divine impact; and the heaviest of the sparks fall downward into exile, dominated now by the demonic *kelippot* (Pynchon's Qlippoth). The great restorative event of cosmic history is to be the *tikkun*, the gathering of these sparks—under the guidance of the Law—back to their proper "home" in the divine Center.[17] Pynchon uses this myth in more than one instance to dramatize the obsession of the *twentieth* century's alienated with the notion of "Return" to a lost harmony and centrality, and to suggest the specifically gnostic problematic that such a notion raises.

Having established that Pynchon himself quite consciously links the cabals of early Judaeo-Christian Gnosticism to the scientistic cabals of his own century, we may return to a consideration of the comprehensive schemata that Jonas and Voegelin derive from this linkage. Despite the fact that they approach their subject from different perspectives—Jonas as a scholar of ancient Gnosticism, Voegelin as a political philosopher—their basic conclusions are revealingly similar. Both find the prelude to much of twentieth-century history in a sense of alienation from nature, a denial of transcendental imperatives, and a belief that values are created in a private psychic economy rather than discovered in an ontological ground; and both find in this metaphysic a recrudescence of "ancient nihilism," as Jonas terms the original Gnostic movements (TGR, p. 320). In attempting to suggest corrective norms, Jonas stresses reintegration into nature and Voegelin the restoration of the imperatives; but it is precisely the gradual resolution of these two vectors into one that provides—I will argue—the normative thrust of Pynchon's fiction.

Jonas locates the ground of existentialism in the nihilistic assumption that the universe is indifferent to "human aspirations"—a "silence . . . which constitutes the utter loneliness of man in the scheme of things" (p. 322). It is the ability to conceive of this alienation that makes the alienation inevitable:

[Man] alone in the world thinks, not because but in spite of his being part of nature. As he shares no longer in a meaning of nature, but merely, through his body, in its mechanical determination, so nature no longer shares in his inner concerns. Thus that by which man is superior to all nature, his unique distinction, mind, no longer results in a higher integration of his being into the totality of being, but on the contrary marks the unbridgeable gulf between himself and the rest of existence. (pp. 322–323)

The memory, or imagination, of a time when no such gulf existed breeds a nostalgia a la Adams: "Gone is the *cosmos* with whose immanent *logos* my own can feel kinship, gone the order of the whole in which man has his place. That place appears now as a sheer and brute accident."

The rather ominous corollary of nature's indifference, for Jonas, is that "nature has no reference to ends":

With the ejection of teleology from the system of natural causes, nature, itself purposeless, ceased to provide any sanction to possible human purposes. A universe without an intrinsic hierarchy of being, as the Copernican universe is, leaves values ontologically unsupported, and the self is thrown back entirely upon itself in its quest for meaning and value. Meaning is no longer found but is "conferred." Values are no longer beheld in the vision of objective reality, but are posited as feats of valuation. As functions of the will, ends are solely my own creation. (p. 323)

The way is thus opened for the Nietzschean reduction of the world to "a mere manifestation of power," a world that "also admits toward itself—once the transcendent reference has fallen away and man is left with it and himself alone—nothing but the relation of power, that is, of mastery" (p. 324). Jonas's name for posttranscendent man is *homo absconditus*, a brilliant pun on the *deus absconditus* of the Deists that suggests the void left when a presence marked by sanctioned values and psychic immediacy is reduced to a neutral power locus.

There is much here already that bears upon modernity according to Pynchon—the desolate inscrutability of a cosmos without transcendental referents, the nostalgia for these referents, the systematic extirpation of the human in the name of power. When Jonas turns to his exploration of the ancient Gnostics in the light of existentialism, yet other links emerge—links that are peculiarly valuable because they suggest a rationale for the demonic animism so incongruously present in Pynchon's "scientific" world of molecules, rockets, and entropy. Jonas is able to make his turn because existentialism and Gnosticism share a common essence: "a certain dualism, an estrangement between man and the world, with the loss of the idea of a kindred *cosmos*—in short, an anthropological acosmism" (p. 325). The Gnostic movement—actually, movements—flourished in the first three centuries of the Christian era, a time that Spengler saw as analogous to our own.[18] Its cosmogony held that the world was created not by the Supreme God, but by an inferior demiurge of tyrannical propensities. Nature is the handiwork not of a knowledgeable and benevolent creator, but of one who acted out of "ignorance and passion":

The world, then, is the product, and even the embodiment, of the negative of *knowledge*. What it reveals is unenlightened and therefore malignant force, proceeding from the spirit of self-assertive power, from the will to rule and coerce. The mindlessness of this will is the spirit of the world, which bears no relation to understanding and love. The laws of this universe are the laws of this rule, and not of divine wisdom. *Power* thus becomes the chief aspect of the cosmos, and its inner essence is ignorance. (pp. 327–328)

The one spark of spiritual enlightenment in this moral darkness is provided by the *pneuma*, the inner human self that reflects the Supreme God, the *deus absconditus* who is otherwise unreflected in creation. It is this component of spirit that makes possible man's knowledge of "self and of God"—knowledge that "determines his situation as that of the potentially knowing in the midst of the unknowing, of light in the midst of darkness, and this relation is at the bottom of his being alien, without companionship in the dark vastness of the universe" (p. 328).

This last point is a crucial one. The spiritual element in man not only constitutes his otherness, but awakens him to this otherness. He becomes aware that the cosmos is an insidious prison and that his "natural" psyche—the "soul" designed by the demiurge to enshroud the spirit—is "the involuntary executor of cosmic designs" (p. 329). This horror—that man cannot even trust his own nature—adds to the overpowering sense of dread that permeates the Gnostic consciousness. The way out of this enslavement is through gnosis, the liberating knowledge that can open a path back to God for the spirit; but this privileged doctrine asserts the impossibility—indeed, the undesirability—of healing the breach between humanity and its enveloping conditions:

Since the *cosmos* is contrary to life and to spirit, the saving knowledge cannot aim at integration into the cosmic whole and at compliance with its laws. . . . For the Gnostics . . . man's alienation from the world is to be deepened and brought to a head, for the extrication of the inner self which only thus can gain itself. The world (not the alienation from it) must be overcome; and a world degraded to a power relation can only be overcome through power. (p. 329)

Despite the difference between the Spartan metaphysic of existentialism and Gnosticism's elaborate theology, there exists "an ontological similarity" in the "formal fact that the countering of power with power is the sole relation to the totality of nature left for man in both cases" (p. 330). From this ontological similarity there flows an ethical one. Nietzsche's proclamation of God's death is equivalent, in certain crucial ways, to the Gnostic proclamation that the true God is absent from creation. In each case, the corollary is the extirpation of any transcendental ground for values within the terms of creation. The resentful contempt that the Gnostic feels for nature is also focused upon natural law, as well as upon the political and moral laws that ultimately derive from his demiurgic masters. His only obligation to these laws is the negation implied by gnosis—to ignore them, or even to break them, in the interests of a perfected alienation from the natural order. This hostile imperative can be construed, ironically, as a sort of negative transcendental that serves to differentiate the demonized Gnostic cosmos from the neutrality and silence of an existentialist void that knows no imperatives.

It is precisely the play of difference and similarity in these two metaphysics that constitutes their value in the synthesis of a grid for Pynchon's fiction. If we use the term gnosticism, with a small g, to embrace their similarities, we may then distinguish between cabalistic gnosticism and existential gnosticism. The former is based upon the premise of a conspiracy that is cosmic in its pretensions if not in its actual scope. It seeks control over nature in general and humanity in particular, and is capable of manipulating the course of world history so insidiously that it acquires a quasi-transcendental status—which is to say that it becomes the seemingly ubiquitous and omnipotent ground of historical process. A terrible coherence is born, a causal nexus so fiendishly engineered that human freedom of choice is effectively negated. Existential gnosticism, on the other hand, jettisons metaphysical coherence and transcendental apparatus in favor of a cosmos defined by the very absence of sentient controls and thus by an infinity of choices that is—ironically—intimidating. The term coined by Heidegger to express this sense of human existence is Geworfenheit—"having been thrown"—a concept that dramatizes the accidental, contingent nature of human origins, and also of historical process. Now the nightmare of the arbitrary replaces the nightmare of the inevitable, and the oppressive omnipresence of Control gives way to an oppressive solitude. This new condition, a sort of aleatory loneliness, tends to engender a nostalgia for transcendentals—even those of a demonic nature.

The absence of a locus for the transcendental breeds a deep spiritual confusion in those Pynchon personae who have no cabalistic alternatives to pursue. This disorientation is dramatized in Gravity's Rainbow by the "grimed brick sprawl" of a hospital:

a lengthy brick improvisation, a Victorian paraphrase of what once, long ago, resulted in Gothic cathedrals—but which, in its own time, arose not from any need to climb through the fashioning of suitable confusions toward any apical God, but more in a derangement of aim, a doubt as to the God's actual locus (or, in some, as to its very existence), out of a cruel network of sensuous moments that could not be transcended and so bent the intentions of the builders not on any zenith, but back to fright, to simple escape, in whatever direction. (p. 46)

Henry Adams found incarnate in the Gothic splendor of Chartres—as we shall see in the chapter on *V.*—an ultimate spirituality, the life-affirming mystery of the Virgin; but Pynchon finds in the cathedral's Victorian parody the bitter fruits of an antitranscendental sensuousness, a one-dimensional materialism that cannot accommodate the notion of a spiritual "zenith." To be trapped in this dimension is to experience the apotheosis of its "cruel" reductiveness: a mechanical, dehumanizing nightmare of "industrial smoke, street excrement, windowless warrens, shrugging leather forests of drive belts, flowing and patient shadow states of the rats and flies" (p. 46). Denied the "chances for mercy" available to their predecessors, who projected winding Gothic paths toward the Virgin's benevolence, the Victorians flee through secular labyrinths of their own creation in a desperate attempt to avoid the consequences of a pure secularity that is equivalent—in the paradoxical matrix of existentialist gnosticism—to a negative religion.

Cabalistic gnosticism corresponds, in Pynchon's terminology, to the condition of "paranoia," while the existential variety represents "antiparanoia." One of Tyrone Slothrop's meditations in *Gravity's Rainbow* makes the distinction, and its ensuing nostalgia, clear:

> If there is something comforting—religious, if you want—about paranoia, there is also anti-paranoia, where nothing is connected to anything, a condition not many of us can bear for long. Well right now Slothrop feels himself sliding onto the anti-paranoid part of his cycle, feels the whole city around him going back roofless, vulnerable, uncentered as he is, and only pasteboard images now of the Listening Enemy left between him and the wet sky.
>
> Either They have put him here for a reason, or he's just here. He isn't sure that he wouldn't, actually, rather have that *reason*.... (p. 434)

The "pasteboard images" are Nazi propaganda posters used as a makeshift ceiling to keep the rain out of a battle-damaged building. They depict an ominous "cloaked figure" in a "broad-brimmed hat, with its legend DER FEIND HÖRT ZU" (p. 433).

The symbolism of the passage is intricately constructed to elaborate the antithesis between the two modes of gnosticism. If, indeed—as the German warning insists—"the enemy is listening," we have a paradigm in which a look toward the heavens reveals a threatening, mysterious host of identical auditors. The overtones of cosmic malignancy in this vision are enhanced by the status of "Feind" as a cognate of "fiend." The vision itself, however, is subverted by the blatant artificiality of "pasteboard" and the deliberate ambiguity of "legend." The "Listening Enemy" is too insubstantial to hold back the rain, which "drips through in half a dozen places" as evidence that the sky's purely impersonal assault is the final truth of things. Thus the linkage of "roofless" with "vulnerable" and "uncentered" as Slothrop temporarily refocuses his sense of universal oppression on an existential specter, the prospect of total unconnectedness. Slothrop's tentative preference for Control over vacuity is echoed by Jonas in a salient contrast between Gnosticism and existentialism: "Gnostic man is thrown into an antagonistic, anti-divine, and therefore anti-human nature, modern man into an indifferent one. Only the latter case represents the absolute vacuum, the really bottomless pit" (p. 338). It is possible, and useful, to plot the development of Pynchon's fiction as the exploration of animistic—i.e., cabalistic—alternatives to such a "pit."

Such a plotting must include, of course, the "onto-epistemological question," which may now be seen more clearly in the context of the religious dialectic from which it emerges. Slothrop is torn between the possibility that he is "here" for a "reason"—that his actions and whereabouts are almost totally controlled by a mysterious and quasi-omnipotent cabal—and that he is "here" gratuitously, anonymously, without appeal. Even though his predilection at this particular point for the conspiracy option has implications—as I hope to show—for the novel's normative structures, it should not blind us to the very real terror that accompanies contemplation of this option in the rest of the novel, and in Pynchon's previous work. To suspect that a shadowy, powerful network with totalitarian intentions is manipulating historical process, even down to the level of individual mind control, is to experience the impingement of an unspeakable impotence and vulnerability, as well as anguished uncertainty about the truth of the suspicion. It is an anxiety that leads Pynchon's successive protagonists on urgent quests in which the "real" stakes are nothing less than an adequate sense of reality.

The current critical consensus seems to be, as I have indicated, that these quests are epistemological missions impossible, finally foundering—as they must—in undecidability; and that the gradual revelation of this cul-de-sac, along with intimations that a provisional middle ground can be found and occupied, constitutes the unifying theme of Pynchon's fiction. The postmodern secularity of this reading, however, does violence to the complex religious dialectic that serves as the fiction's metastructure. Pynchon's universe is a gnostic trap in which the human victims scuttle back and forth between an inhospitable vacuity and a suffocating paranoia. In a profound sense this is Hobson's choice, since either possibility brings with it a demoralizing alienation from the natural order of things, and pervasive feelings of cosmic insecurity.

Another gnosticizing factor is present, ironically, in the mere *existence* of the epistemological question. To suffer the constant anxiety that mysterious powers *may* be manipulating human life is to be, *de facto*, haunted by demiurgic phantasms, and thus to suffer the oppression that characterizes cabalistic gnosticism, even while the question of its basis in reality remains open. Even if a habitable "middle" appears—e.g., Roger's sustaining intimacy with Jessica in *Gravity's Rainbow*—it is quickly crushed by the churnings of metaphysical force fields that are either indifferent or hostile to human constructs. In the very act of privileging moments of communion, Pynchon reminds us of their fragility and transience in the face of massive dehumanizing forces.

If there is a solution, a way out of the gnostic trap, it involves locating a metaphysic of religious potentiality in which these moments can be grounded, and then obtruding this metaphysic as a *benevolent* term into the malign dialectic that dominates the cosmos of Pynchon's fiction. Because Pynchon *begins* his fictional speculations with gnostic assumptions, we are speaking here—paradoxically—of a gnosis that is ultimately antignostic, of a rebellion against gnosticism itself as the sum of metaphysical possibilities. Such a rebellion might entail the restoration of a humanizing transcendental and of man's union with nature. This projection of a normative religious mechanism emerging, however gradually, from Pynchon's fiction, raises complex questions about the ideal relation between the natural, the human, and the transcendent, and also about the perversions of this relation by the gnostic ideologies that provide Pynchon with his animating tensions. It is precisely these questions that concern Eric Voegelin, and it is here that his ambitious analysis of history, religion, and human institutions is invaluable.

To be human is, for Voegelin, to occupy a middle ground between the poles of raw, undifferentiated natural process and perfectly refined spirituality. Adopting (and adapting) Platonic terminology, Voegelin refers to these extremes, respectively, as *apeiron* ("the indeterminate") and *nous* (i.e., "divine intellection"), while the middle ground is the *metaxy*, the In-Between.[19] *Nous* is associated with the transcendental ground of values embodied in such concepts as the Judaeo-Christian God or the Platonic Good—in both cases, a mysterious and inaccessible Beyond in which psychic participation is nonetheless possible for man. This participation takes the form of asking what Voegelin calls "The Question." According to Eugene Webb, one of Voegelin's most lucid exegetes, this is a "term for the tension of existence in its aspect of a questioning unrest seeking not simply particular truth, but still more the transcendental pole of truth as such: 'not just any question but the quest concerning the mysterious ground of all being.' "[20]

The literal existence or nonexistence of the pole is not at stake here so much as the edifying influence of its projection in the guise of a spiritual paradigm. The very attempt to understand and emulate this ultimately incomprehensible and inimitable ordering *produces* the psychic, ethical, and social orderings that characterize the *metaxy*, the humanity-defining tension between the subhuman *apeiron* and the superhuman *nous*. The connection between the transcendental ground and human destiny enables the questioner-participant to entertain simultaneously the notion of what Wallace Stevens calls "our perishing earth,"[21] with its rhythms of growth and decay and its inevitable imperfections, and the notion of a divine revelation that encourages love and reverence for this earth, even while it incorporates an unremitting imperative for the sanctification and ordering of our earthly life.

Concepts such as "revelation" and "transcendental ground" present—to say the least—considerable problems in the current poststructuralist climate, as does Voegelin's privileging of the human subject; so much so that it would seem wise, at this point, to offer a digressive apologia. The drive to jettison the entire apparatus of metaphysics has involved not only the axiomatic discrediting of religious onto-epistemological models but—as Fekete has pointed out—the rejection of their secular analogues. In the place of these classical paradigms we have the attempt on the part of the poststructuralist sensibility that Charles Levin calls "the sociological ego" to substitute an emphasis on formal relations (linguistic codes, economies, etc.) between phenomena, and to dismiss a concern with subjects and objects themselves as "unintelligible, indeterminate, and probably illusory as well (in modern parlance—specular, ideological, fantasmatic, metaphysical . . .)."[22]

But this realm of the unintelligible and indeterminate, not to mention of the metaphysical, is the realm of the animating *mysterium* where what is at least experienced as transcendental and revelatory (or "magical thinking," in Levin's formula) has its habitation (p. 58). This inescapable "aesthetic dimension" of the pysche, which Levin identifies with the imagination, acts constantly to subvert the antimetaphysical focus on the purely relational: "In the macroscope of the sociological ego, the subject and the object may lack solidity relative to the unmoving precision of relational models. But in the microscope of the aesthetic, relations themselves lose intelligibility in the obscure encounter between the subject, the other, and their bodily substances" (p. 29). I am not for a moment suggesting that Levin's psychoanalytic rationale for values is itself a metaphysical *excursus* à la Voegelin; merely that both theorists locate a vital and vitalizing plexus of mystical possibility deep in the core of human experience.

From a very different angle, considering value as produced by the "dynamics of some economy," Barbara Herrnstein Smith grants at least the feasibility of such a plexus.[23] Since "value judgments do not have but also do not need truth-value in the traditional sense," she is willing to admit the possible "social value" of "theories and models that work very badly or not at all" by positivist standards of verifiability (pp. 7, 13). Among the examples she gives are "various ancient and modern cosmological models, including more or less 'mystical,' 'metaphysical,' and primitive ones" that "may come to figure as especially fertile metaphorical structures" (p. 13).

The concession may be a patronizing one, but it opens a crucial door for Voegelin's metaxic model of the human. It is after all Nietzsche—patron saint of perspectivism, sworn enemy of the transcendental—who asserts that "the falseness of a judgment is not . . . necessarily an objection to a judgment. . . . The question is to what extent it is life-promoting, life-preserving, species-preserving, perhaps even species-cultivating."[24] But what if the concept of a transcendental polarity—beyond truth and falsity—is one of these "life-promoting" judgments in the sense that it is humanity-enhancing or even humanity-defining, what if it is inseparable from some crucial species of inwardness and ennobling self-conception?

Moving to firmer ground, the historical perspective that Voegelin establishes over many volumes, we can say that it was at least *seen* to be so by the humanistic tradition deriving from Judaeo-Christian theology and Platonic philosophy, and maintaining even after its modernist secularization what Jean-François Lyotard perceives as "nostalgia for a sublime transcendent."[25] It is the human as it is understood in light of this tradition, I argue, that is shown degenerating into the nonhuman in a novel such as *V.*, and which a Pynchon afflicted by modernist nostalgia undertakes to regenerate through the Orphic naturalism of *Gravity's Rainbow*. If, then, we do not insist upon verifying the notion of a transcendental polarity according to some strict ontology, there would seem to be a strong case for the application of Voegelin's paradigm to Pynchon's fiction.

But it is not only the polarity used to define the human that has become problematic in the poststructuralist milieu; it is the very concept of the human itself as it is framed by the ideology of humanism. Jacques Derrida sums up the case of things in a subtly invidious pairing of humanistic analysis with deconstructive *jeu*:

> There are thus two interpretations of interpretation, of structure, of sign, of play. The one [the humanistic] seeks to decipher, dreams of deciphering a truth or an origin which escapes play and the order of the sign, and which lives the necessity of interpretation as an exile. The other, which is no longer turned toward the origin, affirms play and tries to pass beyond man and humanism, the name of man being the name of that being who, throughout the history of metaphysics or of ontotheology—in other words, throughout his entire history—has dreamed of full presence, the reassuring foundation, the origin and the end of play. The second interpretation of interpretation, to which Nietzsche pointed the way, does not seek . . . "the inspiration of a new humanism."[26]

Perhaps the first thing to notice here is that Derrida, as he follows Nietzsche in depriviledging the notion of a metaphysical or onto-theological origin, nonetheless finds it as central to the concepts of "man" and "humanism" as Voegelin does; the difference is that Derrida is anxious to jettison the humanistic baby along with the epistemic bathwater. He seeks to "pass beyond" the human in order to negate the transcendental; he seeks a sort of negative transcendence. It is futile, in the face of this nihilistic lucidity, to turn the Nietzschean arsenal upon its own position and argue that even "dreams" of discovering a ground for "truth" may constitute a "life-promoting" prerequisite for the human, since the human is synonymous with the falsity that must be subverted in the name of a dissolve into the pre- (and post-) human relational, into a primordial *regressus* of signification.

Derrida is not, of course, alone in his radical revaluing of what William V. Spanos has called the "privileged status" accorded to "Man."[27] Michel Foucault, for instance, after heralding "the shift of language towards objectivity" and "its reappearance in multiple form. . . . with greater and greater insistence in a unity," asks if this epistemic change is not "the sign . . . that man is in the process of perishing as the being of language continues to shine ever brighter upon our horizon," and even if we ought not to "give up thinking of man."[28] Tzvetan Todorov goes so far as to call "anti-humanism" the "dominant tendency of American criticism."[29] It is, at any rate, dominating enough to occasion an involved and judicious survey of its exponents from Alan Wilde, who cites Spanos, Bové, and numerous others in order to present the counterthesis that a "modified . . . humanism can and does persist in the work of writers" who are nonetheless "attuned . . . to the passing of modernism and its values"— an undertaking obviously related to Fekete's attempt to "humanize" post-structuralism.[30]

One of those cited by Wilde, Thomas Docherty, is of particular relevance here because he undertakes (as does Spanos) to appropriate Pynchon for the poststructuralist camp. Docherty's "opposition to humanism" is based partly, in Wilde's summation, on humanism's "valuing of depth, individuality, continuity, and explicability" (p. 13). It is, presumably, these modes of pyschic and historical coherence that Docherty sees Pynchon devaluing:

> Twentieth-century fiction . . . has seen a move away from an aesthetic which says that unity is a desirable thing in itself, and indeed has favored multiplicity and fragmentation. The multiplicity of plots in Pynchon, say, cohere if at all only in a preposterous manner. . . . In terms of characterization, plots can actually serve to dehumanize the characters, rendering them inanimate. . . . The kind of plot . . . that Pynchon flees . . . is actually the ultimate "Realist" plot, the plot of reality which has God as an author. Realist plots . . . take the reader to a point of final equilibrium (judgement, perhaps), an end where all has fallen into a just and meaningful order.[31]

To suggest that "multiplicity and fragmentation" are desiderata for Pynchon is to fall into the simplistic equation of form and theme that so often vitiated the early criticism of *Ulysses*, and to miss the complex tension in his fiction between a collapsing "ontotheology," the growth of cosmic anomie, the prospects of gnostic Control, and nostalgia for a benevolent natural unity. To put it another way, the "multiplicity of plots" finds a thematic coherence in what we might call the metaplot of an urgent drive to discover what unity or disunity is imposed on humankind by the cosmic case of things, not to subvert the possibility of this unity in an ecstasy of poststructuralist *jouissance*. Certain forms of multiplicity, at least, are aspects of the gnostic malaise, not of the cure, and actually tend to function—in Pynchonian mechanics—as part of the dehumanizing forces.

Nonetheless, the belief that Pynchon is somehow sympathetic to this dismantling of a human center remains deeply rooted in the current scholarly milieu. In a recent article in *PMLA*, Marc Redfield sets Pynchon's fiction up as the paradigm case of the "postmodern sublime."[32] Since the sublime "operates to console and empower a subject threatened with being decentered," it follows that a postmodern sublime "would imply a double gesture of illusion and demystification":

> The double gesture exacerbates not only the coercions of specular structures of identification but also the rudimentary quality of the scene's participants, forcing them past the possibilities of representational language. The dynamics of identification pursue their course, leaving us to confront purely linguistic entities. Pynchon's oeuvre performs that gesture persistently and deliberately, returning repeatedly to a zero-point fantasy that grows increasingly more theatrical, more manifestly figurative, without sacrificing the libidinal or linguistic energy that terms like *the sublime* seek to describe.

In other words, we are to suppose that Pynchon himself undertakes to deconstruct the identifiably human into a linguistic relationality that is more or less synonymous with the sublime in its postmodern guise, i.e., successive waves (a la Kroker) of pure, libidinous *frissons* deriving from "terror and exhilaration" (p. 152).

It is ironic that Docherty, in the passage quoted earlier, should object to the phenomenon of dehumanizing as yet another inadequacy of the "Realist" plot, since humanism in general and the Cartesian "constituting of the re-cognizable human individual" in particular are aspects of the episteme he is opposing.[33] The irony is compounded if we examine Pynchon's attitude toward at least one example of the infrahuman relationality by which poststructuralist thought undertakes to negate this individual and the troublesome baggage of subject/object dichotomies and onto-epistemological dilemmas that accompanies him.

Late in *Gravity's Rainbow*, as preparations are being made to launch the 00000 Rocket that will carry Blicero's catamite Gottfried to a sacrificial death, we learn that the young German will be encased in a "film" of Imipolex G. This notorious plastic represents, throughout the novel, the apotheosis of a perverse chemical synthesizing that is not only unnatural but antinatural, and inextricably associated with dehumanization in the name of Control. After a coldly technical discussion of the beam-scanning apparatus needed to render the "Imipolectic Surface . . . erectile," the Swiftian projector touches on the question of "What lies just beneath," only to conclude that "we need not dwell here on the Primary Problem, namely that everything below the plastic film does after all lie in the Region of Uncertainty, except to emphasize to beginning students who may be prone to Schwärmerei, that terms referring to the Subimipolexity such as 'Core' and 'Center of Internal Energy' possess, outside the theoretical, no more reality than do terms such as 'Supersonic Region' or 'Center of Gravity' in other areas of Science" (p. 700).

This "What," this "Uncertainty," is a living human being whose complex, unique subjectivity is airbrushed out of existence by subsumption in the "Subimipolexity"—a relation in the purely relational economy of Imipolex. To imagine otherwise, to attempt to reprivilege the human at least as some sort of "Core" or "Center," is to indulge in idle adolescent fantasies. The thrust of Pynchon's satire should be obvious here: it is not the concept of the "re-cognizable human individual" that is being ironically exposed, but that of the unrecognizable, deindividuated cipher of the posthumanist episteme.

If, then, this episteme seems quite congruous with the entropic, scientific, and bureaucratic world of Pynchon's fiction, it is because—from the standpoint of Voegelinian dynamics—both episteme and world operate as radical perversions of a humanizing *metaxy*. The clearest paradigm of this perversion is furnished by *V.*, where Henry Adams's Virgin is a transcendental prototype grotesquely distorted into a mechanical, life-denying force—a distortion that in turn warps the existence of Herbert Stencil and other questers for "the mysterious ground of all being." Similar parodic structures can be located in the existential alienation of the early stories, in the dialectic between Oedipa Maas and the Tristero, and in the bizarre quests that center upon the Rocket. In all cases, as we shall see, the sense of cosmic well-being attendant upon the metaxic tension between the pure immanence of the *apeiron* and the pure transcendence of *nous* is shattered by attempts to destroy or usurp this transcendental status.

Voegelin's collective term for the metaphysical systems that undertake these destructions or usurpations is *gnosticism*, a usage that brings his analysis into fruitful linkage with that of Jonas. What Voegelin means by the term is a "type of thinking that claims absolute cognitive mastery of reality"—that claims a *gnosis*, or exclusive knowledge, so definitive that it is "not subject to criticism." Gnostic movements are "religious or quasi-religious" in nature, and can take either "transcendentalizing (as in the case of the Gnostic movement of late antiquity) or immanentizing forms (as in the case of Marxism)" (EV, p. 282). The phenomenon of "immanentizing" is, for Voegelin, the attempt to reduce the transcendental Beyond either to an ostensibly realizable scheme of earthly perfection or to the status of a ghostly illusion. In the first instance we end up with totalitarian ideologies, in the second with existential nihilism. Both reductions effectively subvert the spiritual orderings that emanate from a transmundane paradigm: "If man exists in the *metaxy*, in the tension 'between god and man,' any construction of man as a world-immanent entity will destroy the meaning of existence, because it deprives man of his specific humanity. The poles of the tension must not be hypostasized into objects independent of the tension in which they are experienced as its poles" (A, p. 104).

If this hypostasis—this objectification of the immaterial in space and time—occurs, the polarities that define the human are reduced to

> symbols of alienation. . . . The "world" we discern in the perspective of our existence to partake of both time and the timeless is dissociated, under the pressure of the mood, into "this world" of existence in time and the "other world" of the timeless; and as we "exist" in neither the one nor the other of these worlds but in the tension between time and the timeless, the dissociation of the "world" transforms us into "strangers" to either one of the hypostasized worlds.[34]

We end up, in other words, alienated not only from the discredited realm of the transcendental, but from the natural realm that this discrediting was supposed to privilege. It is here that Voegelin's analysis explicitly intersects that of Jonas; we are faced once again with cosmic homelessness and nihilistic anxiety, and with the violent assertions of arbitrary value systems that attend them.

Cabalistic gnosticism, then, undertakes to counter existential despair, anxiety, and chaos by affirming its own gnosis as a substitute for the transcendental ground; but the attempt, because it negates the metaxic equilibrium, is doomed to reintroduce these very maladies into the utopia it dreams of shaping. Voegelin's observations on the "psychopathological" structures that produce these ironies are extremely useful for examining similar structures in the world of Pynchon's fiction.[35] One of these is the distinction between the elite and the preterite, between the "saved" and those abandoned to damnation, that runs through that world. Pynchon draws this dichotomy from Calvinist theology, which Voegelin specifically identifies as a gnostic ideology, and which we will examine as such in the chapter on *Gravity's Rainbow*.

The point here is that this cosmic invidiousness is inherent in the gnostic paradigm, which insists that "the *gnosis* of the . . . visionary is special information possessed only by the few, not the universal tension of existence . . . in which all are involved whether they realize it consciously or not" (EV, p. 206). The corollary of this axiom is that "gnostic movements tend to divide mankind into an elite (the knowers and masters of technique) and the masses, the nonknowers, who at best can be followers of those who know." The elite are the cabalists, the master conspirators who seek to mold reality itself into the form dictated by their privileged vision, while the masses are simply an aspect of the raw, in-

choate given that is to be molded. It is just such hubristic, Faustian assumptions that underlie the insidious plot of V. and her decadent allies
against the entire realm of the animate, and that we find behind the world-
historical manipulations of the Tristero and the Cartel's dream of Control.

If we consider the cynical violence that accompanies the operations
of these cabals, we are led to another corollary of the arrogant self-sufficiency of gnosis: the claim that gnostic activism transcends conventional
moral judgment. According to Webb, such activism

> frequently takes the form of what in "The People of God" Voegelin has called
> "eschatological violence," an attempt to force the wheel of history to turn by
> deeds that violate ordinary morality but are considered to be beyond good
> and evil because they will secure the transition from a world of iniquity to
> a world of light. Even sheer destructiveness and terrorism are interpreted
> from this point of view as . . . the breaking in of the New Age. (EV, pp. 206–
> 207)

Certain that the *eschaton*, the destiny of mankind projected by their gnosis,
is both inevitable and desirable, the true believers mount a ruthless assault
upon the real human present in the name of an imagined human future.
Ironically, however, it is the very concept of humanity that is sabotaged
by the destruction of the metaxic tension. This ironic perversion of a goal
or value into its antithesis is typical of what happens when gnostic concepts are subjected to praxis, but the phenomenon itself—which I have
termed *gnostic slippage*—is inherent in the perversion of Voegelin's paradigm.

It is worth taking the trouble to understand the mechanism of this
slippage because it helps to explain in turn the genesis and functioning
of Pynchon's complex, ambiguous value structures. In *Anamnesis*, Voegelin predicates a sort of ontological hierarchy that provides a convenient
measure of human progress and human regress:

> Divine Nous
> *Psyche*—Noetic
> *Psyche*—Passions
> Animal Nature
> Vegetative Nature
> Inorganic Nature
> Apeiron—Depth. (A, p. 114)

Man, according to Voegelin, "participates" in all of these levels, with the
result that "his nature is an epitome of the hierarchy of being." The substitution of a finite, purely "human" *eschaton* for the infinitely receding
nous means the negation of the spiritual (noetic) quest that produces the
real order of the human. The metaxic tension collapses, and man is pulled
by apeirontic vectors through lower and lower levels of his being—animal

appetite and violence, vegetable passivity, inorganic oblivion—in the name of an illusory order that ultimately represents the dissolution of order.

Two other modes of slippage inherent in the noetic distortions of gnosticism are peculiarly relevant to the metaphysical force fields of Pynchon's cosmos: the instability of the elite-preterite dichotomy and of the distinction between secular and religious constructs. For the gnostic elite, as we saw in an earlier quotation from Jonas, the alien world is a thing to be "overcome"; and a "world degraded to a power relation can only be overcome through power" (see above, p. 11). In relation to this looming complex of forces, the elite experience, ironically, a preterite paranoia that drives them to seek mastery through their elite gnosis; but in so doing they define a new preterite in those who are *not* privy to this plexus of knowledge and power, but are pawns to be manipulated in its service. This preterite, in turn, can escape preterition only by adopting the power techniques of their masters; but in the very act they naturally tend to become—in Wordsworth's phrase—"Oppressors in their turn."[36]

This cycle of oppression remains unbroken because its participants refuse to be contained by the human *metaxy*, with its limiting transcendental—a refusal for which Foucault provides an explicitly antihumanist context:

> Humanism invented a whole series of subjected sovereignties: the soul (ruling the body but subjected to God), consciousness (sovereign in a context of judgment, but subjected to the necessities of truth), the individual (a titular control of personal rights subjected to laws of nature and society). . . . In short, humanism is everything in Western civilization that restricts the desire for power: it prohibits the desire for power and excludes the possibility of power being seized.[37]

Here, a relentless and corrosive relationality is seeking its Nietzschean apotheosis. Only by the removal of *all* transcendental or quasi-transcendental restraints on power can the human overcome soul, consciousness, and individuality—at which point, of course, it blends into the monistic force field of *der Wille zur Macht* and is no longer the human. It would be hard to find a more unabashed example of the gnostic pipedream, or an axiomatic statement more replete with the seeds of apocalypse.

The important slippage in the elite-preterite antithesis lies in the shifting vectors of moral valuation. In Pynchon's ethos, it is the Masters of Control who are to blame for the perversion of natural process and the denial of all that defines the human; in seeking to control the Masters, the victims are threatened with the loss of the moral highground that their preterite status had—in Pynchon's framework—entailed. Gnostic victimization, inseparable from gnostic alienation and paranoia, establishes a cycle of cosmic anxiety and reciprocal retribution that amounts to a closed system and that makes the establishment of an effectual, antignostic norm difficult and unlikely.

The destabilizing of the antithesis between secular and religious value systems is a result of substituting a finite *eschaton* for an open-ended spiritual quest. A secular goal pursued religiously, and regarded as the termination of historical process, inevitably engenders a priestly apparatus, a self-determined morality, and an immunity to criticism. Claims of universality, definitiveness, and absolute mastery invest the principles of the cult with a quasi-transcendental status and an aura of religious mystery that in turn produce "conversions" and fanatical devotees. These considerations help us to understand the atmosphere of imminent revelation, contaminated by false spirituality and evil, that surrounds the machinations of Pynchon's conspirators.

This notion of a conceptual slippage inherent in gnosticism is ultimately useful in charting Pynchon's own relation to the gnostic grid I have elaborated. The English major versed in engineering physics who writes the early stories basically accepts the neutrality of an existentialist cosmos, but he hints at demonic conspiracies that may taint this neutrality. In either case, as we have seen, his own standpoint is a gnostic one, and he is forced in some sense to respond to the alienation and paranoia inherent in this standpoint. To put it another way, gnostic pressures produce—in the Voegelin paradigm—a spiritual deformation of existence that in turn tends to produce a distorting of the lens through which existence is viewed. The viewer (Pynchon) becomes increasingly aware of a flawed perspective, but is not able to escape entirely its jaundicing, negative effects. I believe that this complex perspectival trap goes a long way toward explaining the difficulties in separating Pynchon's implicit norms and hopes from what often seems a prevailing (and corrosive) skepticism, a negating of all onto-epistemological foundations; and thus toward explaining the equally puzzling deformation of apparently serious questers and quests into cartoon characters and farces.

It is precisely such deformations that concern Michael Seidel in his study of *Gravity's Rainbow* and its satiric machinery. Because Pynchon is able, by the time of writing this novel, to get a clearer metaperspective on his own gnostic viewpoint, it will help us to leap ahead temporarily and examine the complex structure of ironic distortion into which Seidel's inquiry opens:

Having de-formed, satire takes as its subject the very deformity it has produced. . . . Rabelaisian monstrosities—misbirths—move through narrative worlds whose paths distort what once were recognizable as paradigmatic wanderings, quests, trials, thresholds, penetrations, resolutions, and revelations. Through such paradigmatic experiences, heroes are initiated, tried, and perhaps encultrated. But satiric narratives perform the opposite—they dehumanize heroes and debase heroic inheritances.[38]

For Seidel, then, "satiric heroes are victims; they are disallowed the luxury of human choice or even self-determined motive because the promiscuous contingencies of the narratives in which they appear are so oppressive to the shapes of humanity, so enervating, that the only relief is in the loss of will, the loss of distinction" (p. 201).

This cogent schema helps us to understand not only Pynchon's place in a long-standing satirical tradition, but the particular functioning and products of the satirical machinery in *Gravity's Rainbow*. Seidel's blueprint for that machinery, however, needs one major adjustment. The "promiscuous contingencies" that warp the "shapes of humanity" in Pynchon's novel are not necessarily all that promiscuous or all that contingent. There is considerable evidence to suggest that many of them are vectors of force specifically designed by some mechanism of gnostic Control to automate a particular character, or at least emanating from that mechanism with a general dehumanizing intent. It is the demiurgic manipulators *within* the novel who bring to bear the distorting, deforming pressure normally applied by the satirist from *outside*, who bring about a world that encourages the degeneration of its inhabitants into impotent, absurd pawns.

It is significant in this regard that Blicero, the very avatar of gnosticism, is neither impotent nor absurd. He (as a representative of Control) is the warper, not the warped; the satirist-surrogate, not the satirized. It is he who is taken by Pynchon with deadly seriousness; and it is *his* norm that prevails in *praxis* in the world of the novel and serves to turn the preterite, those who do not share his gnosis, into caricatures. And yet he clearly *is* warped if judged on the basis of what affirms humanity and what negates it—a basis provided partly by the transient episodes of genuine human communion and the laments for a lost primordial harmony that Pynchon also excludes from ironic distortion. These and other aspects of metaxic structure suggest a larger norm based upon a modernist nostalgia for the transcendental, an embracing ethos that subverts the quasi-satirist Blicero and Control's nihilistic deformations of human life. At this level, the ironic is deironized and exposed as a bitter, life-negating perversion, not a humanizing corrective.

None of this totally deproblematizes the gnostic problematic inseparable from Pynchon's *Weltanschauung*, but it helps us to understand how a complex, self-conscious irony that constantly subverts its own deformations has all too easily conjured up for many readers a nihilistic miasma in which no norm beyond a generalized iconoclasm is discernible. It also clarifies the role of satirical distortion in Pynchon's earlier works where the gnostic and the antignostic are less clearly differentiated. The "Rabelaisian monstrosities" whom Oedipa Maas constantly encounters in *The Crying of Lot 49*, and whose absurdity seems at times to call the authenticity of that quest into question, appear now as deformations indigenous to the gnostic crucible, not as Pynchon's postmodern subversion of his own plot. The same is true of V., where the quester himself—Herbert Stencil—suffers frequently from a fecklessness and cartoon triviality that have misled a number of critics into dismissing his cabalistic scenarios—crucial to the novel's essential tension—as invalid. It is also in V. that we meet the collection of "monstrosities" and "misbirths" that constitute the Whole Rotten Crew, and who—while they can be read as the targets of a focused social satire on Pynchon's part—need to be perceived at a more profound thematic level as the deformed victims of gnostic malaise. And these victims, in turn, find their prototypes in the spiritually crippled roisterers and social misfits of the early short stories.

To return to normal chronology—and to the line of discussion opened earlier—the integrity of the neutral, barren cosmos that these stories assume, the cosmos of existentialism, is compromised from the beginning by intimations of hostile, sentient forces and world-historical conspiracy. The movement to V. is an attempt to explore the parameters of the gnostic world-view by taking more seriously the cabalistic hypothesis. Pynchon remains, at this point, locked within that world-view; but the exploration reveals a growing awareness of gnosticism's aggressive reductionism, especially with regard to human potentialities. It is a critique of the system from within the system, a metaphysical inquiry replete with intimations of a pregnostic harmony in which spiritual vitality and rapport with the order of nature were still possible.

The next, obvious step is to wonder whether some analogous harmony might not be instituted in the present, and this step is taken in The Crying of Lot 49. The attempt to find some source of spiritual revelation as an alternative to existential malaise, however, is compromised by Pynchon's inability—at this point—to imagine a revelation uncontaminated by the paranoia-inducing mystique of cabalistic gnosticism. The either/or of this novel fails, finally, to escape the basic gnostic duality; but it does succeed in sowing the hope that one branch of this duality, symbolized by the Tristero, may lead to a transcendence of the whole that involves not only a rapprochement with the natural order but the reenfranchisement of the preterite. It is not until Gravity's Rainbow that this intimation is developed into a relatively differentiated, antignostic value structure in the Orphic nature sympathies of the narrator. Even here, however, the path back to an integral cosmos remains a highly problematic journey through a cabalistic labyrinth; and the pervasive, insidious power of the gnostic vision continues to infect the very idea of history as a human unfolding—as a saga of autonomous questers in the freedom and potentiality of the metaxy.[39]

Probing the Nihil

Existential Gnosticism
in Pynchon's Stories

When Pynchon entitled his collected short stories *Slow Learner*, he had in mind chiefly those gaucheries of style that make these beginner's efforts—in his own words—"juvenile and delinquent too."[1] If we examine these stories for evidence of insight into gnostic paradigms, however, we discover that he was a quick study indeed. His characteristic concern with what we might call the cosmic context is already present in persistent intimations that the characters and plots of earth must somehow answer to a mysterious teleology of extrahuman forces. In a succession of six stories—written in as many years—climate and geography become signifiers of metaphysical oppression, demonic urges threaten the psyche's integrity, entropy makes its nihilistic debut, and a malignant cabal seeks to negate humanity itself. The dimension that will lend Pynchon's work the tone of a major inquiry is thus established from the beginning, whatever the artistic flaws that mar its first embodiments.

Preoccupied with these flaws, the author's preface to *Slow Learner* alternates between reticence and apology when it comes to recognizing the embracing themes of his juvenilia. Pynchon's remarks on the earliest of the stories, "The Small Rain," focus primarily on the younger self who wrote it and on the story's more or less unconscious insights into the American class structure. Other than the linkage with the preterite/elect dichotomy that these insights suggest, there is no attempt on the author's part to place the story in the thematic context of his more mature work; indeed, he seems to suggest that this early exercise lies beyond the pale, and should perhaps be granted leniency under some Youthful Offender Act. It is the perverse nature of a thematic study, however, to overlook such apprehensions—no matter how well-placed—and to trace a conceptual continuity that transcends radical changes in style.

In "The Small Rain" this continuity is signaled, ironically, by points of stylistic disjuncture—the very points where the now-accomplished Pynchon detects an incongruous admixture of sophomoric "literary" (p. 4) allusions to *The Waste Land* and *A Farewell to Arms*. What he now thinks of as "a whole extra overlay" of borrowed images mistakenly designed to give the characters and their story some satisfying fullness can more usefully be seen as the apprentice's instinctual groping for a metaphysical dimension—however derivative—that corresponds to his story's larger context as he vaguely perceives it. The "literary" seams that still show here, to Pynchon's chagrin, prefigure the world-historical inquiry that will later be given an original formulation and integrated into the actual artistic fabric of his mature work.

That Pynchon's particular instinct leads him at the very beginning to the early Eliot and to Hemingway as touchstones for this inquiry indicates the *a priori* nature of both his modernist orientation and his gnostic vision, as well as the link between the two. Although neither Eliot nor Hemingway appears to have drawn any traceable sustenance from the modern gnostic philosophers cited by Jonas and Voegelin, the world that each delineates is recognizably the realm of existential gnosticism, with its isolation, alienation, and fragmentation, and its persistent negation of transcendental values. When cosmic forces do manifest themselves, they seem to represent in the first instance the use of animism as an artistic strategy, the nightmarish projection of a massive, indifferent chaos that is nonetheless experienced as something antihuman.

Douglas Fowler, linking Pynchon and Eliot as "Gothic sensationalists," finds in the latter a sense of human consciousness "chained into nature" and forced to "witness . . . its own exquisite torturing."[2] In section five of *The Waste Land* the sustaining order of existence collapses into a surrealistic confusion demonically animated by "bats with baby faces" and "voices singing out of empty cisterns" (ll. 380, 385). The cosmos of *A Farewell to Arms* is at the mercy of random destructive forces vaguely personified as "they" and thus—despite their mainly heuristic function—anticipatory of the "They" who weave the web of Control in *Gravity's Rainbow*. Hemingway's shadowy plexus of malignity appears vigilant in rendering hope absurd; if you "stay around" at all, "they" will gratuitously "kill you."[3] At best, "they" act in the fashion of a halfhearted, blundering "messiah" (p. 328) who ends up destroying the objects of his casual concern.

But these apparently supernatural intrusions inevitably transcend their dramatic functions and change the ontological chemistry of the works in which they occur. They suggest that we have edged into a cabalistic modality and that the authors to whom the young Pynchon is drawn tend—in the actual practice of their art—to destabilize the opposition between the two varieties of gnosticism. This ambiguity reflects not only the dramatic uses of animism but also modernist despair over metaxic collapse. The memory of a sustaining transcendental framework may not be quite as immediate to Eliot and Hemingway, writing in the Twenties, as it was to Henry Adams; but it is still strong enough to evoke an analogous nostalgia. In the two later writers, however, the poignance of despair is tempered by a rebellious, sometimes sardonic stoicism. They inculcate in us a constant awareness of the void that must be filled—or at least dealt with—but also of the enormous loss that the void marks. The human thrown back upon its own resources both laments and attacks the collapsing systems that have condemned man to this peculiar existential heroism; and in the process the unacceptably indifferent cosmos is reanimated by the imagination with hostile demiurgic figures. To understand this nostalgic and reactive creativity in Eliot and Hemingway is to understand it in the century's later child, Pynchon, and to approach the springs of his oddly animistic cosmology.

"The Small Rain," set on and around an army base in the Louisiana bayous, is focused on the aftermath of a hurricane in which hundreds of people have drowned, and on the sterile *amours* of a soldier named "Lardass" Levine. The traces of Pynchon's cosmology in "The Small Rain" are to be sought mainly in the suggestiveness of his settings and in the self-conscious literary jokes of Levine and Rizzo—this latter a reminder that even the ironic throwaways of this author carry in them the seeds of an unironic metaphysic. When Levine expresses his hatred of rain, Rizzo retorts, "You and Hemingway. . . . Funny, ain't it. T. S. Eliot likes rain" (p. 51).

The Hemingway allusion is, of course, to *A Farewell to Arms,* where rain suggests a malevolence deep in the scheme of things, a negation so pervasive that no human construct can escape it. The rain is as inseparable from that novel's scenes of carnage—both public and private—as it is from the mass hurricane deaths of Pynchon's story, where it functions as both cause and integral atmosphere. A soggy landscape dotted with the corpses of the drowned and threatened by massive rain clouds becomes the backdrop for Levine's desolate lovemaking, and for his futile ruminations on the direction of his life. The sexual encounter with Little Buttercup recalls the copulation of the typist and the "young man carbuncular" in *The Waste Land* (l.231), with its mechanical lust and desecrating indifference, while the inability of a soldier nicknamed "Lardass" to find any destiny other than aimless drifting anticipates the "schlemihl" Benny Profane in *V.* The gnostic paradigm of gradual entropic exhaustion under desolate and vaguely hostile heavens is already in place.

This cosmic hostility is, of course, given a perverse twist by T. S. Eliot's alleged predilection for rain, a complication of symbolism that points beyond Rizzo's humorous contrasts to ambiguities deep in Pynchon's early metaphysic—ambiguities that will ripen into gnostic paradox. Levine admits that the rain can be life-affirming in its ability to "stir dull roots"— a direct echo of Eliot's "stirring / Dull roots with spring rain" (ll. 3–4). When Levine stands under the dormitory shower, cleansing himself of the smell of death, it feels like "summer and spring rain" (p. 48).

In *The Waste Land* the entropic malaise is symbolized by a sort of heat-induced inertia and sterility that set the tone for Pynchon's opening:

"Outside, the company area broiled slowly under the sun. The air was soggy, hanging motionless. The sun glared yellow off the sand" (p. 27). This infernal stasis is peopled by an "orderly leaning drowsy against the wall" and "an inert figure in fatigues lying on a bunk." We are not far from the "heap of broken images, where the sun beats, / And the dead tree gives no shelter" (l. 22–23) or from zombielike figures who are "neither / Living nor dead" and know "nothing" (l. 40). Eliot's language, charged with figuration and allusion, expands more easily into a metaphysical dimension; but it is precisely this language that reverberates in Pynchon's description, lending it a significance beyond its immediate function. Some such amplitude of reference, replete with enigma, is suggested by Little Buttercup's suspicion that what is "hazarding" Levine is "deeper than any problem of seasonal change or doubtful fertility" (p. 50).

If we accept that Pynchon's rain/sun symbolism hints at questions of an enveloping context for human existence and perhaps even at questions of cosmic governance, it becomes worthwhile to probe the ambiguities and contradictions involved. Since both the rain's flooding and the sun's drought can create the wasteland of sterility and negation, the cosmos is figured as a double bind in which opposing principles of Control both present themselves in structures inimical to human fulfillment. It is the paradigm, at least in prototype, of gnostic slippage, the no-win situation of the preterite.

The paradigm is further realized—and complicated—by the fact that both rain and sun are necessary, in proper balance, if there is to be fruition. The elementals of beneficence are also the elementals of destruction, and only a precarious equilibrium analogous to the *metaxy* prevents the collapse of the former into the latter. The life-affirming blurs into the life-negating, all within the framework of another unstable polarity, and echoes—in the context of natural process—the moral confusion of the gnostic dialectics: salvation/damnation within victim/oppressor. When we recall that natural process was, for the ancient Gnostics, demiurgic process, the leap from Pynchon's weather to cosmic hostility does not seem so far-fetched; and the same recollection will make clear why Pynchon must eventually revise this devaluation of nature if he is to escape the gnostic cul-de-sac.

For his earliest character, Levine, there is no such escape; he must function amid a chaos of values and sardonic echoes of metaxic collapse. The ceremonies of renewal slip automatically into parody, as in the aftermath of sex with Little Buttercup: "assailed still by stupid frog cries they lay not touching. 'In the midst of great death,' Levine said, 'the little death.' And later, 'Ha. It sounds like a caption in *Life*. In the midst of *Life*. We are in death. Oh god' " (p. 50). As often in Pynchon, the divinity as casual expletive expands to suggest the vacuum of the *deus absconditus* or the crucible of the demiurge.

Unable to find a definitive locus of value, Levine is a displaced person in the gnostic sense. If earth is the arena of an alienation too profound to be alleviated by earthly means, he must wonder in any given place "what the hell" he is "doing there" and whether he will be "wondering this" wherever he goes: "He had a momentary, ludicrous vision of himself, Lardass Levine the Wandering Jew, debating on weekday evenings in strange and nameless towns with other Wandering Jews the essential problems of identity—not of the self so much as an identity of place and what right you really had to be any place" (p. 49). In the universe of Lurianic cabalism, of course, all men are "Wandering Jews," the victims of a cosmic diaspora that has made homelessness a norm and "home" the stuff of prophetic fantasy, the Return to the Center. Denied the doctrine on which to base even a dream of reconciliation, Levine exemplifies the *Geworfenheit* of existential gnosticism in Pynchon's desolate century.

Since the introduction to *Slow Learner* is principally a humorous *mea culpa* for the collection's contents, one has to wonder whether "Mortality and Mercy in Vienna" lies outside the range of the repentable. Pynchon omits it from the collection without explanation or even mention, a mystery enhanced by the conflict between *Epoch*'s claim that this is Pynchon's "first published" story,[4] and Pynchon's own claim that this priority belongs to "The Small Rain."[5] At any rate, the near-simultaneity of their appearance (Spring 1959) makes it likely that Pynchon saw fit to let only one twin live because the same genetic defects were grossly magnified in the other. The network of literary allusions that now brings him chagrin in rereading "The Small Rain" is vastly enhanced in "Mortality" by a metastructure explicitly drawn from Conrad's *Heart of Darkness*—a modernist classic of epistemological ambiguity—and buttressed with the modernist likes of Santayana, T. S. Eliot (once more), Hemingway, and Lorca. But here again, what can be condemned as artistic gaucherie can also be lauded as the beginning writer's ambition to achieve a thematic dimension beyond melodrama; and once again, this dimension reveals itself as a complex frame of gnostic preoccupations.

It is necessary to gloss Conrad's story at some length because "Mortality and Mercy" is so intricately articulated with it. *Heart of Darkness* offers an almost perfect paradigm of metaxic collapse in the face of apeirontic energies, and thus an invaluable model for the atavistic apocalypse that builds and explodes in Pynchon's story. A nineteenth-century amalgam of European *noblesse oblige* and Christian responsibilities constitutes the transcendental imperative that defines humanity for the likes of Marlow and Kurtz and lays out its path of edification. Their imperial mission is also, in theory, a civilizing one, the cultivation of social ideals and spiritual orderings in realms of what they consider to be a subhuman disorder.

Faced with a primordial chaos that seems not only intractable but aggressive, the taut religio-ethical structures of the Europeans begin to slacken and degenerate, metamorphosing into grotesque simulacra of their earlier forms. In the merciless heat of the Congo, an accountant wears "starched collars and got-up shirt-fronts" even as he complains that the groans of a dying native are a hindrance to clerical accuracy.[6] This desperate obsession with sartorial order constitutes the same ludicrous parody of moral order as does the basing of the station manager's leadership on the accident of superior health. In both cases, vital spiritual principles are distorted into gratuitous physical constructs, as a "flabby, pretending, weak-eyed devil" (p. 17) erodes metaxic tension with the temptation of petty rapacity. A typical creation of this "devil" is the "papier-mâché Mephistopheles" (p. 26)—actually, the station brickmaker—who accuses Marlow of being part of the "gang of virtue" that includes Kurtz. This "gang," it seems, consists of those who consider themselves emissaries of "pity, and science, and progress, and devil knows what else" (p. 25).

The demonic imagery here—even the seemingly gratuitous "devil knows"—opens into vistas of demiurgic evil when we move to the case of Kurtz. The radical metamorphosis of the loftiest human idealism, Kurtz's transcendental calling, into an amoral empire of totalitarian exploitation, is the classical gnostic transformation delineated by Voegelin. Kurtz's practice of Control, with the presumption of godlike license, recalls the Rosicrucian maxim "Demon Est Deus Inversus" and brings us to the core of gnostic religiosity.[7] With transcendence jettisoned, the demiurgic arbiter is free to redefine the meaning of earth in terms of an absolutely dehumanizing and self-serving gnosis (recall the Russian sailor's belief in Kurtz's omniscience), and to demarcate his Center with the staked heads of the enemies of "Truth."

The atmosphere in which these horrific transvaluations occur, which in a profound sense leads to them, is one of spiritual desolation, traumatic unfamiliarity, and constant menace. The archetype of the nineteenth-century Congo is the realm of gnostic victimage, a place where ubiquitous cruelty and hostile vistas suggest the malignity of nature and of the powers that originally shaped it. Marlow experiences what Kurtz had presumably experienced before him—the "stillness of an implacable force brooding over an inscrutable intention. . . . with a vengeful aspect" (p. 34) on an earth that "seemed unearthly" (p. 36). It is easy enough to image the transformation of Kurtz as a sensitive, enlightened victim of all this into an oppressor who is both reflection and avatar of the very "horror" in which he had once found his spiritual antithesis.

This slippage is mirrored, inversely, in the native "brutes" whom Kurtz wishes to see exterminated (p. 51) and who attack Marlow and his "pilgrims." Although they seem to be, at first, mere projections of an apeirontic savagery, Marlow comes to realize the "remote kinship" (p. 37) of a common humanity with them and to admire the moral "restraint" (p. 42) of the cannibals in his crew. Even at this primitive level, there is differentiation between the human and the nonhuman, and it has occurred within a natural matrix. It takes the gnostic arrogance of Kurtz and his more ignoble compatriots, denigrating nature and ignoring its implicit boundaries, to deny these aboriginals any spiritual status and to turn them into preterite victims.

This ironic reversal, whereby a perversion of the civilizing mission's noetic thrust enforces a spiritual obscurity denser than that of nature, brings us directly to Pynchon's twentieth-century Washington as an urban heart of darkness. When the enigmatic Lupescu, host of the bizarre party-to-be, hands over his duties to Siegal, he tells the latter that he is going "outside . . . out of the jungle" (p. 199). His last announcement to Siegal is the famous announcement to Marlow: "Mistah Kurtz—he dead." This quotation conjures up not only Conrad's story but also—as Joseph Slade has noted—T. S. Eliot's poem "The Hollow Men," to which it is prefixed as an epigraph that serves the purpose of illuminating one gnostic vision with another.[8] Eliot's Kurtz was, presumably, one of the "lost / Violent souls" of that poem, a man who actively courted (and abetted) "death's other Kingdom" in contrast to the passive human scarecrows who have turned their society into a "dead land" of cactus and broken glass, a place of "Shape without form, shade without colour, / Paralysed force, gesture without motion." This is a vision of spiritual entropy, of available psychic energies dissipating to a "whimper" like Kurtz's final "cry that was no more than a breath."

Pynchon's dead souls are the party crew at Lupescu's, the prototype of the Whole Rotten Crew that sets the tone of cultural malaise in *V*. Their drunken boorishness and desperate hedonism, shot through with the pseudointellectual chatter of dilettantes and "Freudian cant" (pp. 210–211), are the symptoms of wretched lives that are little more than a gratuitous series of petty betrayals and vendettas and resultant bouts of guilt. Forced to listen to their confessions in his role as Lupescu's successor, Siegal realizes that Lupescu was beginning to experience a Kurtz-like contamination from the living death around him:

He wondered how his predecessor had managed to remain as father confessor for as long as he had. It occurred to him now that Lupescu's parting comment had been no drunken witticism; but the man really had, like some Kurtz, been possessed by the heart of a darkness in which no ivory was ever sent out from the interior, but instead hoarded jealously by each of its gatherers to build painfully, fragment by fragment, temples to the glory of some imago or obsession, and decorated inside with the art work of dream and nightmare, and locked finally against a hostile forest, each "agent" in his own ivory tower, having no windows to look out of, turning further and further inward and cherishing a small flame behind the altar. And Kurtz too had been in his way a father confessor. (p. 212)

Although Pynchon articulates no humanizing value system as explicit as that of Conrad's "gang of virtue," it is clear that we are dealing here with the collapse of such a system and with the wasteland as aftermath. If ivory is the currency of worship and reverence, or religious commitment, it must be "sent out from the interior" in vital interchange with some exterior ideal in order to achieve a transcendence of solipsistic sterility. Ignoring this imperative of communion and reciprocity, the crew at Lupescu's have deified their swollen self-images and carefully husbanded idiosyncrasies, and have achieved only the enervating stagnation of the closed system and the nightmarish claustrophobia that attends it. The "hostile forest," the alien earth that impounds the demiurge's anxiety-ridden victims, is glossed in an earlier passage as a psychological landscape:

> the badlands of the heart, in which shadows, and crisscrossed threads of inaccurate self-analysis and Freudian fallacy, and *passages* where the light and perspective were tricky, all threw you into that heightened hysterical edginess of the sort of nightmare it is possible to have where your eyes are open and everything in the scene is familiar, yet where, flickering behind the edge of the closet door, hidden under the chair in the corner, is this *je ne sais quois de sinistre* which sends you shouting into wakefulness. (p. 205)

This is the first description in Pynchon of the gnostic paranoia that will become his hallmark, and it illustrates vividly the pervasive and insidious nature of the infiltration. The familiar is, in a flash, the demonic. Debby Considine, who has lived her life in "terror of the unfamiliar" (p. 210) invading the everyday, tells Siegal that she would "lie awake nights, thinking of him [Paul] crouched up in that tree, like some evil spirit, *waiting* for me" (p. 209). Pynchon very clearly, in this early story, finds the provenance of alienation and paranoia in the diseased psyche of individuals—but individuals who have certain psychological and religious assumptions in common. It is in light of this commonality that he will eventually expand his sense of the malaise and its origins to the course of history itself, and even the course of nature.

The association of "the badlands of the heart," in the passage above, with "Freudian fallacy" (following an earlier reference to "Freudian cant") gives the allusion to Vienna in the story's title a significance quite other than that it derives from its source in Shakespeare's *Measure for Measure*. As Joseph Slade has pointed out (TP, p. 20), Pynchon obviously intends a parallel between Angelo's charge to clean up a corrupt Vienna—whatever "mortality" he must inflict in doing so—and Siegal's decision to let the corrupt bacchanals of Washington find "mercy" in sudden death. But Freudian psychology, as Pynchon construes it, is part of the problem, not of the solution. In his view, it is actually psycho*pathology*, a perverse enhancing and supplementation of the very sickness it is supposed to cure. This reactionary attitude brings Pynchon once again into line with the thought of Eric Voegelin and reminds us that their diagnoses of modernity are linked in some very basic ways.

Voegelin also locates a psychopathology (or, in its metaphysical mode, "pneumapathology") in Freud's analysis of human experience. In *Anamnesis* he includes Freud in a catalogue of gnosticizing thinkers—Hobbes, Hegel, Marx, Heidegger, Sartre, Lévi-Strauss—who distort, in various ways, the notion of a transcendental ground of being. "A Freud," he asserts, "diagnoses the openness toward the ground as an 'illusion,' a 'neurotic relict,' and an 'infantilism' " (p. 102). For Voegelin, Freud is a representative of "the modern *agnoia ptoides*" [ignorant aggressors] who "claim for their mental disease the status of mental health." He goes on to define this "disease" as a disturbance of the balance between *apeiron* and *nous* that constitutes the realm of the authentically human:

> Phenomena in the *metaxy*, of [a] psychological nature, are rashly fused in an act of libidinous transgression with the apeirontic depth in . . . the Freudian symbol of the libido, with the declared purpose of mobilizing the authority of the acheronta against the authority of reason. As the symbol of this revolt, furthermore, the unconscious appears in such variegated contexts as Freud's psychoanalysis [and] Breton's surrealism. (A, p. 108)

Voegelin takes the term *acheronta* from Freud's Latin epigraph to *The Interpretation of Dreams*: "*Flectere si nequeo superos, Acheronta movebo*"—"If I cannot alter the higher realm, I will move the Acheron." As the river of the dead, of the underworld, in Roman mythology, the Acheron serves Freud as a resonant symbol of the unconscious that in so many ways controls the "higher realm" of reason and upon which he can hope to have—as he cannot upon reason—some therapeutic effect. For Voegelin this analysis amounts to a gnostic transvaluation, a privileging of the infernal, the apeirontic depth, over the supernal phenomena of higher consciousness. He sees in the liberation of the unconscious the threat of a contaminating deluge—a psychical analogue to what Virgil's Aeneas sees as he approaches the Acheron: "A whirlpool thick / With sludge, its giant eddy seething, vomits / all of its swirling sand."[9] It is easy to comprehend, in light of Voegelin's interpretation, how Freud's Acheron flows into Conrad's Congo and how this confluence becomes the Potomac of Pynchon's story. The voyage into the primordial license of the libido, away from all spiritual restraint, provokes the psychic demons that destroy not only the humanity of Kurtz, but also that of the crew at Lupescu's.

The reader approaching this early story from the later perspective of *Gravity's Rainbow*, where primordial energies are closely identified with the Orphic norm, must wonder how they can be part of the abnormality against which the story's cathartic denouement is directed. The same ambiguity is present in Pynchon's treatment of the wilderness background of Irving Loon, the Ojibwa Indian whom Debby Considine has "collected" in Canada. Having inverted his *Heart of Darkness* paradigm to find the apeirontic "jungle" in the heart of Washington, Pynchon might be expected to locate in the wilderness some redemptive ordering analogous to Conrad's European ethic.[10] This he does to some extent in his characterization of Irving; but the fuller implications of the Ojibwa's spiritual make-up suggest that the wilderness also contains the dark psychopathogens that make this ordering necessary.

The explanation for these mixed signals seems to lie in the undifferentiated character of Pynchon's early gnostic vision. He is as yet unable to separate his sense that a generalized malaise exists from the possibility that it somehow has its origins in primal nature. One factor in this inability is the value structures inherent in the models he takes over from Eliot and Conrad, both of which privilege quasi-Platonic ideals of civilization over the realm of natural law. Moving instinctively toward the moral rehabilitation of nature, a process which must be completed before the Orphic norm can serve as a counterpoise to gnostic alienation from nature's order, Pynchon makes the wilderness of "Mortality and Mercy" normative as a foil to "civilized" decadence; but it still retains aspects of a hostile, quasi-demonic environment.

The Ojibwa was, if we can believe Debby, "happy back in Ontario" (p. 207), where a life of harvest festivals, "puberty rituals," and other ceremonies produced exactly the sort of cultural-religious communion lacking in the isolate, egocentric "temples" of the Lupescu group. We have here an anticipation of the Herero tribal life described in *Gravity's Rainbow*—a life of (for Pynchon) normative solidarity before the depredations of General von Trotha.[11] That Debby would see in this rich community life only "wonderful local color" for her notebooks is a symptom of the spiritual anemia to which that life provides an alternative. Her dilettantish fondness for his "divine melancholia" and his "poetic, religious quality" (p. 210) is complexly ironic in its reflection of her own inner darkness and its dim perception of the spiritual crisis that she has precipitated in him—a crisis that has some gnostic commonality with her own even as it engenders the hostile "act of god" that she has feared.

Pynchon's description of the perceptions that lead to the "Windigo psychosis" could easily have been written by Jonas or Scholem in their dealings with gnostic antiquity: "for the Ojibwa hunter, feeling as he does at bay, feeling a concentration of obscure cosmic forces against him and him alone, cynical terrorists, savage and amoral deities . . . which are bent on his destruction, the identification [with the Windigo] may become complete" (p. 208). The Ojibwa, not surprisingly, have a harmonious relation with nature during the plenitude of harvest and an adversarial one in times of hardship. In the latter instance, oppressed by "an austere and bleak existence," they turn upon each other with a cannibalistic ferocity that is the ultimate dehumanization and at the same time the ultimate identification with the "savage and amoral deities" that have oppressed them. Conrad's references in *Heart of Darkness* to "the gnawing devils of hunger" and "the devilry of lingering starvation" (p. 42) are given another demonic embodiment in the projection of the Windigo, "a mile-high skeleton made of ice, roaring and crashing through the Canadian wilderness, grabbing up humans by the handful and feeding on their flesh" (p. 208). The point in "Mortality and Mercy" is that Debbie and her crew themselves image the savage and amoral forces that oppress Irving and starve him of his spiritual sustenance—thus, the gnostic reversal by which the victim turns avenger and oppressor, denying the humanity in whose name he had suffered. His mass murder and cannibalism are a barbaric thrust from the heart of nature's darkness against the artificial darkness fashioned by a decadent civilization.

As "father confessor" (p. 212) to these neurotic bacchanals, Siegal grants this carnage the status of ritual purification, compounding the religious ironies already present with an admixture of Christian heresy. The "still small Jesuit voice" (p. 213) in his head—a voice that he associates with Machiavellian *Realpolitik*—urges him to go ahead with the "miracle" that is now "in his hands" by acquiescing in the slaughter. Through a grotesque—and essentially gnostic—reversal of values, he will be bringing "these parishioners . . . a very tangible salvation. A miracle involving a host, true, but like no holy eucharist" (p. 212). This parody of Christian terminology has the same purport of moral confusion as will the parody in *The Crying of Lot 49*, where the descent of a "malign, Unholy Ghost"[12] inaugurates a ritualistic orgy of torture and death. The consecration of the crew as "host" is, of course, a desecration in the name of a religion that unleashes savage forces rather than containing them, and that locates "salvation" in a kingdom of death. Mercy, in this realm of value distortion, consists of engineering mortality among those who inhabit a living hell of compulsive, quasi-Freudian self-analysis. It is necessary to destroy the Greenwich-type village in order to save it.

This conceptual melange of oppressor and oppressed, salvation and retribution, compromises Siegal's attempt to escape the barbarization that destroyed Kurtz, an earlier "father confessor" in his own right. Lupescu, according to Lucy, was already in the process of "going native" (p. 201) when he abandoned his role as the auditor of spirit-subverting confessions. Visible evidence of his atavism is provided when he tacks a pig fetus up by its umbilical cord and glosses the bizarre display as " 'Dada exhibit in Paris on Christmas eve, 1919 . . . used . . . in place of mistletoe' " (p. 198). This dilettantish mockery of natural process is given extra force if we look ahead to Pynchon's droll use of pigs as symbols of preterite innocence in *Gravity's Rainbow* and the identification in *V.* of Parisian avant-garde decadence and the gnostic Kingdom of Death. The Dadaists were dedicated emissaries of randomness, consciously practicing an "anti-art" that aimed at the destruction of meaning and order.

Voegelin, in a passage quoted above (p. 35), identifies the Surrealist movement to which Dada eventually led as a gnostic attempt to lend the "apeirontic depth" ascendancy over the higher human faculties. Their substitution of a dead embryo for an evergreen symbol of regeneration suggests an existence perversely enamored of its degeneration toward inanimate matter. Thus Kurtz, occupying the radical reaches of decadence, can scrawl "Exterminate the brutes" across a manuscript that had outlined a metaxic enterprise of exalting the human; and thus Siegal, fleeing a dehumanizing gnosis, can acquiesce in a gnostic extermination. Pynchon's degree of approval, or disapproval, is unclear. In the paranoic confusion that gnostic slippage breeds, retribution against the forces of darkness is itself compromised by this darkness. The cosmos seems engineered with a perverse ingenuity in which exits from oppression and malaise become reentries.

A year later, in "Low-lands," Pynchon seems preoccupied with locating some still point of refuge and vital connection on an Earth that the first two stories had sketched as an alien and menacing arena—a sign that he is already searching for a way to found a norm in natural process. The menace here does not consist of anything so overtly destructive as hurricanes or Windigoes, but rather of an enervating exposure to cold rationality, bourgeois dullness, and the rarefied air of disillusionment. All of these suggest, in the story's context, an impersonal and antiseptic systemization at odds with the labyrinthine, life-sustaining sprawl of the various "Low-lands" inhabited by the protagonist, Dennis Flange. If we cast this opposition in basic Freudian terms, it turns out to be a conflict between the repressive superego and the irrepressible id—a conflict in which Pynchon, like the early Auden, quite explicitly sides with the latter because it represents subversion in the name of life.

This valuation would seem to represent at least a tentative revaluation on Pynchon's part, a moving away from the Voegelin-Conrad suspicion of the subconscious as a source of apeirontic nihilism and toward a valorizing of natural impulse. Nonetheless, the story embodies a basic ambivalence about the forces that inhabit the depths of the psyche, especially when these forces are construed via Freudian grids. Dennis Flange is under the care of a psychiatrist, Geronimo Diaz, who is himself subject to spells of demonic (if entertaining) insanity. Sympathetic with the goal of psychotherapy, the liberation of human consciousness from life-denying repressions, Pynchon still finds the terminology and approach of "cure" hopelessly tainted with the alienation it is supposed to overcome. Once again, the mode of restoration is eerily inseparable from the mode of corruption, and we are dealing with a form of gnostic slippage analogous to that by which "mercy" is dispensed in the form of "mortality."

The first of Flange's "Low-lands" is his Long Island House:

[It] rose in a big mossy tumulus out of the earth, its color that of one of the shaggier prehistoric beasts. Inside were priest-holes and concealed passageways and oddly angled rooms; and in the cellar, leading from the rumpus room, innumerable tunnels, which writhed away radically like the tentacles of a spastic octopus into dead ends, storm drains, abandoned sewers and occasionally a wine cellar. (p. 56)

Flange feels attached to this "womb with a view" by "an umbilical cord woven of lichen and sedge" (p. 57). Behind the defensive humor of the Freudian parody lies a significant antignostic affirmation—Pynchon's early projection of primordial Earth as beneficent origin rather than neutral (or demiurgic) wasteland. The mystery, multiplicity, and fecundity of this subterranean maze serve as forces of opposition to the sterile, reductive schemes that threaten to make Earth's surface uninhabitable.

The antithesis here anticipates that made by Fausto Maijstral in *V.* as he contemplates his wife and child seeking shelter from German air raids in the sewers of Malta: "But in dream there are two worlds: the street and under the street. One is the kingdom of death and one of life."[13] By the time of *Gravity's Rainbow*, this search for the "kingdom . . . of life" will take Pynchon to the very core of an animate Earth as the planet's surface becomes the charnel domain of Control. The threat is more humorous than apocalyptic in "Low-lands," but the "austere and logical" (p. 61) compulsions of Flange's wife, Cindy, coupled with her suburbanite antisepsis, are serious enough to spoil his fetal contentment and drive him out. Her frenzied animus against Rocco the garbageman and against Pig Bodine— the latter not without its justification—looks toward the antipreterite mentality that forms an altogether more ominous strain of gnostic elitism.

The sea that crashes and slops beneath his bedroom window forms another more or less contiguous lowland for Flange. The psychiatrist Geronimo suggests that it constitutes an even truer mother image than the Earth because life began as sea-dwelling protozoa, and salt water originally served the function of blood. This demonstration that the sea is "quite literally in our blood" (p. 59) has a function more profound than its evident sophistry might suggest. We are led to the sense of a living intimacy between man and the planet of which the sea is an integral part—a marriage so basic that its rupture in forms ranging from urban indifference to environmental rapine also amounts to an assault on the very concept of humanity. This incredibly complex chain of vital organic connections will be central to the valorizing of nature in *Gravity's Rainbow*, and it is possible to find an anticipation of that naturalism's sustaining *metaxy* in the "sustaining plasma or medium" (p. 72) of the sea as it figures in the most vital memories of sailors. This is precisely the medium that supports Flange's cherished imago, the memory of himself as a lusty sea dog in a time before marital decline and suburban compromise. The Pacific, in particular, answers to this edifying function and enjoys a peculiarly cosmic mystique as "the chasm the moon left when it tore loose from the earth" (p. 59)—a mystical connection that will be reiterated, with normative force, in *The Crying of Lot 49*.

In "Low-lands," however, this valuation is compromised by the undifferentiated character of the symbol. The sea is also the converse of the mother, "a gray or glaucous desert, a waste land which stretches away to the horizon. . . . a minimum and dimensionless point, a unique crossing of parallel and meridian, an assurance of perfect, passionless uniformity" (pp. 65–66). This is the vacant, quite literally dispirited cosmos of existential gnosticism, a neutral and neutralizing realm that voids the possibility of a spiritual quest. It is thus the counterpart to the quasi-demonic wilderness of "Mortality and Mercy." It is significant that Flange also finds value in this apparently entropic state of zero energy. One part of him seeks an equilibrium so peaceful, secure, and absolute that it seems indistinguishable from the stasis of gnostic perfectionism. This stasis thus reveals yet another form of conceptual slippage in a complex semiotic of harmony and death, a web of ironic ambiguities inherent in gnostic conceptions of paradise. We will see a similar slippage in *Gravity's Rainbow* when Enzian and the Schwarzkommandos seek the Zero Point, but there the ambiguities are explicitly orchestrated within a differentiated value system. Flange's sea remains a contradictory melange of spiritualized nature and still-point mysticism as Pynchon struggles to achieve a critique of gnostic values from inside a network of gnostic assumptions.

A third lowland, the junkyard, is explicitly paralleled with the sea of the "passionless uniformity" exposition: "in the spiralling descent of Rocco's truck he had felt that this spot at which they finally came to rest was the dead center, the single point which implied an entire low country" (p. 66). The parallel implies that this lowland partakes of the same slippage, between a sustaining idyll that suggests a norm and a deadening stasis that violates that norm; but the normative element is enhanced by some new and seemingly unidyllic positives: detritus and the preterite. Wittily privileging the rejected and discarded in various forms from old tires to human beings, Pynchon projects value from gnostic negations of value. The failure to recycle wastes issues from the same arrogant exploitativeness that relegates human beings to the status of refuse. The garbageman Rocco, the reject Flange, the misfit Bodine, and Bolingbroke—black "king" of the dumpsite—exhibit great human warmth and solidarity in their sea-story communion as they restore to use what society's controllers had cast out. The gnostic wasteland of the later novels, together with its victim-inhabitants, receives a humorously literal anticipation here.

Beneath this lowland is the ultimate lowland, the labyrinth of gypsy tunnels inherited from a group of would-be revolutionaries who styled themselves "Sons of the Red Apocalypse" (p. 75). This humorous suggestion of subversion aimed at a goal of postapocalyptic perfection exactly fits a gnostic paradigm: the thirst of the alienated for the cosmic violence that must precede Return. That dream is quashed almost immediately by the prevailing social structure, but the preterite gypsies continue in a more literal and tenacious mode of subversion. Himself a refugee, Flange finds the goal of his descending quest, at least provisionally, in the subterranean room of the gypsy Nerissa. At three and a half feet tall, she is clearly an indigenous lowlander and also—as Flange's sudden perception reveals—the incarnation of the sea as spiritual center: "Whitecaps danced across her eyes; sea creatures, he knew, would be cruising about in the submarine green of her heart" (p. 77).

Her nurturing attitude, indicative of Flange's successful return to the womb, is grotesquely dramatized by her cradling of the rat Hyacinth. The name, of course, evokes—as Slade observes (TP, p. 30)—the "hyacinth girl" episode of *The Waste Land* (ll. 35–42), with its suggestion of failed fertility rituals. Since some degree of fertility is presumably realized in Nerissa's boudoir, the humor of Eliotic parody and grotesque "motherhood" acquires an ironically positive thrust. Pynchon is able, on the one hand, to distance himself from the stereotypical aspect of his fertility symbols, and on the other, to suggest the seriocomic poignance of a preterite community that links an outcast people to an outcast species. It is a theme to which he will return in V. with the conversion of the sewer rats and in *Gravity's Rainbow* with the conversion of the dodoes. The V. episode is intricately related to "Low-lands" in that it takes place in an "under-the-street" world of tunnels that provide refuge for the alienated and oppressed.

Malaise, as I have argued, is the given in Pynchon's cosmos. The search for its name, its causes, and the symbols to dramatize it is the larger concern of the stories we have examined so far. Drawing heavily upon such earlier diagnosticians as Conrad, Eliot, Hemingway, and Freud, Pynchon finds a pervasive cultural anomie threatening the fabric of human relations and the integrity of the individual psyche. In turn, the degeneration of the psyche feeds anomie; but there remains a larger cause, some enervating vector in the very climate of being. Climatic and geographic extremes—heat, flood, the Washington "jungle"—become metaphors that suggest this shadowy but potent animus, even as they mirror the resultant decline. On the level of social and psychic pathology, a similar function is filled by decadent, inanizing parties, sterile relationships, and hermetic retreat. The relation between the two levels, however, the cosmic and the human, remains vague and problematical.

Pynchon's next story, "Entropy," undertakes to bring these metaphors and levels together in a sort of "unified field" concept that not only explains and symbolizes degenerative malaise, but in a profound sense *is* that malaise. We are speaking, of course, of entropy as it is anatomized by Henry Adams, the pathologist of culture to whom Pynchon turns after Eliot and company. This natural phenomenon is, for both writers, so elemental in character and cosmic in scope that it becomes a negative re-flection of the transcendentals that its scientific provenance has helped to dethrone. Through it, Pynchon is able to extend his causal nexus back beyond psyche, culture, and climate of being to the primordial dynamics of nature. If entropy, the measure of disorder, constantly increases in an isolated system, and if—as Callisto postulates in the story—"galaxy, en-gine, human being, culture, whatever" (p. 87) constitute isolated systems, then existence must culminate in a universal stasis: "He . . . envisioned a heat-death for his culture in which ideas, like heat-energy, would no longer be transferred, since each point in it would ultimately have the same quantity of energy; and intellectual motion would, accordingly, cease" (pp. 88–89).

This comprehensive rationale of decline has complex implications for Pynchon's gnostic framework. If we have essentially no control over the descent of our societies and of our universe into silent chaos, if this descent is the result of inexorable physical law, existential gnosticism is the readi-est of metaphysical responses. Its gnosis entails a pessimistic denial of transcendence in the face of apeirontic apocalypse. As we have seen, however, this gnosis tends to mutate into the cabalistic strain. The very fierceness of the human thirst *for* some sort of transcendental referent, together with the apparition of entropy as a sort of grotesque Final Cause, encourages such a mutation. The impersonal cosmic death urge becomes in effect the demiurge of a savage religion, an orgiastic worship of chaos and death.

This is the strain to be elaborated in the novels, as is its antithesis: a set of transcendental possibilities that incorporate entropy into a larger, life-affirming scheme. But already, at the point we have reached in the early stories, the central dichotomy of Pynchon's ethic is emerging: the opposition between those who serve entropy and those who oppose it. As definitive as this distinction would seem to be, it nonetheless blurs in Pynchon's early gnostic matrix, which—as we have seen—tends to sub-vert differentiation. Those who accelerate the drain of energy and those who attempt to stem it both place themselves in opposition to natural process and in alliance with decadent artifice. The perversity of the en-veloping system is such that the means taken to combat negating forces become part of the negative polarity. What we see here is gnostic slippage accounting for the multiple and ostensibly incompatible implications of entropy, and being itself accounted for by the parameters inherent in a larger systemic unity. The rationale thus established goes at least part of the way toward rebutting David Seed's assertion, aimed at demonstrating the postmodern indeterminacy of Pynchon's fiction, that " 'Entropy' re-mains ultimately non-committal about the applicability of its eponymous central concept."[14]

The story is prefaced by an epigraph from Henry Miller's *Tropic of Cancer* that sets the tone of apocalyptic stasis:

Boris has just given me a summary of his views. He is a weather prophet.
The weather will continue bad, he says. There will be more calamities, more
death, more despair. Not the slightest indication of a change anywhere.... We
must get into step, a lockstep toward the prison of death. There is no escape.
The weather will not change. (p. 81)

Aside from establishing the totality and hopelessness of entropic malaise, this passage suggests at least two other motifs that figure in Pynchon's
vision of universal decline. One of these is the notion of Paris—the setting
of *Tropic*—as the plexus of twentieth-century decadence, the paradigm
site of infrahuman transformations. The other is the derivation of a moral
(or immoral) imperative from the inevitability of decline. That we must
get into a "lockstep" implies ritual acquiescence in a sanctioned morbidi-
ty, an acceptance of negation that somehow puts us right with the cosmos.
The "prison of death" is the grotesque promised land at the end of this
prisoner's progress.

The will to entropy takes the form here, as so often in Pynchon's work,
of a wild party characterized by various manifestations of physical and
spiritual disorder and by a miasma of emotional sterility. The connotations
of triviality normally attached to "party" are misleading in this instance.
The symptoms exhibited by the assembled bacchanti are ominously important as an indication of entropy's cultural dimension; and the fact that
such an assembly is entirely dedicated to the trivial is itself a sign of how
far degeneration has proceeded. Alcohol, drugs, and general neurosis in-
duce an alternation between frenzy and coma that suggests entropic chaos
and its consequent stasis.

The music at the party reflects both stages of degeneration: the decline
into chaos and the fall into silence. As a complexly ordered system of
sound energies subtly tied to a wide range of human emotions, music
makes the perfect vehicle for dramatizing the processes and penalties of
growing disorganization. *The Heroes' Gate at Kiev*, Mussorgsky's sono-
rous war-horse, is played at top volume ("27 watts' worth") over a "15-
inch speaker which had been bolted into the top of a wastepaper basket"
(p. 81). Its auditors are the terminally stoned musical group who produced
Songs of Outer Space: "From time to time one of them would flick the
ashes from his cigarette into the speaker cone to watch them dance
around." Music here becomes mere vibration, a mindless aural immersion
that is also the impetus for the random dance of waste particles. It is, in
fact, intended as part of a sound assault that belongs to the "lease-break-
ing" function of the party. The irony of the music's title is rendered transparent by the sentences from *Tropic of Cancer* that fill the hiatus of
Pynchon's epigraph: "The cancer of time is eating us away. Our heroes
have killed themselves, or are killing themselves."[15] Meatball Mulligan's
guests are clearly associated with cancerous erosion and not with its heroic
victims.

It is ultimately silence toward which entropy's declensions tend, corrupted music giving way to no music. Pushing the horizontal logic of jazz to its illogical conclusion, the Duke di Angelis quartet arrives at the conception of an entirely imaginary music. A soundless pseudoensemble moving its fingers on nonexistent instruments becomes a vivid parody of the harmony, lyricism, and rhythm that somehow mirror our larger orderings. What is finally parodied here is the transcendental pole suggested by the "unheard" melodies of Keats's "Ode on a Grecian Urn."[16] Beauty in its idealized projection plays directly "to the spirit," in Keats's phrase, providing the patterns of metaxic balance. Krinkles, Duke, et al., lost in an anarchy of private musical whim, symbolize the loss of order in the name of gaining it. When Meatball suggests that they reconstruct their notion—"Back to the old drawing board"—Duke replies, "No, man . . . back to the airless void" (p. 96). The dedicated production of nothing, in its most profound sense, could not be more clearly attested.

Reflecting on an earlier, larger arena—Europe after World War I—Callisto finds the prelude to this *nada* in the tango from Stravinky's *L'Histoire du Soldat*. This "sad sick dance" (p. 93) with its minimalist scoring seems to incarnate the decadence of an order irreparably undone by carnage. The "exhaustion" and "airlessness" of the music are the qualities of entropic collapse, and recall the "airless void" that Duke prefers to inhabit. There is also an ironic echo of the nineteenth-century *Heroes' Gate* in the effeteness of this twentieth-century *Soldat*. The dancers themselves anticipate the mechanistic nightmare of V., especially in its Paris manifestation (chap. 14): "what meanings had he missed in all the stately coupled automatons in the *cafés-dansants*, or in the metronomes which had ticked behind the eyes of his own partners?" (p. 93).

Meatball's friend Saul, a partisan of this automatism, cannot figure out why his wife grew upset over his comparison of human behavior to "a program fed into an IBM machine," and vehemently denies the suggestion that it may have been because he himself was "acting like a cold, dehumanized amoral scientist type" (p. 90). At its most ominous and presumptuous, technological gnosis holds that mechanical intelligence can bridge the gap between humanity and the machine, and that to perfect is to dehumanize. Stravinsky's tango suggests that this reductive intuition has infiltrated the modern consciousness to produce a perverted rapport with the realm of the inanimate. This concept of perversion becomes ambiguous, however, in the framework of entropic decline, where it is "natural" to experience the loss of differentiating energies, including those that define the realm of the human.

In this ironic light, it is Callisto and Aubade upstairs, the would-be reversers of entropy, who are unnatural in their attempt to achieve a recycling of energy. Callisto's "hothouse jungle," replete with exotic birds and plants from the tropics, is the essence of artificiality and isolation: "Hermetically sealed, it was a tiny enclave of regularity in the city's chaos, alien to the vagaries of the weather, of national politics, of any civil disorder" (pp. 83–84). Its equilibrium is an explicitly "artistic" one, the movements of its flora and fauna "all as integral as the rhythms of a perfectly-executed mobile." The vision of a beleaguered enclave in the midst of alienation and disorder is as quintessentially gnostic as the response centered around a sterile and artificial perfectionism. Paranoia combines with privileged gnosis to produce an elitist scheme of salvation from hostile cosmic forces.

It is also a futile scheme. Callisto's failure to revive a sick bird with his body warmth leads him to realize that "the transfer of heat" has "ceased to work" (p. 98). Entropy, the enveloping suicide of nature, ensures the death of nature's tiniest components, no matter how highly organized. By smashing the glass of the hothouse, Aubade affirms solidarity with the inevitable course of events and abandons the rearguard action of artificial rearrangement. She is choosing nature, but she is also choosing—ironically—among gnostic evils.

The full exploration of this irony involves recognition of the paradox that realizing one's humanity is an artificial enterprise in the sense that the realm of the human constitutes the locus of the transcendental quest. "Human nature" thus involves a going beyond nature in the striving for transcendental ideals and in the reflexivity by which one's position in nature becomes the object of contemplation and assessment. The same rhetoric that condemns Callisto and Aubade for unnatural, isolate orderings reverses, in this new context, to affirm the spiritual dimension that these very orderings demonstrate. A "perfectly-executed mobile" is, after all, a triumph of conception and creativity. Pynchon's music symbolism confirms this normative aspect of the hothouse. Aubade, whose name means "dawn song," has a peculiar sensibility that turns natural process itself into lyricism:

> In the hothouse Aubade stood absently caressing the branches of a young mimosa, hearing a motif of sap-rising, the rough and unresolved anticipatory theme of those fragile pink blossoms which, it is said, insure fertility. The music rose in a tangled tracery: arabesques of order competing fugally with the improvised discords of the party downstairs, which peaked sometimes in cusps and ogees of noise. That precious signal-to-noise ratio, whose delicate balance required every calorie of her strength, seesawed inside the small tenuous skull. (p. 92)

Aubade's effort here is finally one of spiritual ordering, of significantly structuring her relation to the fecund beauty of nature. The entropic cacophony downstairs rises in a constant assault upon this structure, symbolized by musical "arabesques of order." It is Aubade who must sustain the tension of a *metaxy* grounded at one pole by apeirontic "noise" and at the other by the "signal" of an ideal harmony of being. This desperate struggle for "balance" is the struggle to be human, and it hints, in its privileging of natural process, at the transcendental polarity of *Gravity's Rainbow*.

It is in this same normative light that we must examine the peculiar sentience of Callisto. He is differentiated from the oblivious pawns of entropy downstairs by his highly developed awareness of macrocosmic history, by his talent for acute diagnosis, and by a seasoned, self-reflexive humanity. These are qualities he shares with his "predecessor" (p. 84) Henry Adams and will share with a succession of Pynchon personae: the two Stencils of V. and the narrator of *Gravity's Rainbow*. Adams is really the presiding deity of this story, as he will be in V. Like Adams, Callisto keeps his diary in the third person to gain a more embracing perspective, and like Adams he "realizes" that "the Virgin and the dynamo stand as much for love as for power; that the two are indeed identical; and that love therefore not only makes the world go round but also makes the boccie ball spin, the nebula precess" (p. 84).

A basic gnostic ambivalence is present in the simultaneous admission of love as a powerful structuring element—an understanding crucial to metaxic balance—and the reduction of love to the level of mechanical power. Like Aubade, Callisto must struggle to maintain his human resonance against the vision of bleak mechanistic decline that entropy evokes: "He was aware of the dangers of the reductive fallacy and, he hoped, strong enough not to drift into the graceful decadence of an enervated fatalism" (p. 87). His peculiar mode of balance is "a vigorous, Italian sort of pessimism" (p. 88) that balances human skill and courage—*virtù* in the formulation that Pynchon adopts from Machiavelli—against the blind forces of *fortuna*. The entropic randomness predicted by statistical mechanics weights the scale heavily in favor of thermodynamic *fortuna*, threatening to destroy the balance that is humanity.

Because this growing randomness is part of nature's essence, it becomes problematic to project a transcendental ground from natural process. Dissolution, decay, and disorder hardly provide paradigms of spiritual harmony; rather, they mirror the apeirontic polarity, thus negating the possibility of a creative tension. The attempt of Callisto and Aubade to establish such a tension fails because they seek a natural equilibrium that no longer mirrors nature. Their little shrine to the recycling of energies is the relic of an obsolete religion that has become gnostic in its beleaguered isolation and its desperate artifice. Irony's final twist lies in the efforts of Meatball to keep the lease party from "deteriorating into total chaos" (p. 97). Arbitrating, aiding, repairing, he seems to represent some stubborn vestige of enthalpy—the antientropic tendency *toward* order—that resides even in entropy's hedonistic disciples. It is a human impulse to preserve humanity, the hint of a norm in the face of cosmic futility.

Ironically, it is entropy that continues to energize Pynchon's fiction.

Having appeared there as the definitive vehicle of decline, it never disappears; rather, it takes more sophisticated and insidious forms. The main hint of this evolution in the story "Entropy" is Callisto's reflection on European decadence as a form of energy dissipation. This decadence, in the mode of a cultural death wish and growing automatism, provides the focus of the story "Under the Rose," published a year later. It will be most useful for my purposes to treat this work in conjunction with V., since it forms—in a modified version—the third chapter of that novel. In the interest of thematic chronology, however, it should be noted here that "Under the Rose" establishes not only the world-historical canvas central to Pynchon's later studies in malaise, but also the notion of a widespread conscious conspiracy in the service of this malaise.

The story is concerned with the activities of English and German spies in the Egypt of the 1890s. Their machinations are part of a much larger plot to bring on (or to prevent) a European "Armageddon," a cataclysm that will entail the entropic collapse of civilization. That such an end should be explicitly sought through the manipulation of world politics and carefully engineered dehumanization gives a demiurgic scope to questions of cause and effect and heralds Pynchon's increasing focus on cabalistic gnosticism. In his useful contrast of "Under the Rose" as story and novel chapter, Douglas Fowler points out that human agency is deemphasized in the latter in favor of "history" as "something more mysterious and terrible than human beings could have made it."[17] This is true; but the very investiture of history with demonic shadows creates the possibility of an alliance far more ominous than any between spies. Human collusion in evil acquires the status of cosmic perversity when it expands to collusion with antihuman forces of historical process. The movement from "Under the Rose" to V. glosses just this expansion, and thus suggests a rationale for studying the two works as a single, comprehensive vision.

The last of the stories in *Slow Learner*, "The Secret Integration," is Pynchon's most conventional work of fiction, and therefore his most experimental. What, after all, could be more radical than for one of his stories to appear originally in the *Saturday Evening Post* and to present—at first glance—the ambience of a more erudite Norman Rockwell? The distinguishing metaphysical urgency of his writing seems suppressed here in favor of a narrower social urgency and the cultivation of period-piece nostalgia. The vehement racial prejudice central to the story's theme does not have the overtones of world-historical genocide that sound through V. and *Gravity's Rainbow*, nor is the crucial motif of preterite America linked to the shadowy schemes of the Tristero. It is as though a zoom lens had focused on the peculiar texture of small-town American life to the exclusion of the larger gnostic framework within which Pynchon habitually views this life.

Pynchon himself seems to approve of some such exclusion when he asserts in the introduction to *Slow Learner* that the story represents a "positive or professional direction" unfortunately "forgotten" by the time he wrote *The Crying of Lot 49* (p. 52). This judgment will appear perverse to most readers, a privileging of mediocre realism over gifted fabulation; but seen in this context it provides a valuable clue to Pynchon's structural intentions in the story. He was, he says, finally beginning to hear America talking, and also to perceive its "nonverbal reality" (p. 22). It was the "towns and Greyhound voices and fleabag hotels" of Kerouac's road that absorbed him and that seemed a key to the "deeper, more shared levels of the life we all really live" (p. 21). Sympathetic visions of this life—the skid row scenes, for instance—form a central motif in *The Crying of Lot 49*, where they are given a gnostic dimension by their connection with the Tristero network. Presumably Pynchon felt that "The Secret Integration," free as it was of this explicit machinery, offered a potentially more convincing integration of vision and dimension.

Whatever the case, a dis-integration of the story reveals that the familiar paradigms are present after all, disguised as child's play and casual comment. The gang of boys constitutes a secret, alienated enclave within the hostile macrocosm of adult society. Privileged by access to the gnosis of their leader, the precocious Grover, they plot the disruption of oppressive institutions and imagine an environment of brotherhood and freedom. This gnostic paradigm becomes parody, however, in the particulars of its execution. The "plots" are mainly schoolboy pranks such as flushing explosive sodium down toilets, infiltrating PTA meetings, and dropping water bags on moving cars. The dream of interracial fraternity ends with the banishing of the imaginary black playmate and the return of the "alienated" to cozy domestic rapport with the formerly "oppressive" adults. The subversive function of this parody is to diminish the boys' guilt in perpetuating the gnostic cycle of violence, but at the same time to suggest the futility of their integrative efforts against society's forces. The constant question in Pynchon is how one combats enveloping evil without becoming a part of it, and there is never a clear answer. The cartoonlike antics of the "Counterforce" in *Gravity's Rainbow* will attest to the same dilemma and to the same uneasy mixture of parody and norm.[18]

No such moral ambiguity attaches, however, to less aggressive forms of resistance: a sympathetic awareness of the preterite who have fallen victim to oppression, and the acts of charity that flow from this awareness. When the boys minister to Carl McAfee, the alcoholic and homeless black musician, they become avatars of a normative humanity, of a fellow feeling that transcends its individual focus to comprehend the preterite desolation of the continent. McAfee's tales of transient encounters in lost places are redeemed from oblivion by becoming part of a growing moral consciousness that will, in turn, fabricate an imaginary black child named Carl from "phrases, images, possibilities that grownups had somehow turned away from, repudiated, left out at the edges of towns, as if they were auto parts in Étienne's father's junkyard—things they could or did not want to live with" (p. 192). The secret integration unifies more than black and white; it restores to the commonality all that had been alienated and rejected by the controlling forces. The gnostic dream of Return is realized in an act of imagination that will have crucial implications for Oedipa Maas in Pynchon's next novel and for the narrator of *Gravity's Rainbow*.

In the world of the story, however, as in the world outside it, the forces prevail against the dream. Hostile police take the luckless McAfee into custody, and affectionate parents suborn the young rebels with showers, towels, and goodnight kisses. The truth of adult reality is a relentless fragmentation that invades imagined communions, leaving the boys with "dreams that could never again be entirely safe" (p. 193). This is the early onset of Pynchonian paranoia, that suspicion that potent mysterious forces are shaping a future inimical to humanity. This sense of siege and foreboding lends, in retrospect, a gnostic coloration to certain details of the story. Grover explains that "Operation A," their latest subversion, is a reference to "Armageddon," though Tim had guessed "Abattoir" (p. 155). Together, the terms recall the specter raised in "Under the Rose"—the consciously engineered end of human community. It seems a long way from the mock-heroic antics of children to plots against existence itself, but—as Pynchon wryly points out—"You didn't have to know what initials meant to drill kids."

The gradual and insidious extinction of the human is also reflected in the ascendancy of estate housing and machines. Northumberland Estates, the project where "Carl" is imagined to live, is a nightmare of geometrical conformity and sterile openness. No privacy exists there, no hidden nooks where sustaining fantasies can thrive. Its designers attest the indifference of bureaucracy to the life of the spirit, and thus prefigure the gnostic entrepreneurs of *Lot 49* and *Gravity's Rainbow*. Not surprisingly, it is a junkyard owner who warns of a related danger, the absolute triumph of automatism: "My [Étienne's] father says everything's going to be machines when we grow up. He says the only jobs open will be in junkyards for busted machines. The only thing a machine *can't* do is play jokes. That's all they'll use people for, is jokes" (p. 150). The uniquely human provenance of humor is precisely what makes it valuable as a weapon against machinelike behavior, a fact not lost upon Mark Twain's Satan or upon Pynchon's gadfly personae. Once again, however, we are given the vision of a future in which neither idealism nor humor has availed to preserve humanity from reduction to an apeirontic "joke." Metaxic balance is precarious, the forces of disruption are seemingly inexorable—such is the pessimistic formula that finally emerges from the early stories and that will, in fabulous permutations, inform the later novels.

THREE

Depraved New World

Gnostic History in V.

The movement from the story "Entropy" to "Under the Rose" embodies, as I have indicated, Pynchon's transition from a focus on mid-twentieth-century America to a blatantly "world-historical canvas"; and the novel into which the modified version of "Under the Rose" is incorporated expands this historical focus to metahistorical dimensions, elaborating upon the possibility that consciously antihuman forces play a crucial role in shaping history. The framing of this possibility *as* possibility, as one of two equally feasible alternatives, represents a significant step on Pynchon's part toward differentiating his compact gnostic vision. The binary opposition of existential gnosticism and cabalistic gnosticism is at last made explicit, rather than remaining submerged in the representation of an existential wasteland through quasi-demonic imagery; and the opposition in turn gives rise to an epistemological quandary, the notorious dilemma over which interpretation actually represents the case of things. The dentist Eigenvalue, though an advocate of the existential view, frames the contention elegantly in a complex (and oft-quoted) metaphor:

> Cavities in the tooth occur for good reason, Eigenvalue reflected. But even if there are several per tooth, there's no conscious organization there against the life of the pulp, no conspiracy. Yet we have men like Stencil, who must go about grouping the world's random caries into cabals. (p. 153)

Tony Tanner, in his essay "Caries and Cabals," leaps too quickly to identify Pynchon's view with Eigenvalue's.[1] The bulk of the novel's seemingly serious, dramatic moments are based upon Herbert Stencil's "impersonations," vignettes of cabalistic intrigue that he projects from stray scraps of information. Stencil's credibility will be the subject of later comment; but it is worth pointing out here that unless these projections are taken seriously, as genuine possibilities, they collapse into fodder for a rationalistic debunking of the very notion that history might be shaped by conscious, premeditated agency, and the book's essential mystery is dissipated into rather flaccid satire.

One might go even further and assert that the potent and constantly recurrent presence of V.—the feminine persona (or personae) whose relation to the cabalistic option is more or less that of demiurge, of a malevolent goddess-figure presiding over the dehumanization of history— lends this option a sort of *de facto* preponderance. Even her reduction, under an existential interpretation, to a gratuitous series of women in a series of coincidental appearances, does not prevent the powerful complex of symbolism attached to her from continuing to operate; and in this case it figures a goddess-shaped emptiness, an oddly negative divinity that serves as the genius of a historical process driven by random, antiseptically neutral forces.

Both alternatives—the presence experienced as hostile manipulation and the absence experienced as alienating neutrality—obviously depend for their significance upon the *positive* conception of a nurturing, sustaining femininity that inspirits the cosmos and underwrites our ultimate relation to it. This is the archetypal projection that we sum up in the notion of the "eternal feminine" or—in Jungian terms—the Great Mother. The cabalistic V. represents a perversion of this archetype into something consciously destructive, the existential V. a simple evacuation of it; but both subvert the affirmation that the archetype offers—the centrality of the human to the processes of nature and of history.

One upshot of these considerations is that Pynchon needs to draw upon a powerfully realized version of the archetype in all its positivity if he is to invest its negative variants with the proper significance. Actually, he turns—as his allusions have helped his critics to specify—to a variety of sources for images of a fertile, beneficent femininity;[2] but it is the work of Henry Adams that serves as his really indispensable point of reference. The frameworks of metaphysical suggestion that Pynchon erects in V., using Adams as a foundation, make the corresponding frameworks of his stories—the melanges of motifs from Eliot, Hemingway, Conrad, and others—seem shadowy and provisional.

The Education of Henry Adams and *Mont Saint Michel and Chartres* in particular form a paradigm that enshrouds the novel in a complex, intimate network of touchstones, echoes, and parodies. This reciprocal mirroring, complete with planned distortions, extends from parallels between theories of history and between the personae who enunciate them to particular, crucial images that resonate fully only in their interaction. If Pynchon is, as Joseph Slade asserts, "deliberately mocking Adams" (TP, p. 52), the mockery is in the final event that of a sympathetic parody that ironically reflects the parodic structures of gnosticism. And if we are to accept John A. Meixner's more extreme charge that Pynchon "has been raped by Henry Adams,"[3] it is necessary to see this rape as an oddly fruitful one. Casting Pynchon as an unlikely Leda, perhaps, and the father figure Adams as Zeus, we might end up with V.—a daughter even more degenerate and apocalyptic than Helen of Troy, and invested with the world-historical ironies that Yeats explores in his famous sonnet on the subject.

Pynchon has left his critics no choice but to address themselves to the Adams connection; and the result has been an astute body of comment on Adams's theory of historical process, especially as it projects an entropic decline into a chaotic, dehumanized neutrality. This decline is figured, in the now-familiar symbolism, by the metamorphosis of the life-affirming Virgin into the life-negating dynamo. Pynchon's stroke of inspiration is to personify the latter as a grotesque simulacrum of the former, a mechanized apostle of disorder and death. He is thus able to incorporate in a single symbol the various *stages* of dehumanization, with each stage under the aegis of a correspondingly degenerate goddess. It is, by design, an unstable symbol, one that constantly images the extremes of a divinely sanctioned unity and a demonically sanctioned chaos—and thus becomes the perfect vehicle of gnostic parody. In its various forms it dominates *V.*, from the allusion to Dante's Beatrice on the third page to the image of Astarte on the last.

It is impossible to register the full import of the symbol—and thus of the novel—without examining its context in the work of Pynchon's mentor Adams more thoroughly than has been done so far. This is because, as indicated above, Adams's context so intricately pervades Pynchon's. This interpenetration is most evident—and most crucial—in the polarity that generates the contexts. If we juxtapose Adams's vision of an earlier culture unified by a divine symbol, the Virgin, with his vision of the chaos to come, we have the poles of the *metaxy* that will also lend pattern and significance to the events of *V.*

Adams's Virgin was the avatar of a spiritual norm, a protectress who gave meaning, focus, and redemption to human experience and reconciled this experience to the rest of nature. That such a reconciliation is necessary points us back toward the other pole of the *metaxy*, the one at which all spiritual orderings give way to a mindless anarchy that is the final inanimateness of entropy. Adams sees this "anarchism" specifically as the end result of a centuries-long decline from the unified vision of a human *telos* anchored in divinity through the symbol of the Virgin:

> The assumption of unity which was the mark of human thought in the middle-ages has yielded very slowly to the proofs of complexity. . . . Yet it is quite sure . . . that, at the accelerated rate of progression shown since 1600, it will not need another century or half century to tip thought upside down. Law, in that case, would disappear as theory or *a priori* principle, and give place to force. Morality would become police. Explosives would reach cosmic violence. Disintegration would overcome integration.[4]

This is the classical symptomology of the collapse that attends the loss of the metaxic tension. Robbed of a transcendental ground such as that symbolized by the Virgin, or even of the illusion of such a ground, humanity experiences the dissipation of those ordering structures that define and differentiate humanity, and sinks in a series of violent spasms toward the apeirontic depths—in this case, toward an inanimateness defined by the absence of the incarnate anima.

Adams establishes himself as an existential gnostic by regarding this drift as inevitable, the human dimension of inexorable entropy. The unity based on the Virgin was an "assumption"; the loss of this unity is the result of "proofs." Man is finally seen to be a force among other natural forces, but one peculiarly at odds with the rest of nature, against which he sets his "Will." He gains access to greater supplies of natural force, but this increase is accompanied by a corresponding decrease in ability to control this force through assumptions of unity. Adams's vision of the triumph of undifferentiated, impersonal nature is also a culmination of the gnostic refusal, the rejection (in his case, reluctant) of the transcendental ground necessary for the differentiated life of the spirit. If we know only blind and neutral nature, then we must be prepared for the horror of apeirontic reunion with it—a horror figured for Adams by the fatal illness of his sister Louisa:

> The first serious consciousness of Nature's gesture—her attitude towards life—took form then as a fantasm, a nightmare, an insanity of force. For the first time, the stage-scenery of the senses collapsed; the human mind felt itself stripped naked, vibrating in a void of shapeless energies, with resistless mass, colliding, crushing, wasting, and destroying what these same energies had created and labored from eternity to perfect. Society became fantastic, a vision of pantomime with a mechanical motion. (EHA, p. 983)

It is significant that the "Nature" presiding over this return to the inanimate remains a "her" in Adams's formulation. The Virgin of Chartres and Venus—"Venus *genetrix*," as Lucretius calls her, "life-giving Venus"—have degenerated to a terrifying goddess who promotes suffering and the dissolution of organic form to an inchoate force field. The dynamo, it seems, has its own ruling antispirit, its decreating deity, a figure that can be best projected as a negative of the redeeming Virgin—in short, as Pynchon's V.

If, then, we reverse this projection from the data of a novel clearly dedicated to the depiction of degeneration, entropic and otherwise, we arrive at an implied norm closely related to Adams's Virgin. I am not, of course, suggesting that Pynchon, any more than Adams, is an advocate of Christianity *per se*; but rather, that for both writers there is a nostalgia for human unity with an enveloping order—for a total communion of existence that requires a symbol of feminine nature and procreative power on a cosmic scale, an anima associated with a transcendental ground toward which humanity can look from the discontinuity, uncertainty, and strife of history. Although neither believes that such a symbol is available, in any viable form, to his own time, both look to the humanizing order it once provided as the hallmark by which modern degeneration is defined and measured.

The divine dispensation represented by Adams's Virgin is a peculiarly tolerant one, recognizing and forgiving human imperfection even as it provides the edifying light of moral imperatives. In this sense, she renders the *metaxy* habitable by mitigating divine absolutism in the name of humanity and earthly reality. As John Carlos Rowe puts it in discussing Adams's *Mont Saint Michel and Chartres:*

> The Virgin relies on the participation of the common man in a worship that celebrates temporal as well as eternal love. . . . [She] does not deny the difference and variety of human life with the finality of the Trinity. . . . God is absolute in His Word, the logos itself the origin and end of definition. The Virgin's incarnation is seen as the process of the divine defining itself, the activity of grace in the world and the vital relation of man to the universal. The Virgin's cosmos is full of energies unified in her moving center.[5]

Melvin Lyon's succinct comments on "the Virgin as the Dynamo" serve to reveal both poles of Adams's (and Pynchon's) *metaxy:*

> The Virgin . . . is the greatest symbol man has ever created of his own humanity and the sense of unity which is his essence. It represents man at the zenith of his selfhood. The dynamo represents man at the nadir of that selfhood, his sense of unity almost gone, the reality of chaos on the point of breaking through his humanity. The absolute antithesis of the human Virgin is the nonhuman multiverse.[6]

Temporal love, humanity, selfhood, unity—these virtuous conditions are conspicuous by their rarity in V.; but when they do appear, in some transient manifestation, they quickly acquire a normative function through contrast with the hostility, cruelty, personal dissolution, and chaos that prevail in Pynchon's portrait of modern entropic collapse. Even this function, however, is qualified by Pynchon's sense (one found also in Adams) of an inexorable historical process, an assault of apeirontic energies that reduces the unifying symbol to a heuristic metaphor of no real spiritual moment. Thus, as in Voegelin, history plays its role in eroding the transcendental ground of the *metaxy* and destroying the viability of its symbol.[7]

Pynchon's treatment of the V. myth is basically the record of this erosion; but before dealing with its specifics, we must take into account its mode of transmission in the novel. We learn about the woman called V.— or at least about several women so similar that they fit the V. archetype— from the "confessions" of the poet-engineer Fausto Maijstral, from the epigraph by (presumably) Pynchon himself, and from the conjecturings of Herbert Stencil. Since the bulk of what we "know" comes from the last of these, we are faced with certain problems created by Stencil's character, evidence, and methods. More precisely, we discover that he is a clownish, rather ineffectual character given to severe doubts about the ultimate significance of his search for V.; that he relies upon obscure jottings in his diplomat-father's diary, a few bizarre relics, and hearsay for his data; and that he synthesizes these data into a coherent narrative through a process of "impersonation and dream" (p. 63).

Not surprisingly, a number of critics have detected the titillating aroma of epistemological crisis here, and have tended to join Pynchon's character Eigenvalue and Pynchon's critic Tony Tanner (see above, p. 99) in dismissing Stencil's projections as an illusory "grouping" of "random" events into a cabalistic "conspiracy" against life (V., p. 153). But, as we have seen, the locus of epistemological ambiguity in Pynchon is likely to be the locus of significant mythologizing, the site of an attempt to fabricate a metaphysical grid that will accommodate both existential and cabalistic interpretations of existence in a common sense of religious urgency. A cold, positivistic analysis of the "factual" *premises* of Stencil's visions misses the thrust of the visions, as well as Pynchon's skeptical attitude toward cold positivism. As Peter Cooper astutely puts it,

> Herbert Stencil observes not the micro underpinnings of one Situation so much as the macro motion of Western civilization. The question is not whether he fabricates, but whether his fabrications allow for some insight.
>
> Pynchon did not make Stencil such a complete fool or paranoiac as many readers find him, for to destroy entirely his credibility or threat of discovery would eviscerate the fiction. The crucial and characteristic tension between order and disorder could not exist if Pynchon debunked one possibility altogether.[8]

We must consider also the role played by the quasi-satirical deformations of a gnosticized existence, as outlined in chapter one above. The same force field that—with some regularity—warps Slothrop and his quest to a comic grotesquerie in *Gravity's Rainbow* warps Stencil and *his* quest; but in both cases the onto-epistemological issues involved in these quests continue to constitute the serious thematic core of the two novels. Here it is V. who—like Blicero—is treated nonironically, as a satirist-surrogate, but whose "norm" is flagrantly abnormal in comparison with the humanity-centered values of which the victims Stencil and Slothrop still partake.

Finally, the validity of Stencil's mythologizing must be based not only on these considerations, but on how we interpret the parody of Henry Adams which he obviously represents. To put it another way, we must take his "impersonations" at least as seriously as we take the interplay between the contexts of Adams and Pynchon. It is an issue that will be best addressed when we have examined this interplay more closely.

Since *V.* is a study of dual degeneration—that of a symbol and of the civilization it symbolizes—our best point of entry is Fausto's confessions, which contain an overview of the combined process. Born on Malta, and reared as a Catholic, Fausto has had immediate experience of a feminized transcendental, both as the anima of the island and as Adams's Virgin. The first three stages of his life, as set down in his diary, reflect the degeneration of this composite symbol from unifying Mother to inert matter, while the fourth suggests some vestige of spiritual power that brings him back toward humanity. Fausto I is filled with the "optimism" (p. 310) of youth, much of which is bequeathed to the more thoughtful and consciously poetic Fausto II, who "finds island-love and mother-love impossible to separate" and who thus makes a mystically conceived Malta the equivalent of the Virgin of Chartres:

> Malta is a noun feminine and proper. Italians have indeed been attempting her defloration since the 8th of June. She lies on her back in the sea, sullen; an immemorial woman. Spread to the explosive orgasms of Mussolini bombs. But her soul hasn't been touched; cannot be. Her soul is the Maltese people, who wait—only wait—down in her clefts and catacombs alive and with a numb strength, filled with faith in God His Church. How can her flesh matter? It is vulnerable, a victim. But as the Ark was to Noah so is the inviolable womb of our Maltese rock to her children. Something given us in return for being filial and constant, children also of God. (p. 318)

In yet another diary entry, he discusses his refusal to "dwell on death" not only because he is young but "perhaps more on this island because we've become, after all, one another. Parts of a unity. Some die, others continue. If a hair falls or a fingernail is torn away, am I any less alive and determined?" (p. 319). When we consider also that this Fausto spends a great deal of time crouching underground in Malta's "womb of rock," it becomes apparent that this Virgin symbol is also the symbol of an inspirited "Earth," one that anticipates the transcendental anchorage of *Gravity's Rainbow*, and thus marks another stage in Pynchon's gradual differentiation of beneficent nature from gnostic nature.

The Great Mother, as a composite of the Virgin and Venus *genetrix*, has certain functions: unifying, nourishing, regenerating, protecting, inspiriting. These are perceived as real and effective by the Fausto of stage II, who also finds in the island a timeless identity with his ancestors and their fertility rituals. The sacred, transcendental nature of Malta as Virgin is sealed by its description as "this God-favored plot of sweet Mediterranean earth." Even the term *Mediterranean* is significant in defining the metaxic status of Malta. Albert Camus, himself an analyst of the twentieth century's dehumanizing ideologies, finds incarnate in this area of Europe a very human "Moderation" and a harmony with nature that are anti-thetical to the gnostic violence of German "Excess"[9]—a distinction that the beleaguered Maltese would appreciate. For Fausto, the early days of the siege are the apex of selfhood and unity, a time of heightened poetic consciousness and reverence for existence; and they mark the interval in which he feels himself most obviously the beneficiary of a grace beyond history and its violent processes.

It is, however, these violent processes, in the form of incessant German raids, that finally destroy the sense of a living spiritual center and cause the "Siege" of Fausto and his friends to move from "the quick to the inanimate" (p. 320). The bombings are precisely that humanly controlled energy that in turn controls us by destroying our integrating symbols. Fausto, himself moving more deeply into the inanimate, defines the process as "decadence. . . . a clear movement toward death or, preferably, non-humanity" and associates this movement—surprisingly—with the "mother-rule" of his "matriarchal island" (p. 321). His rationale for this association takes us right to the heart of the link between the degeneration of the Virgin symbol and the growth of existential gnosticism. Mother-hood, once viewed as a mystical ground that animated existence in a unifying pattern, is now seen as an "accident," a "random conjunction of events" that is really no more than a "fictional mystery" (pp. 320–321) perpetrated by conspiring mothers. The purpose of this fiction is to compensate for the mothers' awful realization of the "Truth," which is

> that they do not understand what is going on inside them; that it is a mechanical and alien growth which at some point acquires a soul. They are possessed. Or: the same forces which dictate the bomb's trajectory, the deaths of stars, the wind and the waterspout have focussed somewhere inside the pelvic frontiers without their consent, to generate one more mighty accident. It frightens them to death. It would frighten anyone. (p. 322)

Fausto's explicit association of this accidental and initially soulless "zygote" with the Virgin Birth represents an explicit desecration of the Virgin symbol, while his equation of this symbol's mystique with obscurantist fiction constitutes a demystifying that destroys the attendant concepts of unity, nature, and spirituality. The inanimate becomes the Inanimate, a transvaluation that actually privileges *apeiron* over *nous*, and sets the stage for us to understand V.'s more or less religious devotion to the former. We are witnessing the ascendancy of the Adamsian vortex of impersonal energies, an alien multiverse of pointless atomic collisions in which it is impossible to make a moral distinction between the destructive forces of gravity, entropy, and natural disaster on the one hand and the force of regeneration on the other. The destruction of the transcendental pole of the *metaxy* brings a collapse of the very discriminations and orderings that define the spiritual dimension of humanity, and leaves only the indiscriminate chaos of the *apeiron*. Accident rules, and all accidents are equal. One is reminded of the Marabar Caves in Forster's *A Passage to India*, where the filthiest expletive and the most sublime rhetoric elicit identical echoes.

Fausto comes to regard this nihilistic erosion of values as the result of a conflict between "human law" (p. 322) and divine law, a classical gnostic formulation of the problem of cosmic alienation and divisiveness. If the ordained scheme of things is seen as grounded only in a massive inanimateness and indifference, then the principles by which humanity is defined must ultimately remain in a hopeless state of siege, gradually eroding under the pressure of vast energies unaccountable to any logos. A god with no face becomes equivalent, in dehumanizing, to a god with a hostile face. Without some sort of transcendental pole that calls us to a higher spiritual destiny than the materiality of the *apeiron*, we cannot prevent the slide into the Inanimate. Again, the key is differentiation, of a sort that will find in humankind a complexity of a different spiritual order from that of machines. As Fausto puts it, "I know of machines that are more complex than people. If this is apostasy, hekk ikun. To have humanism we must first be convinced of our humanity. As we move further into decadence this becomes more difficult" (p. 322). Fausto's transvaluation of the machine is indeed "apostasy," and of a peculiarly gnostic variety. It is a falling away from the "true" religion centered upon the spiritual potential of the animate as manifested in humanity, and an embracing of the Inanimate heresy.

It is crucial that a *metaxy*-sustaining symbol such as the Virgin remain transparent in a religious sense, i.e., that it continue to point toward a transcendental scheme of things if it is to remain effective. The moment it becomes opaque and loses its unique power of signifying a higher order of reality, this order itself is called into question. These considerations have a peculiarly urgent relevance to Fausto III, who—as a poet—is "always acutely conscious that metaphor has no value apart from its function; that it is a device, an artifice" (pp. 325–326). The task of the poet, cynically put, is to cloak the "innate mindlessness" of "a universe of things which simply are" with "comfortable and pious" metaphor in order to sustain the illusion of an animate bond between man and his world. If this vision of an incoherent, inanimate universe is taken as axiomatic, then metaphors of vital connection indeed offer nothing but delusion and the "Great Lie," and there is no escape—at least for the self-conscious crafter of these metaphors—from a condition of gnostic alienation. The "street of the 20th Century" (p. 323), with its mindless decadence and its inexorable, solitary endings, waits as our ultimate reality. The refusal to give a deeper assent to the metaphor's linkage, to at least the possibility that the whole is animated by mysterious but real connections, dooms language to triviality and existence to despair.

By contrast, this animistic sense of existence has been preserved in

Mehemet, the xebec captain who continues to recognize the viability (the V-ability) of the transcendental female symbol in the form of Mara, a Maltese fertility goddess. Himself a legendary refugee from the Middle Ages, Mehemet is the possessor of a centuries-old wisdom that marks him as the Jungian "wise old man," an archetypal figure who represents in turn the male pysche's successful assimilation of the archetypal anima, i.e., Mara.[10] "Mara" is Maltese for woman, and this apotheosis of woman is a love deity closely related to Astarte, the goddess who provides the xebec's figurehead and is the Syrian counterpart of Aphrodite. The account of Mara that Mehemet told to Stencil makes it clear that her original function was to nurse men and to teach them the arts of love (it is hardly surprising that she served "the shipwrecked St. Paul" [p. 461] in the former capacity rather than the latter).

An additional function as protectress is added when she saves her Maltese flock from the Turks through a combination of aphrodisiacal and magical powers. More particularly, she restores a eunuch to potency and causes the detached head of a Turkish sultan to spread rumors that break a Turkish siege of Malta. This latter feat was celebrated in song by a "latter-day jongleur" who regarded Mara as "his Lady" and whom "No Renaissance had ever touched" (pp. 464–465). The parallel between his lyric for Mara and the verses produced by medieval French troubadours for Mary is inescapable, and leads us back once again to the metacontext that *Mont Saint Michel and Chartres* provides for *V*. In his chapters "The Three Queens" and "Les Miracles de Notre Dame," Adams analyzes these songs as an aspect of the cult of the Virgin. Like Mara, the Mary of the lyrics and priestly poems does not hesitate to intervene on behalf of her charges at the expense of existing schemata. As Adams puts it, "she upset, at her pleasure, the decisions of every court and the orders of every authority, human or divine; interfered directly in the ordeal; altered the processes of nature; abolished space; annihilated time" (p. 586). It is a paradigm of miraculous intervention that clearly covers Mara's supernatural feats and further links Pynchon and Adams in a common value locus, nostalgia for a feminized transcendental.

Since Mara is the animating spirit of Malta, it would seem fair to take Mehemet's early feelings toward the island as his feelings toward the goddess in his medieval phase. Return to Malta was like a reverential reunion with the living heart of the sea, "something my own heart needs as deeply as a heart can" (p. 457). At this point, then, the goddess anchored a productive spiritual tension for Mehemet. For the Mehemet of 1919, however, this blind trust has given way to an ambivalence that retains the sense of animate relation to nature and to history, but incorporates a new awareness of the animating spirit's fickleness. Thus his warning to Stencil upon arrival in Mara-haunted Valletta—"She's an inconstant city. Be wary of her" (p. 457)—and his earlier warning: "Beware of Mara" (p. 465). It is clear that Mehemet has moved from revering an image of benevolent deity like the Maltese Gaea-Tellus whom Fausto II espoused, to fearing an image of cosmic menace—Venus *genetrix* declined to a capricious demiurge who is finally indistinguishable from the goddess of fortune.

This change is reflected in the contrast between the "living figurehead" (p. 462) of Mara lashed to the bowsprit of the Turkish ship and the wooden sculpture of Astarte, "goddess of sexual love" (p. 456) that serves as the figurehead of the xebec. The former heroically saves her people through the exercise of her powers; the latter leans toward Valletta "as if it were male and asleep and she, inanimate figurehead, a succubus preparing to ravish" (p. 457). The disorder and violence of Malta at this period are symptomatic of just such a ravishing and reflect the degeneration of the feminine life principle into the Jungian archetype of the Terrible Mother— the Medusan opponent, as Erich von Neumann puts it, of "the mobility of the life stream that flows in all organic life," the advocate of "petrifaction and sclerosis."[11]

It is this V. figure in various human guises who structures the novel as a symbol of gnostic declension toward the rule of the Inanimate. She is a counter of twentieth-century history, herself declining toward an automaton even as she presides over a series of scenes that are microcosms of that history's progressive pathology. We first encounter her in Cairo during the Fashoda crisis of 1898, with France and England on the brink of a war in which Russia and Germany would have to become concerned. In the earlier short story "Under the Rose," from which this incident in the novel is drawn, the British spy Porpentine sees Fashoda as the potential spark for a worldwide conflagration: "Not just a small incidental skirmish in the race to carve up Africa, but one pip-pip, jolly-ho, up-goes-the-balloon Armageddon for Europe."[12] It is just the sort of seedbed of apocalypse that V. will be drawn to for the rest of her life, as she moves from being a voyeur of the Inanimate and its forces to being its active agent.

The gnostic element in this progress, or regress, is registered by the increasingly heretical relation of V.—in her manifestation as Victoria Wrenn—to the Catholic religion in which she was reared. Educated in a convent school, she decides to become a nun, but leaves the novitiate "after a matter of weeks" (V, p. 72) because she cannot be the exclusive bride of Christ. This desire, laughable in its naivete, is nonetheless symptomatic of the usurping temperament of gnosticism, of the wish to place one's own self at the plexus of power instead of sharing a divine dispensation with the rest of humanity. She becomes a manipulator and rearranger of her religion, seizing upon the dramatic potentialities of the Mass in order to construct a universe in which a colonialist God battles "an aboriginal Satan" (p. 73). This fantasy of imperialist oppression as the divine logos suggests that the natural (aboriginal) order is evil and that it must be purged or suppressed by an artificial white empire that arrogates to itself cosmic sanction for its dominion—a gnosticizing of history that will become more hubristic and more thorough in the genocide committed against the Hereros, and will reach its maximum metastasis in the Cartel of *Gravity's Rainbow*.

V.'s loss of her virginity to the English spy Goodfellow represents an obvious-enough desecration of the Virgin symbol, but the event is freighted with multiple associations and overtones that link this desecration with the increasing ascendancy of the Inanimate. The most important of these is the connection between the phrase "under the rose" that served as the title of the original short story, and the Rose windows of Chartres. In *Mont Saint Michel and Chartres*, Henry Adams develops at length the relation between the Virgin and a rose symbol in which he senses "Our Lady's promise of Paradise" (p. 474). As Rowe phrases it, "the rose is her [the Virgin's] virtual incarnation and blossoming for the world of man."[13] Both symbols then, the Virgin and the rose, together with their promises of harmony and grace, undergo simultaneous degeneration in the deflowering of V. by an agent dedicated to sub rosa activities. It is apropos, in this connection, that the phrase "sub rosa" itself is thought by lexicographers to stem from the legend that a rose was used as a bribe to keep the indiscretions of Venus—another aspect of Adams's Eternal Feminine—from being revealed.

Earlier in the novel, the phrase is used with explicit reference to the spreading cult of the Inanimate as exemplified in Da Conho's love for his machine gun and Rachel Owlglass's love for her MG: "Love for an object, this was new to him [Profane]. . . . he had his first intelligence that something had been going on under the rose, maybe for longer and with more people than he would care to think about" (p. 23). To sink sub rosa, then, is to sink away from the ordering, spirit-sustaining powers of the Rose and toward the apeirontic depth, the subhuman realm of blind entropic process that constitutes late Adamsian nature. In the Western Rose Window of Chartres, Adams had seen "a confused effect of opals, in a delirium of color and light, with a result like a cluster of stones in jewelry" (p. 472). This epiphany of transcendental hope in the name of the Queen of Heaven stands in parodic contrast to the brutal end of V. on Malta. Transformed by this point into the Queen of the Inanimate, the spokeswoman of death, she has literally *become* artificial gaudiness and bedizenment. Her dismemberment by children who remove a clockwork eye, jeweled teeth, and a star sapphire navel—this last with the point of a bayonet—symbolizes the sterile crucifixion of a false god, a violent death without hope of resurrection; and is, in that very lack, an ironic testament to the preeminence of violence and death in the gnostic religion that she serves with increasing awareness as she approaches her end.

The V. symbol, then, constantly suggests both the apex of human experience and its lowest declivity. It also embodies in its progressive narrowing the process of degeneration by which the former becomes the latter, as we see from the description of the Nile Valley by Waldetar, the Egyptian train conductor: "The point of the green triangle is Cairo. It means that relatively speaking, assuming your train stands still and the land moves past, that the twin wastes of the Libyan and Arabian deserts to right and left creep inexorably to narrow the fertile and quick part of your world until you are left with hardly more than a right-of-way, and before you a great city" (p. 82). The two V's are both here: the tiny inner V of lush, life-sustaining farmland and an encompassing, contiguous V of inanimate wastes. This bivalent figure is the very model of gnostic parody, a simulacrum of creativity and growth that ultimately serves death. Cairo's position at the apex makes the city the unavoidable end point of encroaching sterility, the urban cul-de-sac of twentieth-century decline.

Apical to both desert and lushness, Cairo is an appropriate flashpoint for the "Armageddon" that certain sub rosa agents seek, and still others hope to prevent. According to Christian eschatology, this battle is to be fought on Judgment Day as the decisive struggle between good and evil. The triumph of good is to result in the Last Judgment, which is one of the episodes depicted in the Western Rose of Chartres. Here again, the context provided by Adams penetrates the immediate context of V. to furnish a touchstone by which degeneration can be measured. For Adams, the terrors of the Apocalypse are not only mitigated by the transcendental beauty of the Virgin as Rose, but transformed into forces of her "infinite mercy" (p. 474), assurances of "pardon," "love," and "pity" that ultimately cancel the harshness of God's deserved judgment on mankind. Thus, the metaxic tension is not destroyed by an immanentized terminus of history, but retains its quality as the locus in which the human is continually animated and affirmed.

V., however, presides over a very different version of the Last Judgment. She is a goddess-in-training for the gnostic forces of the Inanimate—forces whose victory at Armageddon would mean the desolation of Earth and the extinction of humanity, all in the one-way time that negates the possibility of redemption. In the "Under the Rose" version of these events, Porpentine—attempting with Goodfellow to prevent the catastrophe—realizes that "Lepsius, Bongo-Shaftesbury, all the others" are not simply extensions of the master spy Moldweorp, with his "rage for apocalypse" (SL, p. 118), but are also part of a massive conspiracy in the service of the Inanimate: "They were all in it; all had a stake, acted as a unit. Under orders. Whose orders? Anything human? He doubted" (p. 134). Instead, Porpentine now imagines the "bell-shaped curve" of a "Gaussian distribution," an impersonal "Force, Quality" (pp. 134–135) constantly exerted against all that is personal and animate. Bongo-Shaftesbury is able to become the coldly mechanical executioner of this "Force" by flipping an electrical switch implanted in his arm, an artificial surrogation that anticipates the automating of V. herself. Conversely, the besieged, ravaged humanity of both Porpentine and the young prostitute attacked by Mold-weorp is shown by their grotesquely flayed skin, a symbol of dehuman-izing assault throughout the novel proper. It is in fact Porpentine's demonstration of humanity that finally results in his death at the hands of the robotic Bongo-Shaftesbury, who considers love, hate, and sympathy reprehensible, and defines humanity as "something to destroy" (V., p. 81). In this conscious animus against all things human, Bongo-Shaftesbury is revealed as the agent of forces more malignant and ubiquitous than the German Empire. Once again, we are dealing with the gnostic project of absolute surrogation, the definitive usurping of an abhorred natural order by what amounts to an empire of death. It is appropriate that this project is imaged by the sterile abstraction of the Gaussian curve, the perfect "god" of "order" for the vortex of random impersonal forces that share a common vector of entropic decline.

Less than a year later, we find V. in Florence, that center of Machia-vellian *virtù*, i.e., of political machination at its most cynical and cunning. It is significant that her nascent political convictions include a detestation of socialists and anarchists. The latter group will come to symbolize, in *Gravity's Rainbow*, a love of freedom and natural process at odds with gnostic designs of control; and V. herself, within the next twenty years, will be in the service of fascistic plots designed to suppress freedom through the cynical and extremist exercise of *virtù*. Fascism is singled out by Voegelin as an example of the modern gnosticism that preaches order while ultimately bringing chaos.[14] *Virtù* as a tool for limited political objectives is not incompatible with metaxic order; carried to hubristic extremes, however, it results in the collapse of this order and becomes the ally, often inadvertent, of entropy and death.

This development in V.'s politics is an outgrowth of the imperialistic brand of Catholicism that she had embraced as a child and that lends itself to a process which conflates politics and religion into an increasingly gnosticized whole. Within the few months since her "deflowering" by Goodfellow, this ex-virgin has slept with three other men for payment, episodes that she regards in her "outre brand" of Catholicism as "outward and visible signs of an inward and spiritual grace belonging to Victoria alone" (p. 167) and as a surrogate consummation with Christ himself. This peculiar sort of hubris, which allows her to invert the normative values of the church for her benefit in the name of a private and unique rela-tionship to deity, is gnostic in nature, as is the air of metaphysical ag-gressiveness implied by "a nunlike temperament pushed to its most dangerous extreme." By pointing out that "in Paris similarly-minded la-dies were attending Black Masses," Pynchon suggests V.'s association with the systematic desecration of sacred symbols and the reconsecration of them in the service of demonic forces. In the case of V.'s increasingly perverted sacrality, such transvaluation will finally amount to the elevating of the entropic vortex over a vital spiritual order and of inhuman stasis over human development.

We have already seen, in the Cairo episode, how Pynchon uses Adams's account of the iconography at Chartres to dramatize this process of perversion. The same device is extended in the Florence section to an elaborate parody through the conjunction of V. and Botticelli's *Birth of Venus*. The theft of this painting is the object of Mantissa's elaborate plot and is motivated by his sub rosa love for a canvas image which is, after all, just as inanimate as Da Conho's machine gun and Rachel's MG. Once again, the material simulacrum has replaced the animating spirit. The chapter title, "She hangs on the western wall" (p. 152), constitutes an explicit link between the painting's position in the Uffizi and the placement of the Virgin's image on the western wall of Chartres. Adams describes her as occupying "the central window" of the three lancets beneath the Western Rose, "with her genealogical tree on her left, and her Son's testimony on her right" (MSMC, p. 465). This "testimony" is the Passion of Christ, with the Crucifixion itself displayed in the middle of the lancet. The parodic degeneration of this symbol is found in the comb purchased by V. in a Cairo bazaar. The five teeth of this grotesque adornment consist of five crucified British soldiers carved in ivory by a Mahdist tribesman in commemoration of the Massacre at Khartoum. Thus it symbolizes a sort of imperialist Passion, exactly in keeping with V.'s own gnosticizing religion and the vicious suppression of native populations that this "resurrected" imperialism will entail in twentieth-century kingdoms of death.

The "genealogical tree" of the Virgin is the Tree of Jesse, the ancestral nexus that leads ultimately to the Annunciation and promises the fullness of time in the birth of Christ. Its parodic counterpart in V. is the hollow Judas tree left in front of Botticelli's *Venus* as part of the robbery plot. Emptiness in the place of fullness is this tree's promise, an emptiness attendant upon the Judas-like betrayal of the illuminating *metaxy* to the blind processes of the *apeiron*. Mantissa reads this desolating potentiality into Venus herself as he watches Cesare slicing the picture from the frame. The goddess of sexuality and fertility is suddenly glimpsed as the malign ruler of a phantom wasteland, "A gaudy dream, a dream of annihilation" (p. 210).

This phrase, and the remembered image of a colorful spider monkey frozen in ice, link the artificial Venus to the Antarctic explored by Hugh Godolphin, and in turn to his fantasy land of Vheissu. The provenance of Vheissu is the most explicitly gnostic of any symbol in the novel. Godolphin finds the decisive clue to the symbol's meaning at the South Pole in a howling barrenness "like a country the demiurge had forgotten" (p. 205). This substitution of the shaping demon of Gnosticism for "God" in the stock description of desolate purlieus sets the stage for an even more significant and ominous usurpation, as Godolphin realizes when he ponders the significance of the "rainbow-colored" spider monkey frozen in the ice thousands of miles from its habitat in tropical Vheissu:

> I think they left it there for me. Why? Perhaps for some alien, not-quite-human reason that I can never comprehend. Perhaps only to see what I would do. A mockery, you see: a mockery of life, planted where everything but Hugh Godolphin was inanimate. With of course the implication... It did tell me the truth about them. If Eden was the creation of God, God only knows what evil created Vheissu. The skin which had wrinkled through my nightmares was all there had ever been. Vheissu itself, a gaudy dream. Of what the Antarctic in this world is closest to: a dream of annihilation. (p. 206)

Godolphin's epiphany reveals the extent of gnostic surrogation. Retroactive to the mythic origins of the race, the cabal's plot substitutes a flamboyant "garden" of death for the fecund plexus of all life. This inverted Eden suggests that in the beginning was the Inanimate, that its logos is decreation, and that its entropic Kingdom is coming to destroy the last illusions of organic vitality. Such is the power of the demiurgic forces that "They" can plant a colorful "mockery of life" at the almost-inaccessible still point of Earth, bringing about through the shock their ultimate triumph: causing the animate to doubt its animateness, to identify with seemingly ubiquitous barrenness. The insidious message of Vheissu is: "V.'s you."

Henry Adams found in the Garden of Eden an epistemological tension between "God who was unity, and Satan who was complexity, with no means of deciding which was truth" (EHA, p. 1083). Thus, if we imagine Satan creating his own Garden, we find primordial harmony replaced by what Godolphin calls the "barbarity, insurrection, internecine feud" of Vheissu, and the fundamental order of creation giving way to a "madman's kaleidoscope" in which "no sequence of colors is the same from day to day" (p. 170). This perpetual singularity—which anticipates the realm of "Westwardman" in *Gravity's Rainbow*—is finally the chaos and randomness of the entropic vortex no longer held at bay by such unifying symbols as the Virgin and Eden.

The question of whether this apparent disorder conceals some spiritual center—a "soul"—is one that had preoccupied Godolphin during his visit. Comparing the flamboyant surface of Vheissu to the "skin of a tatooed savage," he concludes that the country's "music, poetry, laws and ceremonies" are themselves no more than "skin" (p. 170). Since these are principal indices of spiritual vitality and resonance, it seems unlikely that Vheissu has a soul or that its integument conceals anything other than the apeirontic depth of which it is actually part. To fall in love with Vheissu is to become eventually so frustrated by this alien and alienating surface that one prays for "some leprosy" to "flay that tattooing to a heap of red, purple and green debris, leave the veins and ligaments raw and quivering and open at last to your eyes and your touch" (p. 171). But "leprosy" takes us back phonologically to Lepsius, the henchman of Bongo-Shaftesbury, as well as the flayed skin of Moldweorp's victims. This disfiguring process is explicitly identified with the forces of the Inanimate, forces whose ally Vheissu would drive one to become in the name—ironically—of love. The goddess of the Inanimate herself, V., ordains the process during the riot in Florence when Godolphin has to drag her away "from an unarmed policeman, whose face she was flaying with pointed fingernails" (p. 487). "Riot," the description of Vheissu's flamboyant chaos, "was her element," and as such it constitutes the negation of the ordered *metaxy* anchored upon the Virgin.

So absolute and cataclysmic is this negation that it carries us beyond the nostalgic secularity of modernism and into "the postmodern scene" as Arthur Kroker finds it projected in Baudrillard's "brilliant hologram," a scene located at "that rupture where the representational space of modernist perspective dissolves into the detritus of fractals, fuzzy sets, and bodies without organs."[15] Looking for an analogue to the treasure-hunt dismemberment of V.—herself, by that point, a collage of parodic artifacts—and to the orgiastic flayings that are at once both aesthetic and ideological, we arrive at the paintings of Francis Bacon and Alex Colville— works that represent a postmodernity, in Kroker's phrase, "exceeding Baudrillard":

> In Bacon and Colville's artistic productions, the body alternates between its suspension in an infinitely imploded and inertial state of pure hermeticism (Colville) and its dispersion *en abyme* in the exploding detritus of the schizoid ego (Bacon). Here, the pain of the external condition is so overwhelming that the gaze turns inward as the body implodes into the density of a sign with no referent; and there the body is turned inside out—actually peeled open— as its organs are splayed, like negative photographic images, across the field of a dead, relational power. To be buried alive in the perspectival fictions of their own skins, or splayed across the postmodern scene with all their organs hanging out: these are the alternative images presented by Bacon and Colville of panic bodies at the *fin-de-millennium*. (p. 185)

This physiological apocalypse is a symptom, for Kroker, of "the *fatal implosion* of the Cartesian subject. . . . in an ultramodern culture where Mind is exteriorized in the structural paradigm of telematic society" (p. 181). This dissolution of structured human innerness in the name of a relational exteriority is, it will be recalled, the target of Pynchon's irony in the "Subimipolexity" episode of *Gravity's Rainbow* (see above, pp. 19–20). It is clear that as early as *V.*, his imagistic instincts are at work projecting a grotesque, flamboyant archetype of dehumanization that decisively indicts the postmodern scene.

After recounting the Florence episode, Pynchon interrupts the chronology of V.'s career for a number of reasons, some of which will be made clear later. Certainly one of the most pressing is the need to extend the Vheissu theme into a more realistic and ominous dimension through another encounter between V. and Godolphin. Setting this encounter in German Southwest Africa in 1922 gives Pynchon a chance to look backwards toward the genocidal slaughter of the native Hereros in 1904 and forwards toward the Nazi death kingdom that these atrocities anticipated, while 1922 itself provides an atmosphere of Weimar decadence easily related to the encroachment of the Inanimate.

The "siege party" at Foppl's farmhouse is presided over not only by Foppl himself, but also by Lieutenant Weissmann and V. Under the name of Vera Meroving, V. becomes a Queen of the Night to Weissmann's King, anticipating the role that Greta Erdmann will play in *Gravity's Rainbow* as the diabolical counterpoint to Weissmann-Blicero. The siege mentality is focused not only on defense against native attacks, but on a defense against the passage of time. The attempt to turn the clock back to 1904 and freeze it there is symbolized both by the cultivation of earlier settings and rituals (including 1904-style atrocities) and by the clockwork eye with which V. has replaced her natural one in an act of homage to the Inanimate.

V. explicitly equates the year of genocide and the gnostic Garden of Evil when she tells Godolphin that "Lieutenant Weissmann and Herr Foppl have given me my 1904. . . . Just as you were given your Vheissu" (p. 247). The difference is, as Godolphin notes, that the private fantasies based upon Vheissu have been transformed into public realities of a particularly grisly sort, the working out of "three-o'clock anxieties, excesses of character, political hallucinations on a live mass, a real human population" (p. 248). The gaudy "dream of annihilation" associated with "iridescent" spider monkeys and Antarctic wastes is the one literally realized in a desolated Sudwest washed by Antarctic currents and heaped with native corpses "bejeweled green, white, black, iridescent with flies and their offspring" (p. 269). The parody of the gemlike luminescence that overwhelmed Adams before the Western Window of Chartres is grotesquely evident here, as is the parody of the Virgin's universal solicitude by rites of wholesale slaughter. If Godolphin was the inadvertent recipient of a gnostic revelation, Foppl and his guests are its committed executors as they substitute a static Kingdom of Death for the ancient rhythms of native life around them. In the hallucinatory atmosphere created by gnostic magic, the guests relive Foppl's role in the atrocities of 1904, interweaving remembered murder with the very real and present murder (usually by flaying) of Foppl's native servants.

Foppl's love of General von Trotha, who instigated the massacres, has a clearly gnostic basis in that it involves a relief from metaxic tension, which is to say, from the constraints of being human: "He taught us not to fear. It's impossible to describe the sudden release; the comfort, the luxury; when you knew you could safely forget all the rote-lessons you'd had to learn about the value and dignity of human life" (p. 253). The "fear," of course, is the fear of transgressing against the very value system that defines humanity, and that requires a moral posture perpetually aware of the anchoring ideal. But if humanity is redefined in terms of brute, amoral power—a typical value mode of modern gnosticism—it is effectively abolished as a differentiating moral concept, and its enabling posture relaxes in a luxurious sinking toward the apeirontic depth. It is significant that Foppl compares this perverse relief to being excused from memorizing historical dates. What is sought by him and his fellow genocides amounts to escape from a history replete with moral and social determinants into an atemporal freedom, the godhead of unanswerable license.

The desecration is a conscious one and is enhanced by the perversion of ritual and religious symbol. Chained together by cruelly heavy links, a procession of Hottentot prisoners resembles a mural in a German village church: "the Dance of Death, led by a rather sinuous, effeminate Death in his black cloak, carrying his scythe and followed by all ranks of society from prince to peasant" (p. 262). The Dance depicted here functions in a Christian *metaxy* to encourage the maintenance of moral vigilance, not its relaxation, while death itself is a terrifying presence but also a natural, inevitable, and universal one.

Gnostic surrogation on the part of the genocides systematically subverts and inverts this symbolism to produce a Death that is itself the ultimate religious agent, rather than the enemy and spur to that agency. It is also an artificial and arbitrary substitution, consciously engineered and restricted to the helpless preterite mass, who experience the sjambok in place of the scythe. The total parody of a shared religious association is enough to give the "unpopular chore" of herding the prisoners "an atmosphere of ceremony" (p. 262). V.'s earlier heretical fantasy of a colonialist, aborigine-killing God in a "wide-awake hat" has been realized here in a perverted version of "Väterliche Züchtigung . . . fatherly chastisement" (p. 267), the Terrible Mother complemented by the Filicidal Father in an archetypal nightmare world. Since this "Father" is identified not with a transcendental pole of justice and harmony but with the absolute negation of this pole in the name of arbitrary murder, the Ideal is collapsed into the *apeiron*, and the gnostic kingdom reigns supreme.

The metaphysical pretensions of this kingdom, and of the gnostic religious experience it incorporates, become clear when the troopers experience "an odd sort of peace" (p. 264) in killing the rebellious Hottentot and project the same feeling onto their victim. This union of "destroyer and destroyed" produces a sense of universal "pattern: a great cosmic fluttering in the blank, bright sky" that brings all future victims "into alignment . . . a set symmetry, a dancelike poise." This moment of mystical ecstasy is the apprehension of a unity, one based upon a *telos* of murder. Humanity systematically exterminates humanity in defiance not only of life-affirming morality but of the life principles inherent in nature. It is a cosmic usurpation. Man undertakes to supplant the gods and principles that supposedly transcend him, and to destroy the given of creation in an exhibition of both physical and moral ascendancy that is finally an act of spiritual warfare.

This universal surrogation is mirrored in the surrogate universe of Foppl's planetarium, with its wooden planets and wooden sun. The "gold leaf, burning cold" (p. 239) that covers the latter is an index to the parody of nature's life-sustaining processes by dead artifice that informs the novel's structure, while the "coarse cobweb of chains, pulleys, belts, racks, pinions, and worms" that drives the system suggests a nightmare of raw mechanical complexities replete with overtones of sadism. The use of a black slave (a "Bondelschwaartz") on a treadmill to power this "universe" symbolizes perfectly the inhuman basis on which gnosticism's ostensible humanization of the cosmos rests. The truly human—i.e., that mode of being differentiated from the apeirontic mass—is realized only by the recognition of values that transcend this mass. The negation of these values leads finally to such self-destructive and subhuman dichotomies as enslaver and enslaved, two modes distinguishable only by their respective positions in a blind, amoral force field.

Presiding over this field is, once again, a degenerate, artificial goddess—the wooden "Venus" that Hedwig Vogelsang chooses as her dancing partner. Hedwig, sixteen years old, is herself—in her precocious decadence and perverse artifice—an emanation of this goddess and a precursor of Bianca in *Gravity's Rainbow*. In both, the innocence symbolic of the Virgin's transcendental status has given way to a squalid hypersexuality that specializes in the unnatural. Mounted on a Bondelschwaartz, her neck scarred by bondage devices, dressed only in black tights, she mounts a prolonged sexual assault on the scurvy-weakened Mondaugen, attracted by his disease and the accompanying debilitation.

Hedwig is joined in this elaborately cultivated decadence by other guests such as Weissmann, who doubles in transvestism and twists his hands in the hair of Vera Meroving while she flagellates him with the ever-present sjambok. Flaying, that recurrent symbolic assault, is their particular delight and elicits a perversely tender love lyric from Hedwig, who sings of "Caresses" that "tease / cankered tissue apart" (p. 238). Even such a normal biological process as healing is something to be subverted in the name of a grotesque love. Once again it is the organic natural order, together with its supplement of moral restraints and spiritual sublimations, that is targeted by a gnostic enterprise seeking total substitution in the name of Control and in the service of death, whose dance it organizes and accelerates.

Twisted passions are, of course, no less intense for being twisted, and

can even give rise to an equally fierce *nostalgie de la boue*. Foppl, confined
to the bizarre, inhuman desolation of the coast of Swakopmund, escapes
into warm, comforting dreams of death marches and native corpses im-
paled on thorn trees, and into the present reality of a sadistic "affair" with
a Herero woman named Sarah whom he keeps manacled to his bed. He
is ironically oblivious, of course, to the link between his personalized,
concrete sort of inhumanity and the impersonal variety embodied in the
intimidating landscape; but it is precisely this link that provides us with
the novel's most telling insight into the relation between cabalistic gnosticism and existential gnosticism, and shows how one grows naturally out
of the other.

Foppl's own speculations take him to the point of seeing an analogy
between the "bleak, abstracted . . . rather meaningless" shore, with its
"agglomeration" of "female corpses . . . against the unhealthy yellow
sand," and the coming bureaucratization of slavery and death, a mass
enterprise "with a logic that chilled the comfortable perversity of the heart,
that substituted capability for character, deliberate scheme for political
epiphany" (p. 273). What he is foreseeing most immediately, of course,
is the advent of the Third Reich, with its massive, systematic extermination schemes and its coldly logical lunacy. It is a form of gnosticism
diagnosed, as we have seen, by Voegelin and traceable in a peculiarly
Teutonic manifestation to Foppl's atrocity-ridden Sudwest. Once again,
Voegelin's analysis of modern pneumapathology is complemented by that
of Camus, who devotes the early chapters of *The Rebel* to a shockingly
lucid account of how impersonal mass murder and enslavement in the
name of the state find their origins in private, charismatic acts of meta-
physical-rebellion like those "sanctioned" by von Trotha.[16]

Foppl's bureaucratic nightmare will eventually culminate in the Cartel
of *Gravity's Rainbow*, the definitive gnostic realization of Control. The
whole of existence is involved, in one way or another, in the Cartel's
conspiracy to shape a bureaucracy whose power is absolute. It is a matter
to be discussed at length in later chapters; what needs to be emphasized
here is that this bureaucracy's depersonalized, detached, and mainly joy-
less exercise of power is the ultimate fruition of the cabalistic gnosticism
that started, for Foppl and crew, as a highly personalized orgy of quasi-
religious violence. From an imagistic viewpoint, the siege party's animated variant of the "iridescent" Vheissu dream has degenerated into an
African-coast variant of Antarctic bleakness and alienation, the wasteland
in which Godolphin had experienced the final extension of Vheissu's
tentacles. But it is precisely this imagery of apocalyptic desolation that
functions as a correlative for existential gnosticism, with its depersonalized energies and its comfortless, alien version of nature. Henry Adams
would have no trouble envisaging the ravages of entropy, both physical
and spiritual, on "a coast that offered life nothing" (p. 247) in all its
gruesome particulars:

a sun with no shape, a beach alien as the moon's antarctic, restless concubines in barbed wire, salt mists, alkaline earth, the Benguela Current that would never cease bringing sand to raise the harbor floor, the inertia of rock, the frailty of flesh, the structural unreliability of thorns; the unheard whimper of a dying woman; the frightening but necessary cry of the strand wolf in the fog. (p. 274)

Pynchon goes to some trouble to describe the peculiarly menacing and inhuman quality of this wolf cry: "if it were human it could have been called laughter, but it was not human. It was a product of alien secretions, boiling over into blood already choked and heady" (p. 268). Since Weissmann-Blicero's atavism in *Gravity's Rainbow* will take a similarly lupine turn, we can locate yet another link between the cabalistic gnosticism to which he adheres as a member of the Cartel, and the existential mode represented by Foppl's bleak registering of the wolf. Both the demonic activity of the former and the morbid passivity of the latter lead, in the last analysis, to the same result: a dehumanized existence ruled by the Inanimate in its most life-negating forms and geared to the dissolution of all spiritual constructs. Target of conspiracy or not, the world of V. drifts toward inorganic stasis, its goddesses of renewal now identified with the coming sterility.

Another irony in Foppl's perceptiveness is that, in the midst of his inhuman treatment of the natives, he understands the importance of "humanity" as "a nervous, disquieted, forever inadequate but indissoluble Popular Front against deceptively unpolitical and apparently minor enemies" (p. 274). These "enemies" are precisely those abrasive, dehumanizing aspects of the Sudwest coast that make nature appear the product of a hostile demiurge. Foppl, despite his role in destroying the metaxic tension that differentiates the human from the subhuman, has glimpsed the humanistic system that will be increasingly central to Pynchon's norm. What he fails to understand is that it is not our situation in nature that is the enemy, but the construal of that situation in the light of existential gnosticism—a perspective that Pynchon himself, at this point, cannot entirely escape or accept.

Since what nature *is* constitutes a salient religious problem in the novel, we can hardly overlook nature's own testimony in the case. This evidence is, unfortunately, hearsay, since it is filtered through Weissmann; but its possible applications are intriguing and helpful. The engineer Kurt Mondaugen has been recording sferics, seemingly random radio noises in the atmosphere, in an attempt to make sense of them. After stealing Mondaugen's transcriptions of one of those "messages," Weissmann decodes it as the initial proposition of Wittgenstein's *Tractatus*: "The world is all that the case is" (p. 278). William Plater has developed a convincing thesis about the applicability of this proposition and others to the closed linguistic universe of Pynchon.[17]

If, however, we interpret it in light of the novel's gnostic matrix, we discover an ambiguity at least equally fruitful. The sferic utterance can be read as the affirmation of an Ur-nature—a given, a *fait accompli* of accident that is the only primordial truth in a wild whirl of projections, interpretations, and modifications. In this light, nature rather comically reproves the unnatural denizens of Foppl's villa, who are dedicated to supplanting her with an inferior and unvalidated order of being that supposedly "perfects" the original sprawl and casual agglomerations. Spoken by Weissmann, however, the same phrase can easily suggest the *fait accompli* of gnostic powers, i.e., the world is whatever its shapers' means and machinations happen to make it, and one either adapts to this new "case" or lives in fruitless nostalgia for what is no longer the case. Yet another interpretation is that this particular sferic series is no message at all, but random noise twisted into meaning by human mental processes. These multiple possibilities mean that entropy in its communications sense has triumphed, and that no truth that is not hopelessly ambiguous can be extracted from science's gnostic attempt to comprehend direction and thus master nature's voice. Ironically, what the attempt throws an indirect light upon is its own gnostic nature.

V. next appears in World War II Malta as the Bad Priest. This episode not only follows the events at Foppl's villa chronologically, but grows out of them as the apocalyptic finale of German imperialism and of V.'s own decadent surrogations. From the account we get of her, in Fausto's diary and commentary, it becomes clear that she has reached the farthest limits of gnostic death worship—has, indeed, become at the same time its high priest and its symbolically degenerate goddess. Renouncing the last vestiges of the feminine life principle to pose as a "male" priest, she dedicates herself to preaching chastity and abortion in the name of a supposedly God-ordained sterility.

Rumors that she "confederates with the Dark One" (p. 313), and her plea for Fausto's wife Elena to abort her child and become exclusively the Bride of Christ by entering a convent, suggest the heretical obsessions of earlier days in Cairo and Florence carried to a new extreme in the usurpation of traditional Christian symbols for gnostic ends. Sin, which Elena has accepted as a casual phenomenon of life, is portrayed as a demon in V.'s demonic sermons: "the shape of an evil spirit: alien, parasitic, attached like a black slug to her soul" (p. 314). Since Elena's principal "sin" has been the conception of a child outside wedlock, it is easy enough to find a life-negating analogy here between embryo and slug. Another priestly simile comparing sin to "spirit's cancer" has a similar application so that Elena's frightened search for "the metastasis she feared was in her" is really horror at the natural growth of new life.

It is in V.'s teaching of the Maltese children that the cosmic scope of gnostic ambitions is most explicitly and shockingly revealed. The children readily interpret the universe along gnostic lines because they are, in

Pynchon's own words, naturally possessed of "as certain fondness for the Manichaean" (p. 338). Hans Jonas devotes an entire chapter to explaining how Manichaeism represented "the most monumental single embodiment of the Gnostic religious principle" (TGR, pp. 207–208). This sect's elemental point of departure is, in Jonas's quotation of Mani, that " 'Before the existence of heaven and earth and everything in them there were two natures, the one good and the other evil. Both are separate each from the other. The good principle dwells in the place of Light. . . . The evil principle . . . in his land of Darkness' " (p. 210). The warfare that Mani predicates between these realms is figured for the Maltese children by the aerial combat between Spitfires and Messerschmidts. Their Manichaean gnosticism is distinguished from V.'s variety in that it involves identification with the life-affirming good.

As a champion of evil in the form of sterility, V. is automatically identified with the demiurgic forces whose alleged powers over human life are precisely what made it possible to interpret Manichaean doctrines as a variety of gnosticism. Certainly her formula for reshaping nature as a nonregenerative, inorganic mass has the absolutism and the scope of a demiurgic plot. She advises the girls, as she had advised Elena, to forgo sexual activity and reproduction, while preaching to the boys "that the object of male existence was to be like a crystal: beautiful and soulless" (p. 340). Father Avalanche, the Good Priest, speculates on these doctrines in a tone of mild outrage: "God is soulless? . . . Having created souls, He Himself has none? So that to be like God we must allow to be eroded the soul in ourselves. Seek mineral symmetry, for here is eternal life: the immortality of rock. Plausible. But apostasy" (p. 340).

What Father Avalanche perceives here is nothing less than a massive gnostic subversion of the metaxic tension that makes humanity possible. Eternal life is a projection into an indefinite future of both Catholic spirituality and nature's God-sanctioned cycles of reproduction. In both cases, since it is an ideal transcending the mortal, earthly lifetime of the individual, it appears as part of the infinite fulfillment that makes up the constantly deferred "fullness of time." As the perfection of soul, in the classical Christian interpretation, God anchors the *metaxy* with the edifying model toward which humanity strives in its struggle to realize the potentialities of the human.

The gnostic surrogation here is total and thus cosmically determinative. A soulless God is an implicit indictment of human spirituality, which—in grotesque emulation—must allow itself to erode toward the purely material *apeiron*, with its "mineral symmetry." To become "rock" is to know (or, more accurately, to fail to know) the paradoxical immortality of eternal death. Asymmetrical, transient humanity is precisely that which disgusts the apostles of gnosticism and leads them to assault both God's nature and God's soul with "corrective" schemes that will ensure their own godhead in an artificial Kingdom of Death.

It is just such a scheme, on the personal level, that drives V. to replace her living organs and appendages one by one with decorative artificial devices. She is the premature embodiment of the gnostic surrogation praised by Yeats during one of his periodic rages against natural decay:

> Once out of nature, I shall never take
> My bodily form from any natural thing,
> But such a form as Grecian goldsmiths make
> Of hammered gold and gold enamelling.[18]

Not yet out of nature, V. attempts nonetheless to attenuate her relations to it with a bizarre eclecticism undreamed of by Yeats: golden feet, false hair, tattooed scalp, glass clockwork eye, jeweled teeth, and sapphire navel. Appropriately enough, her disassembly comes at the hands of the children to whom she has preached her antithetical gospel, while she herself lies wounded from a bombing raid that is the long-term fruit of Sudwest gnosticism.

Fausto, who administers Extreme Unction, sees her as a "suffering" and "foreshortened" Christ (p. 343). The grisly irony of the comparison is appropriate in light of V.'s attempt to co-opt Christian symbolism in order to undermine both spirit and nature. If Christ was the Word made flesh who dwelt among us, sent into the world to redeem the world, then V. was the Word made artifice, an antithetical Logos of death dedicated to preempting rather than redeeming. "Suffer little children to come unto me," Christ had commanded, "for of such is the Kingdom of God."[19] V. suffers the children in a horribly literal but fitting way, since she had envisaged a sterile kingdom based upon the suppression of childbirth. The "crucifixion" of this death goddess by the avatars of future life exactly reverses the circumstances of the spirit-affirming Christ, and symbolically seals the character of the increasingly gnosticized century with which V. has become identified.

Having shown V. at the extremity where her death coincides with her maximum gnostic decadence, Pynchon is concerned in the two remaining "V." episodes with flashbacks that place this decadence in new social, psychological, and religious perspectives—perspectives that juxtapose her human emotions with the dehumanizing actions that they breed. That this *femme fatale*, whose fatalism operates on a world-historical level, can proceed in good faith as a largely unconscious servant of the Death Kingdom is yet another irony linking the sentient conspiracies of cabalistic gnosticism with the blind entropic determinacies of the existential strain.

"V. in Love" is set in the Paris of 1913, an atmosphere ripe with avant-garde decadence in both art and life on the threshold of the apocalyptic war promised by Fashoda. V. is in the grip of a lesbian obsession with a fifteen-year-old dancer named Melanie l'Heuremaudit, whose appearance at one point in a kimono "translucent and dyed rainbowlike with sun-

bursts and concentric rings of cerise, amethyst, gold, and jungle green"
clearly links her with the congeries of iridescent Vheissu images and thus
with the Inanimate. This linkage is multiplied by her sexual manipulation
of an insensate lay figure and by eyes that have the "dead" color of "freezing rain" (p. 394). Paradoxically, this deadness gives her eyes the quality
of a demonic mirror in which the gazer sees a terrifyingly alien "ghost"
of himself that either galvanizes him to flight or freezes him in morbid
narcissism. Again, it is a comprehensive gnosticizing that is at stake, the
fabrication of a hostile universe.

Itague speculates on the permeation of the entire world by this demiurgic presence: "Cast in the image of what? Not God. Whatever potent
spirit can mesmerize the gift of irreversible flight into a grown man and
the gift of self-arousal into the eyes of a young girl, his name is unknown.
Or if known then he is Yahweh and we are all Jews, for no one will ever
speak it" (p. 399). Itague admits that one of these names may be l'Heuremaudit—"Cursed Hour." This conjunction of spiritual danger with names
of supernatural potency, especially in a Jewish context, links Melanie as
demiurge with Merkabah mysticism, one of the varieties of early Jewish
Gnosis investigated by Gershom Scholem. In this ancient sect, the "secret
Names of God, or pictures imbued with a magical power" are used as
protection from attack by "angels of destruction" (K, pp. 17–18). Since
Melanie herself is such an angel, the power of this magic is malignantly
reversed. More precisely, it functions to subvert the male-female polarity
that is crucial to the processes of nature and—where the benevolent Virgin
figure is involved—to the tension of the *metaxy*. Instead of finding in the
woman a fertilizing animistic complement to the power-centered male
principle, men see only the sterile reflection of their egotistical drives,
while women see their own luxurious potential without the world that
would give realization and significance to this sense of self. It is all consonant with the solipsistic, static "paradise" to which gnostic hubris ultimately leads in its constant repression of nature and spirit.

Just such an idyll manifests itself in the lesbian love affair of Melanie
and V. The narcissism of the former perversely complements the fetishism
of the latter in a relation that constitutes an orgiastic celebration of the
Inanimate. All possible permutations of voyeurism are inherent in the
mirror-filled apartment where V. watches her dehumanized love object
watching herself and watching her watcher. This complex reciprocity of
mere images is the most sterile of surrogates for the reproductive forces
that animate nature, and is thus—as Pynchon makes explicit—a sexual
augury of "the Kingdom of Death," a realm "served by fetish-constructions
like V.'s, which represent a kind of infiltration" (p. 411).

He is also at pains, however, to clear V. of any conscious complicity
in the advent of this kingdom. Had she known that she was involved in
a "conspiracy leveled against the animate world," her reaction would have
involved "an ambiguity." The uncertainty would have arisen not from

any vestiges of nostalgia for spirit and nature, but from the refusal to accept her own death as part of the conspiracy's success. Paradoxically, the two directions that this reaction could have taken both lead toward further immersion in the Inanimate. She might have constructed an apparatus of self-control so repressive that she became "a purely determined organism, an automaton, constructed, only quaintly, of human flesh." She would thus fulfill the prophecy of SHOCK and SHROUD, the robots who try to convince Benny Profane that the entire human race will eventually become as mechanical as they. Pynchon's description of this mechanistic rigidifying as "Puritan" echoes Eric Voegelin's linkage of Calvinism and gnosticism—a linkage we will explore in depth in the chapter on *Gravity's Rainbow*. Conversely, V., reacting against this puritanism, might have journeyed "even deeper into a fetish-country until she became entirely and in reality . . . an inanimate object of desire." Certainly Pynchon suggests that, for V., all roads lead to the Kingdom of Death, even those intended hypothetically as detours; and that her life is, however unconsciously, a gnostic exemplum encouraging this kingdom's advent.

Pynchon's most immediate reason for discriminating among the vectors of V.'s motivation is to show that she is, indeed, hopelessly and blindly in love with Melanie. The fact that lesbian fetishism is one of love's "strange displacements" has nothing to do with the intensity or sincerity of the emotion. V. would fancy herself to be, in this affair, not a destroyer of noble emotional orderings but an affirmer of them. But the irony of fervent commitment, within a gnostic frame of values, lies precisely in the fact that it is directed toward a despiritualized objective that is finally antithetical to the very notion of human nobility. In the name of rising, such "love" constitutes an apeirontic descent in keeping with the parodic *metaxy* of gnosticism. Anchored by Melanie as degenerate Virgin, this simulacrum of divine tension serves to destroy the very sources of tension in the slide toward the Inanimate.

It is, in fact, an inanimate phallus in the form of a pointed pole that defiles Melanie and kills her during the performance of "The Rape of the Chinese Virgins." That this grotesque crucifixion is accidental is ironically appropriate in a ballet where randomness reigns supreme. As one of the automaton handmaidens runs amok, Melanie experiences her final bloody spasms of dance music in which "all tonal location had been lost, notes screamed out simultaneous and random like fragments of a bomb: winds, strings, brass and percussion were indistinguishable" (p. 414). The performance thus constitutes, like the musical aberrations of the early story "Entropy," a sort of entropic ceremony, a parodic ritual in which violent disorder becomes an antirationale denying the Logos of Chartres and of all other spiritual orderings.

Dissonance and desecration are combined in yet another ceremony, the Black Mass attended earlier by V. with yet another young girl. Although we are shown only the exhausted aftermath of the service, we

learn that it had been accompanied by Porcepic's harsh experimental po-
lyrhythms and that Hosts, the consecrated symbols of Christ's body, lie
"scattered" (p. 403) about a room that contains both sleeping and copulating worshippers. According to Gerhard Zacharias in *The Satanic Cult*,
the Black Mass has its roots in Gnostic cults of the first century A.D.,
especially in the practices of a group known as the Phibionites. This sect
indulged in ritual copulation similar to that involved in Porcepic's Mass,
but one of their prime concerns was the sterilization of the act so that the
amount of life on Earth would not be increased—an obsession that led
even to the slaughtering and ritualistic devouring of embryos. The connection with the antireproductive obsession of V. as Bad Priest is clear
enough, as is the analogy between V. and Barbelo, the "negative, devouring
aspect of the Eternal Feminine" with whom the Phibionites identified.[20]

In Paris, by the late seventeenth century, these rites had been refined
into elaborate ceremonies involving the consecration and elevation of the
Host over a supine naked woman who served as an altar, followed by
sexual practices involving some rather imaginative deviations.[21] In the
Paris of 1911 the young sculptress, without lingerie, lies pillowed upon
V.'s breasts while V. burns the phrase "ma fetiche" into her skirt with a
cigarette and while the writer Gerfaut hymns the sexual proclivities of a
thirteen-year-old girl. Outside, the rainclouds that refuse to burst, and
diffuse "an exhausted yellow light" (p. 403), suggest the Waste Land's
final entropic stasis. The link between the ritualistic defiling of the Virgin
and the reign of the Inanimate is thus reinforced and placed in an ominous
perspective of gnostic tradition.

Itague, who was present at the Mass, relates this question of the Inanimate to the question of the nature of history—an issue raised in varying
contexts throughout the novel. He delivers his insights, which have a
normative ring, in response to the historical optimism of the socialist
Kholsky, who argues that "History" has "basic rhythms" that are "measurable"—rhythms that make the "tide" of "Socialist Awareness . . .
irresistible and irreversible" (p. 405). That history may be a "woman" of
"mystery" does not mean, for Kholsky, that one cannot predict her cycles.
Itague's analysis of this theory suggests distorted truths among its illusions. To Kholsky's insistence that socialism represents a "rising" rather
than the "falling" of decadence, Itague replies, "A decadence is a falling-
away from what is human, and the further we fall the less human we
become. Because we are less human, we foist off the humanity we have
lost on inanimate objects and abstract theories."

Itague's specific reference is, of course, to Kholsky's socialism, which
conceptualizes people as "point-clusters or curves on a graph"—a charge
that Kholsky admits without the slightest perturbation and that he ramifies
by discoursing dreamily on such mechanistic phenomena as the decline
of brain cells and the collision of atoms. We are back in the bleak and
depersonalized universe of Henry Adams's prophecies, but with the en-

tropic spread of the Inanimate disguised as a vital political ascendancy, an ostensible rising that is really a falling. The construing of dehumanization as human progress, and an avid devotion to that degenerative process, bring us back to the same gnostic illusion embodied by V. in love. If history is indeed a woman, it would appear to be a woman like V., the antithesis of the Eternal Feminine and her promise of life abundant. As such, history offers no "measurable rhythms" but instead—in Itague's withering retort—"the jitterings and squeaks of a metaphysical bedspring." To gloss this figure, we have only to compare Mondaugen's sferics, the apparently chaotic collection of "clicks, hooks, risers, nosewhistlers and . . . warbling" from the atmosphere (p. 230). In the case of both "metaphysical bed spring" and radio noises, the medium is the message in all its opacity and randomness. The world is all that the case is, and the case—in V., at least—is the constant decline of pattern and meaning as "History" becomes mere history and slides toward the apeirontic silence.

This concern with the course of twentieth-century history is continued and dramatically elaborated in our next account of V., an account that also constitutes the concluding episode of the novel. On Malta in 1919, she is reunited with Sidney Stencil, a veteran diplomat whose richness of experience and mellow sophistication have now made him into a Marlow-like commentator. It is precisely this complex and seasoned perspective on V.'s politics and their historical role, together with V.'s reciprocal awareness of Stencil's position, that gives the novel's conclusion its ominous and far-reaching suggestiveness.

Stencil is at the end of a long and harrowing career that has also been a quest for the truth about historical process. In the course of it, he has seen comparatively civilized rules of diplomacy and the efficacy of Machiavellian virtù give way to barbaric expediency and complex causal nexuses that seem to defy the most skillful manipulator. His suspicion is that this crescendo of anarchy is the result of a "disease" contracted by the world "sometime between 1859 and 1919" (p. 461). After renewing his intimacy with V., he finds that suspicion has become belief: "There were no more princes. Henceforth politics would become progressively more democratized, more thrown into the hands of amateurs. The disease would progress" (p. 489). If such progressive degeneration has, indeed, afflicted the twentieth century, it means the growth of social and cultural entropy and the end of polity in a random political splintering. Pynchon gives us a foretaste of this anarchic melange in his description of eight Maltese factions in the "Situation" of 1919, with eight divergent aims (pp. 471–472).

As a student of such "situations" over the years, Stencil has come to understand that each "takes shape from events much lower than the merely human," from several "thousand accidents" of the "inert universe" (pp. 483–484) to which are added the complex idiosyncrasies of the human participants. What this means, finally, is a loss of human control over human events, as the inert, sublogical universe—which is to say, the Inanimate—more and more dictates the course of history. Metaxic collapse in the aftermath of the failure of *virtù*, and of the animating ideal that *virtù* served, gives us once again the multiverse of Adams—the dynamo run amok, the human negated in the absence of a humanizing transcendental tension.

In the light of such considerations, Stencil has developed a theory of "Paracletian politics" (pp. 479–480) that not only links V. with the increasingly chaotic course of history, but grants her the status of a demonic spirit presiding over the birth of entropy's Kingdom:

> The matter of a Paraclete's coming, the comforter, the dove; the tongues of flame, the gift of tongues: Pentecost. Third Person of the Trinity. None of it was implausible to Stencil. The Father had come and gone. In political terms, the Father was the Prince; the single leader, the dynamic figure whose virtù used to be a determinant of history. This had degenerated to the Son, genius of the liberal love-feast which had produced 1848 and lately the overthrow of the Czars. What next? What Apocalypse?
>
> Especially on Malta, a matriarchal island. Would the Paraclete be also a mother? Comforter, true. But what gift of communication could ever come from a woman.... (p. 472)

Pynchon's ultimate source for this theory is the writings of a thirteenth-century monk, Joachim of Flora, who turns out to be—in an ominous twist worthy of Pynchon's own fiction—one of the pioneers of modern gnostic thought. It is Joachim who first sets up the trinitarian division of history's stages in an attempt—according to Voegelin—"to endow the immanent course of history with a meaning that was not provided in the Augustinian conception" (NSP, p. 119). More specifically, Joachim conflates the course of secular events with that of divine events, endowing the former with the *eschaton* of the latter in a gradual progress of humankind toward spiritual perfection.

This progress culminates in the "third age of the Spirit" (NSP, p. 111)—the age of the Paraclete—when the "divinization" of society makes possible the withering away of the now-superfluous Church. It is no coincidence, for Voegelin, that this utopian prophecy anticipates the Marxist dream of the withering away of the State. Even though Joachim remains loyal to the belief that utopia has a transcendental origin, later theoreticians would insist upon a complete "immanentization of the *eschaton*," thus paving the way for those gnostic movements that undertake an enforced perfection in the name of "History." One of these is Nazism, a political philosophy with which V. is at least indirectly involved, as we have seen, from its inception. For Voegelin, the "National Socialist Third Realm" represents the third stage in "the concrete application of the trinitarian schema" to German history—the attempt to realize a Hitlerian "millennial prophecy [that] authentically derives from Joachitic speculation" (NSP, p. 113).

If we subject Stencil's version of this schema to what we might call a Voegelinian extension—and the schema's theological origins invite that— it becomes a historical theory in which the Father represents the transcendental charismatic figure who anchors the *metaxy* and incarnates *virtù* in the form of a history-determining Logos. The order of the secular state mirrors as best it can a projected City of God—the *civitatis Dei*— and receives its progressive modifications from perceptions of this higher ordering. At a later, increasingly gnostic, stage, this projection and the metaxic tension that accompanied it give way to what Stencil contemptuously terms "the liberal love-feast," democratic experiments in human self-sufficiency that produce violent revolution in the name of social harmony and brotherly love. The final era of history—terminal, perhaps—is symbolized by the descent of the Holy Ghost, whose gnostic analogue inaugurates a politics of demonic anarchy similar to that described in Yeats's prophetic poems. All notion of an authoritative center quite lost, the humanizing polity dissolves into a riotous chaos of movements, each claiming the sanction of some divine voice that is incomprehensible to the others, and to the world that must suffer the fanatical ravagings licensed by the assumed mandate.

That this descending and inflammatory Ghost might be feminine, a mother, leads Stencil to a conventional sexist linkage between woman as adept comforter and woman as inept communicator. It is the latter trait, of course, that he fears as a source of political anarchy, a welter of fervent, confused directives completely antithetical to the clear Logos of the Father. When we consider this matriarchal Paraclete as the Terrible Mother, however—the Maltese cult of the feminine in its negative aspect— we find gnostic reversals that put a very different face on both comfort and communication, and lead us directly back to V. as an incarnation of this figure. Just as V.'s comforting of Hugh Godolphin in the Florence of 1899 had been a ploy, whatever its emotional vectors, to gain information about Vheissu, so her arranging of a comfortable retreat for Stencil on Malta works to her political advantage.

The "hothouse" of nostalgia undermines Stencil's last vestiges of *virtù* in the combined cause of Maltese peace and the British Empire; later he will conclude that V. kept him "only as long as she had to" (p. 492). Paralyzing Stencil's sense of the present with memories, V. also indulges fantasies of a "lovely rainbow or wardrobe . . . of different-hued, different-sized and -shaped feet" (p. 488). It is the Vheissu syndrome once again, the concealing of the Inanimate beneath seductive variegations and—in this case—beneath the pseudoanimation of memory. The final result is a sort of psychic inanition equivalent to the heat-death of the story "Entropy":

To enter, hand in hand, the hothouse of a Florentine spring once again; to be fayed and filleted hermetically into a square (interior? exterior?) where all art objects hover between inertia and waking, all shadows lengthen imperceptibly though night never falls, a total nostalgic hush rests on the heart's landscape. And all faces are blank masks; and spring is any drawn-out sense of exhaustion or a summer which like evening never comes. (pp. 486–487)

This Paraclete's "gift of tongues" takes an entropic form—that of incitement to riot. Stencil's fears about the chaotic results of feminine communication are ironically realized in an extremely effective communicator who happens to be dedicated to "Absolute upheaval" (p. 487). Associated with banditti who sew the severed genitals of their murder victim in the victim's mouth, stirring up mobs in the ultimate service of Mussolini's fascism, V. brings violent disorder in the name of an illusory order that is, in the long run, identical with the Inanimate.

In his article on the novel's Pentecostal aspects, W. H. Lhamon, Jr., finds an ambivalence in Pynchon's attitude toward the "tongues of fire" and in his corresponding attitude toward V. As Bad Priest, she is "profane . . . an embodiment of inanimateness," but she is "also sacred: the Paraclete, the communicator, a significant totem in a world otherwise devoid of meaning."[22] Lhamon sees in this sacred voice hope for "the radical transfiguration of the world," the possible fulfillment of "a longing for transcendence" (p. 74). In the context of *Gravity's Rainbow*, which Lhamon several times invokes, this affirmation might conceivably be justified as the revelation of a freedom transcending gnostic Control; but even there we are confronted with the unmitigated evil of Blicero's "transcendence" and of his Cartel's plan for the "transfiguration of the world." In the gnostic modality, the language of religious experience constantly subverts itself. *Transcending* becomes a *descending*, a sliding downward from our higher potentialities; and *transfiguring* is a *disfiguring* of the world that had made the human possible. At the apocalyptic extreme, these two movements produce the apeirontic triumph of the Inanimate, the spectral *eschaton* that haunts the novel and speaks through V. with fiery tongues.

These considerations help us to understand Stencil's apprehensive amazement that V. is able to resolve "by some magic" the two extremes of "The street and the hothouse" (p. 487). The "intolerable double vision" of this century is, for Stencil, that "the Right can only live and work hermetically, in the hothouse of the past, while outside the Left prosecute their affairs in the streets by manipulated mob violence. And cannot live but in the dreamscape of the future" (p. 468). This last phrase captures exactly the air of unreality surrounding the projections of the gnostic "magic" decried by Voegelin; but for V., both violence *and* nostalgia are exercises in gnostic *virtù* toward a common end not fully understood even by its expediter: the advent of the Kingdom of Death.

Lhamon finds—quite correctly, I think—a correspondence between the eras of Stencil's Paracletian theory and the stages of V.'s life; but here again, the peculiar ironies inherent in gnostic principles serve to subvert both the distinctions between the eras and any affirmative aspects of these distinctions. As a practitioner of *virtù* in Cairo and Florence, V. manages successively to alienate the Father for good (her own father, Sir Alastair) and to unman him (in Hugh Godolphin's pathetic unburdening). This Terrible Mother's earliest projections, as we have seen, were of exclusive union with the Terrible Father in a fantasy of imperialist Control. When we add to this the affinity with "riot" revealed in Florence and her growing alliance with the forces of the Inanimate, it becomes clear that her *virtù* is directed toward gnostic orderings that lead finally to massive disorder, and as such undo the very shaping principles that constitute *virtù*. In this case, *virtù* is really the Paraclete's apocalyptic instigations, symbolized by the "triangular stain" that swims "somewhere over the crowd" in Cairo "like a tongue on Pentecost" (p. 92) and links V. with the awful potential of Fashoda.

If we connect the next era, the "liberal love-feast," with V.'s Parisian amour, we can locate the turmoil of 1848 and of the Bolshevik revolution in the symbol of aesthetic insurrection; but the theme of liberal politics becomes explicit in Kholsky's fantasy of a socialist future, which is revealed with equal explicitness as a gnostic fantasy of the Inanimate. The link between this fantasy and V.'s own fetishistic love-feast with Melanie has already been explored, as has their common terminus in the Kingdom of Death. That this feast does, in fact, represent the deterioration of Machiavellian skills, and the movement to the second stage of Stencil's theory, is made clear by Pynchon himself: "The Florentine spring, the young entrepreneuse with all spring's hope in her *virtù*, with her girl's faith that Fortune (if only her skill, her timing held true) could be brought under control; that Victoria was being gradually replaced by V.; something different, for which the young century had as yet no name" (p. 410).

The suggestion here seems to be that V.'s attempts—however self-defeating—to order and control the chaotic unfolding of events are giving way, by the time of Paris, to an increasing identification with this chaos in the guise of the apeirontic Inanimate toward which it tends. Her "love" of Melanie as object is actually a subversion of the very humanity that is defined and enhanced by the spiritual enthalpy of love. It would thus appear that the final stage of Stencil's theory, the Paracletian descent of tongues, is merely the apocalyptic fruition of gnostic tendencies already immanent in both V.'s *virtù* and V.'s love feast, and ironically subversive of the well-wrought polity.

It has been necessary to trace the degeneration of V. in detail because this process parallels the gnosticizing of the century—from a youthful stage that has "no name as yet" for V. to a midpoint that has no choice but to find one. It is V.'s life as comprehensive myth that lends significance to the mid-century antics of the Whole Rotten Crew. Pynchon's nonironic, in-depth exploration of this life provides the metasatiric effect—the machinery of which we have examined—of ensconcing an abnormal "norm" that in turn distorts the relatively harmless lives of Benny Profane and other relatively innocuous characters into the stuff of cartoons. Simultaneously, however, V.'s world-historical machinations provide these cartoons with a mythic context. It is this context that produces a larger thematic redemption of the buffoonery that opens the novel, and of the banal partying and "yo-yoing" that make up the Crew's existence.

The V. myth is a myth of more or less systematic profanation and of simultaneous reconsecration in the spirit of gnosticism; thus Benny Profane, the exemplary victim and register of these processes. "Fat" and "amoeba-like," his very appearance incarnates the metaxic slackening, the slide toward the subhuman. The *virtù* that creates tension has given way entirely to the passive appetite, a vague and perpetual adolescent "wanting." He is thus part of the drifting chaos once ordered and given meaning by the Virgin and her analogues.

The degeneration of the Virgin toward the Inanimate is reflected in the ceremonies of desecration that surround Profane from the first page of the book. Christmas Eve in the Sailor's Grave sees a carol celebrating the Virgin birth interrupted by the "atheist" Pig Bodine, and the parodic celebration of "Suck Hour" at a foam-rubber breast (pp. 15–16). In the same episode we learn of a set of false teeth, unnaturally sharpened, being applied to the derrière of a barmaid named Beatrice, who thus becomes a comic profanation of Dante's virginal guide to Paradise. The equation of artificial body parts and sacrilege is established here in a farcical mode that will later give way to deadly seriousness in the account of V.'s surrogations.

It is not as though the Eternal Feminine failed to exert its ordering wiles on Profane. Rachel Owlglass comes the closest to giving some shape and purpose to his life in her constant urgings that he acquire shape and purpose. She exists as the direction of available spiritual energy, as love and meaning. Even so, she is herself a victim of love for the Inanimate in the form of her MG, and it is she who gets Profane a job that involves demoralizing contact with the Inanimate in the form of the automata SHROUD and SHOCK. Also, her own involvement with the Whole Rotten Crew represents a form of social entropy that compromises any regenerative powers she might possess. When the virgin Fina, den mother to the street gangs, offers herself in good faith to Profane, he turns her down. Her subsequent defilement by the gangs suggests not only Profane's spiritual inadequacy, but the power of "the Street," the apeirontic arena, to destroy metaxic symbols. Capable of turning the gang's murderous hostility into a "summer-mild" harmony that is "Christian, unworldly and proper" (pp. 144–145), she is finally reduced to a hollow-eyed object and presumably executed by her own brother, the avenging "Angel" of the Street. The destruction of the Virgin is the end of the brief "peace" enjoyed by Profane, who must now return to the "dream-street" (p. 151) of twentieth-century alienation.

This failure of every possible symbol of spiritual dynamism means that Profane is perpetually the victim of the Inanimate—in his own term, a "schlemihl." For him, the Inanimate is a constant and ominous presence, a hovering demonic force ready to seek revenge or to present him with the gnostic *fait accompli*—a sudden turn into "alien country" where "nothing else lived but himself" (pp. 20–21).

This "country" is "the mercury-lit street" (p. 40) which throws even his own animateness into doubt as he imagines himself lying down there and turning into concentric ivory artifacts. It is the "single abstracted Street" of Profane's nightmares, bound to the goddess of entropic riot and dehumanizing metamorphosis by the description of its lighting: "overhead, turning everybody's face green and ugly, shone mercury-vapor lamps, receding in an asymmetric V to the east where it's dark and there are no more bars" (p. 10).

What Profane fears, without having the understanding to name it, is the Kingdom of Death; and what this same lack prevents him from perceiving is that this kingdom has its roots deep in the assumptions of his social circle, the Whole Sick Crew. Their decadence is connected explicitly with that of Mondaugen's Sudwest by Herbert Stencil, who sees them as "linked maybe by a spectral chain" in a Dance of Death that recalls the manacled Hottentots, and also as reflections of the bizarre, literally rotting "Crew at Foppl's" (p. 296). Their corruption of "Art" and "Thought" fits the pattern of entropic decline and demonstrates the vitiation of the very activities that should heighten the metaxic tension and refine its differentiations. Their "artists" spend much more time talking about art than they do producing it, and the few works actually realized suggest an abject poverty of spirit: a series of "Cheese Danish" paintings, works that reflect "technique for the sake of technique—Catatonic Expressionism," and "parodies on what someone else has already done" (p. 297).

The defeat of organic conception by mechanism, of vitality by catatonia, and of creativity by sterile dabbling could hardly be more explicit; nor is there a more salient characteristic of gnosticism than enslavement to a sterile theory that pretends to the very animation it replaces and negates. The same sterility attaches to the Crew's "philosophical" conversations, which depend upon the constant rearranging of a finite number of fashionable concepts. The link with entropy theory is forged explicitly by the dentist Eigenvalue's realization that if no new energy in the form of intellectual originality enters the closed system, stasis is inevitable: "This sort of arranging and rearranging was Decadence, but the exhaustion of all possible permutations and combinations was death" (p. 298).

There is one important exception, however, to this dearth of creativity. Herbert Stencil, Sidney's son, is the inheritor of his father's quest for pattern in history, which he has transformed into a quest for V. This transformation is the result of historical vectors peculiar to the twentieth century—vectors dramatized by the occasional ironic distortion of both quest and quester and reflected in the orientation of young Stencil, who was "Born in 1901, the year Victoria died," and was thus "in time to be the century's child" (p. 52). The fact that he was "Raised motherless" is one that Pynchon chooses to dwell on, suggesting some awful mystery associated with the mother's sudden disappearance. The equation of the quest for V. with the quest for the Mother is thus a natural one, and fits exactly the gradual revelation of the degenerate Virgin figure as goddess of the Inanimate.

It is appropriate that "the century's child" experience this particular revelation as part of a maternal obsession so deep in his psyche that he himself is puzzled by the fixation—a drive that brings him the only "animation" he knows. His father, Sidney, reinforces this symbolic role for V. when he expresses the hope that the shipfitter Maijstral is indeed having an affair with Sidney's old "love," V., "if only to complete a circle begun in England eighteen years ago. . . . Herbert would be eighteen" (p. 489). Did it not seem likely from Sidney's conversation with V. in Malta that the Florentine episode was their last meeting, one would be tempted to project from this train of thought a more literal motherhood for V.[23] As it is, her seduction of Sidney in 1899 is close enough to Herbert's birthdate to provide a significant maternal analogue, and the ominous gestation of the century to come.

It is precisely this gestation that Henry Adams had in mind when he asserted, in a passage cited earlier, that "the child born in 1900 would . . . be born into a new world which would not be a unity but a multiple" (EHA, p. 1138). Adams's sense of his own historicity as nineteenth-century man, "a citizen of Quincy, born in 1838" (EHA, p. 1176) and now stranded in an alien century, links him with his fellow gentleman-historian-diplomat Sidney Stencil, as well as with Herbert, the twentieth-century man whose alienation in his own century Adams predicts. Pynchon makes an additional, explicit connection when he compares Herbert to "Henry Adams in the *Education*" (p. 62) as an author who refers to himself in the third person. Young Stencil describes his extension of this technique as "forcible dislocation of personality," a complete self-projection into the consciousness of another person.

These projections involve elaborating and dramatizing bits of information picked up about V. from his father's diaries and from various conversations. The result is nothing less than the crystallization of the V. myth, the organizing (or disorganizing) myth of contemporary history:

> Around each seed of a dossier, therefore, had developed a nacreous mass of inference, poetic license, forcible dislocation of personality into a past he didn't remember and had no right in, save the right of imaginative anxiety or historical care, which is recognized by no one. He tended each seashell

on his submarine scungille farm . . . carefully avoiding the little dark deep right there in the midst of the tame shellfish, down in which God knew what lived: the island Malta, where his father had died. (p. 62)

This rich, seemingly random process of accretion is something that compels Stencil absolutely and that he cannot dismiss as a detached scholarly quest. Instead it is "simple-minded" and "literal," the pursuit of V. as a "beast of venery" (p. 61). Such libidinous immediacy is the very stuff of myth, which relies on a compelling sensuality to convey its urgent, basic significations.

Pynchon's metaphor for myth formation also has its source in *The Education of Henry Adams*, in an elaborate figuration that provides us an invaluable touchstone for delineating both the origins and the significance of the V. myth:[24]

As history unveiled itself in the new order, man's mind had behaved like a young pearl oyster, secreting its universe to suit its conditions until it had built up a shell of *nacre* that embodied all its notions of the perfect. . . . The woman especially did great things, creating her deities on a higher level than the male, and, in the end, compelling the man to accept the Virgin as guardian of the man's God . . . [She] conceived herself and her family as the center and flower of an ordered universe which she knew to be unity because she had made it after the image of her own fecundity. . . . Neither man nor woman ever wanted to quit this Eden of their own invention, and could no more have done it of their own accord than the pearl oyster could quit its shell; but although the oyster might perhaps assimilate or embalm a grain of sand forced into its aperture, it could only perish in face of the cyclonic hurricane or the volcanic upheaval of its bed. Her supersensual chaos killed her. (pp. 1138–1139)

If the pearl of Adams's oyster is a myth that orders existence as a living, fecund unity and makes humanity possible, the pearls of Stencil's "scungille farm" constitute a myth of disorder, of the dissolution of humanity into the "supersensual chaos" from which its unifying constructs had once differentiated it. Adams illustrates the life-affirming order of his nacreous "Eden" by quoting a Latin hymn in praise of Venus, and in so doing dramatizes the vital link between the pagan goddess and the Virgin as feminine aspects of the generative Logos. The subsequent usurpation of the Eternal Feminine by V. is the usurpation of Eden by Vheissu, of nature by artifice, of organic vitality by entropic stasis; and Stencil is the compulsive, obsessed mythologizer of the process. He is also, in his fractured twentieth-century mode, Voegelin's quester after "the Question." That his constantly receding object is an ironic incarnation of the century's anti-spiritual vectors does not negate the essential spirituality of the impulses that drive him to seek the mysterious logos behind these vectors.

The "little dark deep" of Malta is not so much a gap in Stencil's V.

myth as its terrible center, the animate penetralia "in which God knew what lived." Piqued and enlightened by Fausto's diary, he overcomes his fear enough to visit the island and drag more of its relevant mysteries into the light of consciousness. One of his discoveries, the death of V. as Bad Priest, would seem to cap his quest; but it continues as he pursues her glass eye, now the property of another V., to Stockholm. Like other dis-membered deities, V. lives on in dispersal, presiding over the fragmen-tation of the human through her reincarnate fragments.

It is signficant that the narrative frames of V.'s Maltese episodes are not based upon Stencil's impersonations. The first episode, recounted in Fausto's diaries, provides an elaboration of V.'s activities entirely consis-tent in spirit and purport with these impersonations. The second gains its autonomy, and authority, from being designated an "Epilogue" to the entire novel and from being narrated—presumably—by Pynchon himself. This distancing and objectivity make possible a stark, dramatic coda in which the novel's tension between history as infrahuman process and history as Inanimate conspiracy is resolved in a common vision of gnostic alienation.

This vision is focused most intensely in the death of the elder Stencil, which ends the novel as a sort of coda to the coda, bringing the tension described above into significant conjunction with malign female presences of the V. archetype. It is Veronica Manganese's limousine that appears on the dock as Mehemet's xebec begins its fatal voyage, and her disfigured driver who waves goodbye "with a curiously sentimental, feminine mo-tion of the wrist," the gesture of the degenerate goddess dismissing Stencil from the realm of the animate: "Veronica Manganese had kept him only as long as she had to. His eyes kept dead astern" (p. 492). Stencil has, in other words, begun to be transformed into her inanimate image as he has recently observed it: "the live eye dead as the other, with the clock-iris" (p. 487). The driver, Hugh Godolphin, is himself the victim of an inanimate implant, as part of plastic surgery that has undermined his face's organic structure. Their result is a grotesque peeling of the skin that links this final episode to V.'s appearance in Cairo, when the similarly afflicted Porpentine becomes an early martyr to the assault of the Inanimate.

The other symbols of the degenerate feminine, Mara and Astarte, have been linked earlier in the threatening wooden figurehead of the xebec. Mehemet's warning to Stencil that "She [Mara] will find ways to reach out from Valletta" turns out to be the prophecy of Stencil's death in a waterspout that occurs within the same "invisible circle centered at Xagh-riet Mewwija" (p. 462) identified as her special domain in the Turkish episode. The image that presides over this disaster, presumably the last image that Stencil sees, is "Astarte's throat naked to the cloudless weather" (p. 492). This dead figurehead is the Inanimate figuratively an-imated, prevailing with such force and finality that it is seen as a sort of negative life become stronger than the positive.

This is the final gnostic vision of V.—a massive alienation in which cosmic indifference shot through with grotesque coincidences is indistinguishable, at least in effect and in psychic repercussions, from cosmic hostility. The animating symbols of unity and harmony, belied and eroded, become nightmare personifications of the Inanimate. Thus it is that Stencil, already feeling "like a sacrificial virgin" (p. 63), must die because he is—like Porpentine—the symbol of a humanized vision grown obsolete. The deadly waterspout is, inevitably, shaped like a "V." As a destructive phenomenon of nature, it represents the collapse of the regenerative Virgin symbol into Adams's vortex of chaotic impersonal forces, a hollow gnostic simulacrum suggestive of entropy and death.

FOUR

Closures and Disclosures

The Quest for Meaning in
The Crying of Lot 49

Pynchon's gnostic vision reaches a sort of nadir in V. in a radical extrapolation of Henry Adams's entropic nightmare. It is the cosmic underwriting of this nightmare that appalls. The decline of humanity toward the Inanimate is symbolically sanctioned by the degeneration of divinity itself from the Virgin to V. The conspiracy—if it exists—to abet this decline seems beyond the possibility of full comprehension, much less effective opposition. Nonetheless, the perception of conspiracy does—as we have seen—animate both Stencils, giving them a sense of history as something informed by changing modes of spirit, and thus instigating a religious consciousness. The problem is that this change takes the form of a dehumanizing descent, and that the consciousness must be increasingly debilitated by despair over the degeneration of its object. The animation of the characters thus seems somewhat incidental and as ultimately futile as the characters themselves in the face of the overwhelming Inanimate.

The case is very different, however, in Pynchon's next novel, *The Crying of Lot 49*. The central figure, Oedipa Maas, must deal constantly with the shadowy quasi-presence of the Tristero conspiracy, the possible existence of which is somehow bound up with the possible existence of a "transcendent meaning" (p. 136). Because we are never out of *her* presence, the charging of that presence by the Tristero revelation puts the question of enhanced religious consciousness at the heart of the experience offered by the novel. Edward Mendelson has explored this question with considerable insight in "The Sacred, the Profane, and *The Crying of Lot 49*," one of the first articles to recognize the importance of sacrality in Pynchon's fiction. For Mendelson, the Tristero is a possible locus of transcendental values that could offer a redemption of the quotidian chaos and banality of modern life, and Oedipa's increasing awareness of it constitutes a "hierophany," a sacralizing revelation that edifies her consciousness.[1] This reading, however, for all its trenchancy and usefulness, finally makes Tristero more normative than the evidence will support.

Thomas Schaub raises precisely this objection in his "Open Letter" to Mendelson, emphasizing the "dark, rough edges" of Oedipa's "information surplus,"[2] e.g., the Tristero revelation, and its "ominous, paralytic aspect" (p. 95). Schaub finally goes so far as to identify Tristero as Oedipa's "own death . . . the price of freedom" (p. 100) from the otherwise exitless tower of modern banality.

What is finally at stake here is the determined sacrality of Mendelson's interpretation and the determined secularity of Schaub's. Reading *Lot 49* as he reads Pynchon's other fiction, Schaub finds it to be a "parable of perception" (p. 96) that ultimately privileges "ambiguity" and the search for pattern rather than any "patterns"—including religious ones—revealed in the text. Oedipa's searches for such patterns, he insists, "are fraught with maybes, dim visions, and the persistent possibility that it is all a joke woven by Inverarity into his will." Mendelson, on the other hand, admits the possibility of Tristero's nonexistence—at least as a transcendental phenomenon—but finds contextual reasons for deemphasizing this possibility in the face of the crescendo of revelation upon which he centers the novel.

Both critics, it would appear, affirm separate elements of a binary opposition that Oedipa experiences as limiting and oppressive, as a contretemps that might have been avoided:

> Perhaps she'd be hounded someday as far as joining Tristero itself, if it existed, in its twilight, its aloofness, its waiting. The waiting above all; if not for another set of possibilities to replace those that had conditioned the land to accept any San Narciso among its most tender flesh without a reflex or a cry, then at least, at the very least waiting for a symmetry of choices to break down, to go skew. She had heard all about excluded middles; they were bad shit, to be avoided; and how had it ever happened here, with the chances once so good for diversity? For it was now like walking among matrices of a great digital computer, the zeroes and ones twinned above, hanging like balanced mobiles, right and left, ahead, thick, maybe endless. Behind the hieroglyphic streets there would either be a transcendent meaning, or only the earth. (CL49, p. 136)

Schaub discreetly (and accurately) points out that "Oedipa objects to the binary structure itself, one term of which is the Tristero which Mendelson finds so heartening" (p. 95). Believing himself true to the spirit of this objection, he nonetheless goes on to deny the availability of "transcendent meaning" to the lives of Oedipa and others. The truth, it seems, "is never present to our knowledge; it is always destroyed by the action it empowers. The action itself remains meaningless, the Message undecoded." The only freedom he can find for Oedipa is the Tristero of "Death" (p. 101). In the name of antibinary ambiguity, Schaub ends up choosing an option that destroys that tension in favor of the meaningless sprawl of

San Narciso and its replications, "only the earth" of arbitrary power dis-
tributions and spiritual confusion.

The difficulty of both critics is understandable. What would it mean
to void the binary opposition presented here as the closed set of choices?
One answer, proposed by Alan Wilde, is to find in Oedipa's heroic *waiting*,
in her refusal to rush the process of choosing, one of the "middles" that
are supposedly "excluded." The development of this possibility leads
Wilde to the unorthodox conclusion that *The Crying of Lot 49* is, among
Pynchon's novels, "the one that most authentically discloses to us the
universe of postmodern quandary."[3] This authenticity is based, for Wilde,
upon Pynchon's "willingness"—in this particular fiction—"to accept randomness, contingency, and uncertainty as part of the very nature of things"
(p. 94), whereas in *V.* and *Gravity's Rainbow* "the postulated middles
[e.g., the acceptance of indeterminacy] reveal themselves . . . to be no more
than so many markers of desire and intention, which the novel's deeper
impulses (in phenomenological terms, their intentional structures) parody
or subvert" (p. 5).

I agree with Wilde that the "middles" of these two novels are to various
extents "subverted," but not that this subversion is solely phenomenological; it is, rather, an aspect of a conscious thematic structure that com-
prehends *all* of Pynchon's novels in a demonstration of how gnostic
religious vectors undermine the domain of the human. Oedipa's "waiting"
is not a stoical acceptance of perpetual metaphysical uncertainty, but an
anxious interval before the "crying" of some Pentecostal revelation. Even
Wilde, arguing for a purely "secular Tristero" to support the postmodern
secularity of his analysis, admits that there "is much in *Lot 49*" that
supports a religious interpretation à la Mendelson (p. 98).

If there is a way out of the religio-secular binarities that constitute this
novel's problematic, it would seem to involve the retention, somehow, of
both "transcendent meaning" *and* a recalcitrant earth, a ground of apeirontic chaos; and with that duality we are returned to the concept of the
metaxy as we have seen it developed—an in-between in which humanity
is to some degree illuminated by spiritual possibility without losing its
base in the opaque materiality of natural process. Oedipa's yearning for
an "excluded middle" can be construed as a form of modernist nostalgia
for the vanished metaxic tension of human and sacred that rendered the
gnostic desecrations of *V.* significant. It is impossible for Tristero to serve
as the transcendental pole of this *metaxy* because it is—as I hope to argue—a gnostic phenomenon. As such, it finally dissolves the redeeming
tension in a hubristic assertion of absolute dominion on its own terms.
Oedipa's fear of being "hounded" into joining Tristero is a fear of ab-
sorption into a totalizing system that would destroy her sense of humanity
and earth—fear of a revelation that threatens to "grow larger than she and
assume her to itself."

Mendelson's discomfort with the notion of this revelation as a wholly benevolent one causes him to enter a qualification that implicitly recognizes this gnostic modality: "The frequent associations of the Trystero with the demonic do not contradict the Trystero's potentially sacred significance: the demonic is a subclass of the sacred, and exists, like the sacred, on a plane of meaning different from the profane and the secular" (p. 122). My only quarrel with this is that it fails to recognize the *dominance* of the demonic in Tristero's machinations, or at least what we know of them. When Mendelson asserts that "the foils to Trystero are always associated with sacrality gone wrong" (p. 117), he obscures the important datum that Trystero itself has just this association. It practices assassination and mind control in the name of its own self-righteous gnostic usurpations, and is explicitly identified by one group as the demiurgic hierarchy responsible for a fallen cosmos.

This identification provides the paradigm case for the gnosticism of Tristero, not only because it fits the ancient Gnostic paradigm so well, but because it gives Tristero an undeniably metaphysical dimension. It is a precept of the Scurvhamites, a seventeenth-century sect of "most pure Puritans" (CL49, p. 116) who have apparently gone to the trouble to bring out a doctored edition of Wharfinger's play *The Courier's Tragedy*, mainly so they can modify one of the couplets to read: "No hallowed skein of stars can ward, I trow, / Who's once been set his tryst with Trystero" (p. 52). According to Professor Bortz, Wharfinger's editor, "Nothing for a Scurvhamite ever happened by accident, Creation was a vast, intricate machine. But one part of it, the Scurvhamite part, ran off the will of God, its prime mover. The rest ran off some opposite Principle, something blind, soulless; a brute automatism that led to eternal death" (p. 116). It is with this "brute Other," the "clockwork" principle (p. 117), that the Scurvhamites identify Tristero, a demonic conglomerate so powerful that even "God's will" cannot save those who have an "appointment" with it.

Tony Tanner characterizes these Scurvhamite beliefs as "somewhat Manichaean,"[4] thus identifying them with one of the principal Gnostic sects. Certainly the division of universal dominion between good and evil deities corresponds to a central doctrine of Manichaeism; but the idea of a clockwork precision in the domain of evil does not. According to Jonas, Mani himself describes the movements of matter in this domain as "disorderly motion," and the Darkness that rules the domain is seen as constantly "raging within itself" (TGR, pp. 211–212). We can find a much more accurate analogue in the doctrine of what might be called orthodox Gnosticism of the Jewish and early Christian varieties. Here, in Jonas's words, the fallen *cosmos* is an "order with a vengeance, alien to man's aspirations. . . . The blemish of nature lies not in any deficiency of order but in the all too pervading completeness of it. Far from being chaos, the creation of the demiurge, unenlightened as it is, is still a system of law" (p. 328).

It is impossible to miss the analogy between this aspect of the

Scurvhamite universe and the antipathetic universe symbolized by the clockwork eye of V. The "brute automatism" that is "blind" and "soulless" and leads to "eternal death" is another version of the Inanimate, destroying the *metaxy* where vision and soul define the human, and expediting the Kingdom of Death. Tanner, in effect, recognizes the perverse gnostic consecration of natural decline when he speaks of the Tristero as "the process of entropy-turned-Manichaean, stealthily at work bringing disorder and death to the human community" (p. 43). In this demiurgic capacity, Tristero parallels V. and *her* shadowy organization as a complex of forces so profoundly life-negating that it appears to belong to a cosmic mythology.

The Manichaean can also turn entropic, however, which is to say that cabalistic terror can become existential despair—a principle that Pynchon demonstrates in the carefully tuned ambiguities of both novels. The decline of what we might call the sense of the sacred in our century may be construed as the loss of a revealed truth about existence, or else as the loss of an obfuscating superstition—although the irony that it is loss in either case is one that we must explore. Just as Herbert Stencil must face the possibilities that the V. who anchors his myth is nothing more than a woman—or series of women—with a penchant for intrigue, and that history is merely random occurrence sprinkled with coincidence, so Oedipa is forced to wonder whether Tristero is a spurious revelation, a string of clues planted by Pierce Inverarity as a hoax that parodies revelation. If this is the case, she would seem to be left with "just the street" of San Narciso, that part of the binary opposition that opens into the wasteland of existential gnosticism.

But it is precisely at this point that we come across an irony central to Pynchon's epistemological ambiguity and, finally, to the sense of the religious that informs his work. A hoax set up to resemble an elaborate conspiracy is in itself an elaborate conspiracy; and insofar as it aims to control the whole sense of reality of its victims, it is gnostic in design. If Inverarity has indeed gone to the trouble to manipulate, bribe, and suborn so many coconspirators posthumously, then the Tristero really does exist as a reflection of his own power mania, the mania for artifice and dehumanization that has produced San Narciso, Yoyodyne, Fangoso Lagoons, and other insults to the "tender flesh" of the land. His vast, shadowy enterprise would appear to be a precursor of the gnostic Cartel, as would the Tristero; in fact, that enterprise may be an *aspect* of Tristero. The notion of a gigantic, powerful conspiracy with its own laws and morality, moving toward unguessable degrees of control, begins to acquire a religious significance not dependent upon a Scurvhamite cosmology or even upon Tristero's autonomous existence.

Another way of putting this is to say that Oedipa's newfound sense of revelation and of a religious dimension to human existence remains valid even with the decline of Tristero to secular status, and possibly even to the status of a trick. The portion of the novel that describes the receding of "paranoia" (p. 124) about Tristero's supernatural powers, and the discovery of a "secular Tristero," is dismissed by Mendelson as a "potted history" that offers the possibility of seeing the Tristero as "merely a symbol, merely a way of speaking with no hieratic significance in itself" ("The Sacred," p. 121). It is a possibility that Mendelson rejects as inconsistent with the thrust of Oedipa's experience, and he is right. We should not, however, gloss over the larger significance of this movement from the religious to the secular, a significance that becomes clear only in a gnostic context that radically destabilizes this antithesis. In this context, ironically, the secular *becomes* the religious if it presumes enough scope and power to challenge the preeminence of the latter. The opposition is never stable because the gradual assumption (or renunciation) of a metaphysical dimension by various value systems tends to create a quite unbinary spectrum.

Even Thurn and Taxis, a secular cartel presumably free of Puritan fanaticism, comes to see its Tristero opponents as possessed of demiurgic potency, "something very like the Scurvhamite's blind, automatic anti-God" (CL49, p. 124); and even when this force, thought to be of transcendental provenance—"a historical principle, a Zeitgeist"—is understood to be "secular," the demonic qualities of "Power, omniscience, implacable malice" continue to be attributed to it. The possibility that Tristero staged the French Revolution for its own ends suggests that this "secular" power amounts more or less to control over human history. The ultimate purport of the secular transformation is that the loss of belief in a literal supernatural machinery in the universe, a loss consonant with modernity, need not mean the loss of religious awe and terror. These emotions can be transferred to a natural machinery that aspires to the metaphysical sway abdicated by the gods, both good and evil.

The circumstances under which the "historical" Tristero was formed and the attitudes of its founders suggest a clearly gnostic origin. Alienated and ostensibly dispossessed by the Thurn and Taxis postal system, Tristero y Calvera "styled himself El Desheredado, the Disinherited, and fashioned a livery of black for his followers, black to symbolize the only thing that truly belonged to them in their exile: the night" (p. 120). He then begins "a sub-rosa campaign of obstruction, terror and depredation along the Thurn and Taxis mail routes." Actually, this brief history encapsulates both the original Gnostic sense of alienation in a hostile realm controlled by a superior but illicit power and the later shift by which the oppressed gnostics become the oppressors, thus creating a new—and paranoid—oppressed. As Jonas puts it in a passage already quoted, "the world (not the alienation from it) must be overcome; and a world degraded to a power system can only be overcome through power." Exiled from the realm of light by what it sees as a demiurgic usurpation, Tristero responds by extending its own realm of darkness so as to encroach upon the prerogatives of the other; in other words, by becoming itself more demiurge than victim.

We are witnessing once again the slippage that the larger gnostic context, as established by Voegelin and Jonas, brings to binary oppositions. When there is no ontologically transcendent power, no "Savior" to break into "the closed system from without" (TGR, p. 328) as there is in Judaeo-Christian Gnosticism, then the disinherited must attack from within, setting up their own closed system with the aim that it will become the subsumer rather than the subsumed. Gnosticism as process thus tends toward a dialectic in which the empowered and the powerless jockey for ascendancy amid a generalized sense of alienation. For the original Gnostics it was nature at its most general, the created cosmos, that was hostile and antispiritual. In the Voegelinian extension, however, this role may be assumed by secondary, artificial "nature," a ubiquitous, pervasive *system* that breeds paranoia—in Pynchon's sense—among the victims of Control so that they themselves seek gnosis and power, and thus partake of the salient, identifying attributes of the oppressors.

This conceptual slippage, inherent in gnosticism as an organizing category, explains the seemingly contradictory aspects of Tristero as an ominous system of demonic control on the one hand and a conduit of spiritual enlightenment on the other. Insofar as Tristero is the beleaguered minority, defending itself against the hostile, enveloping system symbolized by San Narciso and the U.S. Postal Service, it becomes the champion of Pynchon's beloved preterite, the "passed over" derelicts and victims most obviously excluded from the system and oppressed by it. Not only does it provide them with a secret communication network—a system of gnosis—for those deep and unofficial emotions that cannot be entrusted to official channels, but it also offers the possibility of a revolutionary impetus that may open up the System, bringing some hope for spiritual renewal in the San Narciso wasteland. It is precisely this arena of action that is suggested by the clandestine mail service's acronym, W. A. S. T. E.—We Await Silent Tristero's Empire—as well as the preterite, discarded nature of the clientele. In this sense Tristero is enthalpic, taking the silent human "waste" left by social entropy and using it with the energy of vital exchange. Thus, the old sailor can write to his wife, the mother to her son, with a candor and power that must otherwise be suppressed.

The other side of the gnostic opposition, however, is invoked by the "Empire" aspect of Tristero, implying as it does that the ominously "Silent" oppressed "Await" their turn to institute their own system of absolute control. This maneuver is anticipated by Konrad, the seventeenth-century Tristero agent projected by Professor Bortz. Konrad suggests that an alliance between Tristero and Thurn and Taxis would produce a monopoly on communications that would result in complete power over military and commercial movement and over potential competitors. The "so long

. . . disinherited" would then become "the heirs of Europe" (p. 123). This element of threat and suppression is present in a second Tristero acronym, DEATH, which is unpacked as "DON'T EVER ANTAGONIZE THE HORN" (p. 90). One of the definitive characteristics of gnostic empire, according to Voegelin, is its self-proclaimed immunity to criticism or questioning of any sort. Peremptory dealings with those who would open the System by calling its rationalizing gnosis into question are the stratagem by which the System seeks to remain closed, and thus impermeable.

In a modern gnostic modality, then, the blurring of the line between the virtuous and the vicious tends to be at least partly the result of the axiom that demonic force seems called for in disrupting demonic process. When this reciprocal violence grows so widespread and unlicensed that moral boundaries are obscured, it finds its literary correlative in the Jacobean drama—in this case, the spurious *Courier's Tragedy* by the spurious Wharfinger. One episode in particular, the murder of Domenico by Ercole, serves as a vivid example of this ethical indeterminacy and of its roots in Pynchon's gnostic vision. Ercole, a "good" character defending Niccolo—the "rightful" heir to the dukedom of Faggio—finds it necessary to silence Domenico before he betrays Niccolo to certain (and certainly horrible) death. His chosen method of dispatch is to trap Domenico's head in a black box, bind him, tear his tongue out with pincers, stab him, pour a powerful acid into the box, and castrate him, along with other "goodies" (p. 47). This treatment hardly meets the requirement of minimum force; it serves instead to confer upon Ercole a demonic status made explicit by his own mocking speech:

> Thy pitiless unmanning is most meet,
> Thinks Ercole the zany Paraclete.
> Descended this malign, Unholy Ghost,
> Let us begin thy frightful Pentecost. (p. 47)

This taunt, screamed out while the disembodied tongue is waved about on a rapier, connects Ercole with the "malign" manifestation of V. as Paraclete. Herbert Stencil's vision of a history increasingly determined by forces so insidious that they seem a single demonic spirit dictating messages of anarchic violence is anticipated by Ercole's self-image here, a parodic reflection of the Holy Ghost as gnostic demiurge. In the latter case, however, the gift of tongues is not the wild cacophony of competing imperatives to violence, but the "gift" of no-tongue, the infrahuman silence that follows the last disorderly attempts at ordering. In this light, Domenico's "tongueless attempts to pray" (p. 46) appear as desperate, hypocritical nostalgia for a metaxic harmony destroyed partially by the demonic forces with which he has allied himself. The now-ubiquitous violence brings him the antiword that prefigures the wordless *apeiron*.

The gnostic revelation, then, is a vision that destroys; it is the "truth" about a world in which "spirit" is dedicated to the eradication of the spiritual, and thus of the human. Once this desolate—and desolating— picture is viewed with full force, the seer becomes its victim in that he (or she) is permanently traumatized by the ascendancy of the demonic. Coleridge's mariner and Keats's "palely loitering" knight are essentially victims of gnostic revelations, as are various other Romantic isolatos. Pynchon's works are replete with examples, but perhaps the most notable is Hugh Godolphin, whose Vheissuvian vision in Antarctica may fairly be said to have wrecked his repose in humanity. The reverberations of this experience continue throughout the novel *V.* and finally into *The Crying of Lot 49*, where they become a part of the dying sailor's hallucinations as projected by Oedipa: "She knew that the sailor had seen worlds no other man had seen if only because there was that high magic to low puns, because DT's must give access to dt's of spectra beyond the known sun, music made purely of Antarctic loneliness and fright" (p. 96). In the polar wasteland of his delirium tremens, the old drunk has had a vision of the ultimate alienation, of the static and dehumanized Kingdom of Death.

This appalling macrocosm is the limit toward which the tiny particles of decay, "dt's" as the time differentials of calculus, tend. Each is a "vanishingly small instant in which change had to be confronted at last for what it was . . . where death dwelled in the cell . . . at its most quick" (pp. 95–96). Thus, there is metaphorical "truth" in the baseless fantasies of the sailor's delirium as he glimpses the awful figurative vistas building behind the mathematically demonstrable intervals of change. It is the same sort of truth experienced by other visionaries—in Oedipa's catalogue, saints, clairvoyants, true paranoids, and dreamers—who are acting in special relation to "the word, or whatever it is the word is there, buffering, to protect us from" (p. 95).

This word is, presumably, that "act of metaphor" which "was a thrust at truth and a lie, depending where you were: inside, safe, or outside, lost" (p. 95). Once again, the gnostic matrix plays havoc with dichotomies. To be "inside" and "safe" in a gnostic vision such as the sailor's delirium is to experience the dehumanizing isolation of the extreme outsider and the existential insecurity that accompanies it. The sailor is one of the preterite, and therefore "blessed" with both the normative status of victim and the "divine" revelation of his preterition. Oedipa seems on the edge of a similar dispensation with her glimpses of the sailor's Antarctic and of the Tristero. Although the latter provides the sailor with a means of mitigating his isolation, its gnostic qualities enhance—for Oedipa, at least—the paranoid sense of pervasive menace, of a crucial but unfathomed factor in everyday experience.

Nonetheless, Oedipa finds the prospect of gnosis irresistible, especially insofar as there is promise of the definitive revelation, "the direct, epileptic Word, the cry that might abolish the night" (p. 87). Her fear is that this "central truth" is something "too bright for her memory to hold; which must always blaze out, destroying its own message irreversibly, leaving an overexposed blank when the ordinary world came back" (p. 69). This dream of a magical formula that will reveal the penetralia, the last cosmic secrets, is the one dreamed by the Lurianic cabalists in relation to the mystical names of God, and carries with it the same notion of a potency so overwhelming—as we saw in the previous chapter—that humanity is strained and threatened by the very concept.

If Oedipa is indeed unable to assimilate this revelation, she is left in the spiritually unenlightened state that Schaub's strictures suggest, and must continue to roam the San Narciso wasteland. If, on the other hand, the "Word" is fully comprehended, she risks being assimilated by that which speaks it, being bound through gnosis either as participant in or victim of a possibly malevolent system. Certainly the absolute disjuncture between the "overexposed blank" of this mysterious Word and the "ordinary world" makes it problematic that the former exists in any edifying relation to the latter. In metaxic Christianity, the Word that was God is made flesh and dwells among us in order to exert a constant redemptive function upon the nontranscendent ordinary. A remote, inaccessible Word, its aura emanating more menace than love, cannot easily duplicate this function.

The possibility of the Tristerian Word's possessing a beneficent aspect cannot be ruled out, of course, since Pynchon's transcendental ground remains undifferentiated in the cosmos of *Lot 49* and since the preterite are apparently served by its functionings; but Oedipa's lot remains one of hopeful and apprehensive frustration, spiced by a voluptuous terror. To submit to the possibility of a conscious demonic force at work behind events is to submit to the thrill of such life-endangering situations as high balconies, roller coasters, and feeding carnivores—"any death wish that could be consummated by some minimum gesture" (p. 87). The ironic duality of gnostic "redemption" could hardly be caught more vividly. The animation of what had seemed to be the existential wasteland by sentient powers may be in itself a ground for rejoicing and worship; but if these powers serve in their turn the Kingdom of Death, submission to their sway constitutes the death worship that Voegelin finds inseparable from gnostic movements. Yeats's apocalyptic observation that "the worst are full of passionate intensity"[5] brings its irony to bear directly upon Pynchon's apocalypse, in which the conspiracy against the animate is prosecuted with the fiercest animation.

This antipathy between gnostic Word and vitalizing spirit is absolutely central to Pynchon's thought, and will constitute—in the assault of various language-sanctioned conspiracies on primordial nature—one of the main dialectics of *Gravity's Rainbow*. In *Lot 49*, we find it explicitly realized in the life and death of Randolph Driblette, the director of *The Courier's Tragedy*. Oedipa's hope that he can provide some point of textual authority to validate the Tristero is thwarted by Driblette's denial that such authority exists. For him, words (and thus The Word) are nothing but "rote noises" (p. 56) to stimulate actors' memories. The living reality, the significance, lies solely in the spirit of the interpreter—in this case, Driblette himself—as he projects the "closed little universe" of the play from its true matrix, his own imagination. Even facts, the things words express, are nothing but dead "traces, fossils," without the animation provided by this private psychic magic.

Whatever the momentary attraction of this creative energy, it finally amounts to an imprisoning solipsism like that of the women in the Remedios Varos murals that had saddened Oedipa in Mexico, the world as a tapestry embroidered by captive maidens who can know only their own embroidery. Driblette's denial of all transcendental givens and restraints in favor of the individual as the legislator of significance fits exactly the pattern of gnostic existentialism as Jonas describes it in yet another passage quoted above: "the self is thrown back entirely upon itself in its quest for meaning and value. Meaning is no longer found but is 'conferred.' Values are no longer beheld in the vision of objective reality, but are posited as feats of valuation." In the absence of the Word, the Logos, man arrogates the absent authority to himself, and thus effects what is finally—according to Jonas—a gnostic alienation from the natural order of being.

The great attraction of Tristero for Oedipa is that it offers, as potential Word, the hope of an imperative transcending the arbitrary embroideries of the tower, with its isolating magic. For Driblette, however, imprisoned in his own existential hubris, Tristero is merely "The Adversary" (p. 56) of Wharfinger's play—possibly based upon history, but with no more present reality than other "traces" and "fossils," and "without value or potential" in itself. It is as though this dismissal of the demonic Word and its power evokes the Word's retribution in the form of Driblette's death by drowning. The moment of suicidal madness that leads him to walk out into the Pacific in costume from a play involving Tristero may well have been instigated—as Oedipa suspects—by Tristero itself in its relentless "stripping away" of the "men" (p. 114) who might have helped her. The existential alternative, assuming the absence or nonexistence of Tristero, is a suicide based upon the despair accompanying the perception of the arbitrary, of the gratuitous nature of a life without the imperative of any word. In either case, the gnostic bifurcation involves a common ground of alienation and metaxic collapse.

It is ironically appropriate that Driblette, the denier of transcendental values, should drown in the ocean that constitutes a possible locus of such values. Oedipa invests the Pacific with a positive religious significance in much the way that Pynchon will valorize Earth as a whole in *Gravity's Rainbow*. She believes "in some principle of the sea as redemption for Southern California . . . some unvoiced idea that no matter what you did to its edges the true Pacific stayed inviolate and integrated or assumed the ugliness at any edge into some more general truth" (p. 37). Her larger meditation grants the Pacific an explicitly cosmic dimension—"the hole left by the moon's tearing-free"—as well as the status of a mystical force field: "You could not hear or even smell this but it was there, something tidal began to reach feelers in past eyes and eardrums."

The notion that this aura arouses our brains in ways that transcend the subtlest detection devices of science looks forward to *Gravity's Rainbow*, with its tension between mysticism and gnostic technology. In *The Crying of Lot 49*, the Pacific as spiritual plexus stands in contradistinction to the San Narciso wasteland, with its sweeping suburban sprawl and its seacoast effluvia of "surfers, beach pads, sewage disposal" (p. 36) and other pollutants—again, the social modality of apeirontic degeneration. Oedipa, however, stops short of affirming "inviolate" (p. 37) Nature as the transcendental pole of a *metaxy*; her dream of Pacific redemption still is only an "arid hope." This tentativeness, together with those normative aspects of Tristero that also offer some hope of redemption, suggests that Pynchon has not yet managed to differentiate, in *Lot 49*, a religious norm that stands in clear antithesis to the several varieties of gnostic alienation.

The hope that the Tristerian Word has manifested itself in a sort of enthalpic miracle and that she can participate in this redemptive spirituality leads Oedipa to seek out John Nefastis and his spurious antientropy machine. This device, which had existed only as a heuristic, highly theoretical concept of the physicist Clerk Maxwell, has supposedly been realized by Nefastis as a box with a piston inside and a picture of Clerk Maxwell on the outside. Concentration on this picture by a "sensitive" is supposed to evoke Maxwell's Demon (in this case, presumably an emanation of Maxwell himself), the phantasmal agent that sorts fast and slow molecules in order to sustain perpetual motion in a heat engine, thus circumventing the Second Law of Thermodynamics. It is precisely the entropic homogenization of the molecules, the decline of energy potential, that yields the information necessary for the Demon to prevent the homogenization. In the classical formulation, information entropy—the decline in amount of information delivered—decreases as thermodynamic entropy increases. This information is, without some intervention that can use it, the message arising from decay, the word of apeirontic decline becoming clear only as the decline approaches a terminal stasis. In a significant sense, it is thus the desolate Word of existential gnosticism that sounds through Pynchon's early entropy-centered fiction.

The redeeming intervention will take the form later, in *Gravity's Rainbow*, of cyclical renewal, a natural enthalpy that can postpone the final stasis indefinitely. In the world of *Lot 49*, however, there is only the spurious gnostic Demon, a man-made (or, at least, man-conceived) entity designed to interfere—through a kind of magic—with natural process. Insofar as this intervention defeats the generalized Death immanent in heat-death, it obviously has a normative function; but this function is compromised, as are all gnostic "positives," by antinatural means and demonic provenance. In the latter regard, Maxwell's photograph suggests to Oedipa an ominous set of "hangups, crises, spookings in the middle of the night [that] might be developed from the shadowed subtleties of his mouth, hidden under a full beard" (p. 78). The origin of the picture, the Society for the Propagation of Christian Knowledge, carries its own overtones of religious conspiracy and reminds us of the usurping growth of the Gnostic heresy within its Christian host.[6] All of this prepares the final irony that Oedipa's failure to operate the machine may be seen as an affirmative symptom, a sign of her incompatibility with the deranged world of Nefastis and finally with the forces of the Adversary.

It may well be that Pierce Inverarity, even after death, is in some way a member of these forces. Oedipa connects him explicitly with Maxwell's Demon as "the linking feature in a coincidence" (p. 89) that could easily be part of Tristero's designs upon her. Certainly the episode in which this connection is made, Oedipa's reunion with the anarchist Jesús Arrabal, provides us with a portrait of "the dead man" that suggests transcendental evil. That this moral judgment is made by a champion of the poor named "Jesús" is enough to suggest that Pierce represents a Satanic archetype, but the religious tensions here are more characteristically Pynchonian than those in the basic Christian antithesis. Pynchon's sympathy for anarchists such as Arrabal is based partly on their feeling for the preterite and partly on their championing of an absolute freedom that is the very antithesis of gnostic restraint—and that involves a dream of natural beneficence which anticipates the naturalistic norm toward which he is working.

What *this* Jesús has in effect set up is an anarchist *metaxy* anchored by a transcendental pole—"another world" of "spontaneous and leaderless" revolutions in which "the soul's talent for consensus" (p. 88) makes possible an effortless and automatic functioning of the masses. Pierce represents the other pole, the image of iron control and entrenched, unmitigated elitism that is finally unthinkable in the ordinary human realm of mixed good and evil, where even "the privilegiado is always, to a finite percentage, redeemed—one of the people" (p. 89). Jesús, faithful to the concept of metaxic tension, can therefore account for Pierce—if Pierce is serious—only as a "miracle," an apparition of pure evil as supernaturally terrifying as "a Virgin appearing to an Indian." In this case, the "Virgin" is the male analogue to the Bad Virgin in *V.*, an ominous gnostic figure who aims at the absolute dominion of all that is antihuman and antinatural. It might not be too much to say that in Pynchon's world of religious simulacra, Pierce is to the Virgin of Chartres (or Guadeloupe) as the American CIA is to its anarchist namesake, the Conjuración de los Insurgentes Anarquistas.

The situation is given the true gnostic twist by the fact that Jesús apparently receives his "anarcho-syndicalist" newspaper through the Tristero service. The normative function of its title, *Regeneración*, is humorously compromised by the delivery of the paper some sixty years late, a lapse that has obviously permitted degeneration to proceed. Another irony, this one more ominous, is the paper's date, 1904—the Annus Horribilis of the novel V., the year of von Trotha's genocidal rites in the Sudwest. An additional convolution is provided by Jesús's humble acceptance as a "footsoldier" of a ludicrous contradiction, an anarchist hierarchy: "The higher levels have their reasons" (p. 89). It is no wonder that Oedipa carries this thought "back out into the night with her," since it fits so well the image of another mysterious and arbitrary wielder of power, the Tristero. The possibility that Tristero is abetting "regeneration" by helping those who would help the preterite is severely mitigated by all of these considerations, with their dark gnostic cast. The final turn of irony's screw is the conflict between Pierce's role as possible Tristero initiate and his role as Adversary of the anarchist cause that Tristero serves. Again, the conceptual slippage inherent in gnosticism produces a complex moral dialectic that opens into spiritual ambiguities and their concomitant terror.

One result of this terror is a constant pressure on the metaxy, the domain of the human. This pressure, which takes the form of alienation or demonic menace, is translated into a paranoia that may seek relief from the stress by either confrontation or retreat. The former involves a movement of usurpation or identification toward the transcendental ground; the latter an illusory denial of this ground that serves as anodyne and evasion, and is apeirontic in direction. Both are abdications of the metaxic responsibility for human balance. Both Mucho, Oedipa's husband, and Hilarius, her psychiatrist, are involved in such abdications, and their experiences serve to instruct Oedipa in the importance of maintaining this balance in the face of Tristero's pressure.

Hilarius's involvement at Buchenwald with the Nazis and his continuing involvement with Freudian psychology give him a sort of dual gnostic citizenship. We have already examined how Voegelin's analysis of both Nazism and Freudianism in the light of gnosticizing tendencies bears upon Pynchon's earlier fiction. Now Pynchon brings together, in the person of Hilarius, both these examples of what Voegelin has called "modern radical deformations of consciousness" (A, p. 107). Another of Voegelin's references to Freud—quoted earlier in connection with "Mortality and Mercy in Vienna"—is particularly useful here. His assertion that "the Freudian symbol of the libido" has "the declared purpose of mobilizing the acheronta against the power of reason" provides a powerful metaphorical link, in the case of Hilarius, between the "Acheron" of the subconscious and the dark, infernal river of fascist impulses. In both cases the lucid "middle" of humanitarian moderation is forsworn in favor of a licentious, tension-destroying descent toward the anomie of the apeiron, and we are back in the intoxicating "freedom" of Foppl's Sudwest—the seedbed of Nazi genocide.

Hilarius's job at Buchenwald was to drive Jews insane on the theory that a "catatonic Jew was as good as a dead one" (p. 102). This perversion of what is supposed to be a science of human restoration—psychiatry— into mind-destroying, dehumanizing techniques of Control provides a paradigm linkage between gnostic reality-manipulation and the Kingdom of Death. Distortion of the stabilizing natural order, the key to the requisite alienation, is undertaken by means of Brechtian vignettes, operations, drugs, backward-running clocks, and other radical restructurings of ex- periential givens. The initial irony is that a gnostic project of Control is used to produce the sort of alienation and disorientation identified with the experience of the gnostic as victim. This is in fact the victimization inseparable from gnostic power-dislocation and redoublings. The subse- quent irony is that Hilarius himself falls victim—years later—to this ter- rorism and projects around him the paranoiac demons he had once invoked for others. Voegelin's construction of the gnostic enterprise as being ultimately an exercise in insanity finds a personal focus in the instance of Hilarius's breakdown.

This fit of violent irrationality—which culminates in an armed con- frontation with the police—represents the sudden failure of a rationalizing evasion, a Freudian schema that has "no Buchenwalds in it" (p. 102). Hilarius has sought desperately, as an act of penance, to believe in a denatured and exorcized nursery world where the ovens of Auschwitz "would be converted over to petit fours and wedding cakes, and the V-2 missiles to public housing for the elves." As in the case of Randolph Driblette, the denial of transcendental evil seems to have unleashed a demonic assault from the sources of this evil. The dark forces embodied earlier in Nazi exterminators, the rampaging denizens of twisted and long- suppressed hatreds, are externalized in Hilarius's paranoiac hallucina- tions as avenging "angels of death"; and a central Voegelin axiom—that gnostic orderings breed apeirontic disorder—is further corroborated.

Although he has been more or less destroyed by the demonic fantasies he tried to suppress, Hilarius has discovered the value of fantasy on the one hand and the danger of absolute suppression on the other. He reads, like a good Blakean, a normative lesson into his extreme experiences. His warning to Oedipa to "Cherish" her fantasy and to protect it against "Freudians" and "pharmacists" (p. 103) is in effect a warning to preserve her private sense of the transcendental from the mania for a monistic materialism—one form of gnostic immanentization. If she loses this sense, she will "begin to cease to be." The threatened process is one of apeirontic decline, the loss of the delicate human equilibrium between matter and spirit in favor of the former. The irony that her "fantasy" is focused upon the Tristero brings us back to the novel's central paradox, the adumbration of a spiritual norm strongly tainted by the demonic. The insidiously com- plex and pervasive nature of gnostic spirituality compromises even the search for a redemptive antithesis to gnosticism.

Another of Hilarius's formulations for the balance that has—ironically—eluded him, is "relative paranoia" (p. 101). This concept, which Pynchon will grant some degree of normative status in Gravity's Rainbow, involves a clear distinction between one's own identity and that of "others." Put another way, the belief in autonomous external sentience, if only in the form of individual egos, is necessary if one is to function sanely in the world. At the level of transcendentals, the "other" in the form of the Word—an imperative from outside the individual consciousness—is crucial if a metaxic equilibrium is to be inhabited and the megalomaniacal doom of Driblette avoided. An absolute paranoia would mean the usurpation of human effectuality and freedom by the spiritual, i.e., demonic, pole in the triumph of cabalistic gnosticism, while a complete absence of paranoia would mean the triumph of the existential variety—the solipsistic nightmare of the arbitrary, a state of total unconnectedness.

It is this latter condition of obliviousness to the integrity of reality's givens that Hilarius associates with the taking of LSD, a drug that causes egos to "lose their sharp edges" by blurring the distinction between "me" and "the others" (p. 101). This hallucinogenic evasion, which is much like Hilarius's own misguided attempt to sanitize the dark corners of the unconscious through Freudian psychology, is Mucho's chosen form of coping with—i.e., denying—the complex discreteness of things. Under the influence of this drug he is, according to his employer French, "losing his identity," becoming "less himself and more generic. . . . a walking assembly of man" (p. 104). This colleague's derisive name for this humanoid melange is "the Brothers N," an abstract variable reflecting the dehumanization that Mucho's loss of identity actually entails. In the name of catholicity he achieves only dispersion and shallowness.

Mucho's multiple identities are closely tied to the novel's parody of Pentecost. He speaks in myriad tongues, but this glossolalia culminates in a Babel of quasi-mystical nonsense, thus marking him as a gnostic apostle of entropy. He subverts the Word by breaking it down into presemantic components of frequency and harmonics that suggest the inchoate apeiron rather than the humanely structured metaxy. By doing away with differences in time of utterance ("arbitrary") and in speakers ("the different power spectra are the same, give or take a small percentage"), he reduces the complex spirituality of all human speech to a single voice, a "big, God, maybe a couple hundred million chorus saying 'rich, chocolaty goodness' together" (p. 106). The commercial banality of this pronouncement is so extreme as to effect a parody of the "God" voice involved— again, much as the Marabar Caves of Forster's A Passage to India deflate the most exalted religious pronouncements to a meaningless echo. The Logos is caricatured here as a mindless aural wallowing that signposts only chaos. The disguising of this chaos as spiritual unity returns us to the elemental irony of gnostic pretensions. Mucho imagines that a fullness of being has been gained, when in fact a degeneration into aimless "power spectra" has occurred. Oedipa realizes with reluctance that her earlier parting from him "was the day she'd seen Mucho for the last time. So much of him already had dissipated" (p. 108).

In one of the contradictory doublings that we have already encountered, Mucho uses his gnostic fantasy to flee a corresponding gnostic nightmare. His dream of "rich, chocolaty" unison serves him as an anodyne against an earlier dream in which he would be menaced by the sign over his used-car lot announcing membership in N.A.D.A., the National Automobile Dealers' Association: "Just this creaking metal sign that said nada, nada, against the blue sky. I used to wake up hollering" (p. 107). The mere use of the word *nada,* Spanish for "nothing," in an American work of fiction invokes its paradigm gloss in Hemingway's "A Clean, Well-Lighted Place," where it carries the same burden of existential alienation and dread as it visited upon Mucho. In both cases, *nada* is the vacated spiritual center of a "secular" gnosticism that shares the desolating effects of its demonic counterpart. This overlap is especially striking in the parodic prayer of Hemingway's waiter, which could so easily apply to the life-negating presences of V. and their Inanimate empire: "Our nada who art in nada, nada be thy name thy kingdom nada thy will be nada in nada as it is in nada."[7] The old man in the waiter's cafe is fleeing in alcohol and private ritual the debilitating insight that "It was all a nothing and a man was nothing too," just as Mucho seeks to fill the mocking emptiness of "the blue sky" with the pseudoprofundities of LSD.

The other gloss on "nada" is Pynchon's own, and arises from the description of the used cars bought and sold beneath the N.A.D.A. sign. These rusting, defective machines, filled with the poignant detritus of their preterite owners, constitute a bleak existential revelation for Mucho, an automotive version of entropy's "unvarying gray sickness" (p. 5). The only nourishment offered the spirit is "a salad of despair, in a gray dressing of ash, condensed exhaust, dust, body wastes." These awful residues are indices, like the stains on the old sailor's mattress, to the tawdry, "futureless" lives from which they emanated, and open into the same Antarctic vistas of hopeless alienation. The drug in which Mucho seeks escape from these vistas has, of course, been prescribed for him by Hilarius, whose blatant manipulations qualify him as a sort of psychiatric demiurge. Once again, the labyrinth in which the victim of a gnostic revelation seeks refuge is itself revealed to have a gnostic coloration.

Oedipa is in flight from a vision of America similar to Mucho's and faces the same problem of a tainted alternative. Because she chooses, as Hilarius points out, to remain in the open-minded and balanced posture of "relative paranoia" and because she is unwilling to abandon her human identity, she cannot participate in Mucho's self-destructive evasion. Rather, she must head deeper into the only real choice the binary opposition has left her, the Tristero, and hope that its mechanisms of Control will leave some space for the exercise of a peculiarly human spirituality—

for a mode of transcendence that is not demonic or absolute. If Tristero permits such a mode, the possibility surely arises from the link between the exile of the organization and that of the preterite who have also lost their portion of the American legacy, and whom Tristero serves as a conduit of vital interchange. In one fantasy of largesse, Oedipa imagines using her capacity as executrix to spread Inverarity's "legacy among all those nameless," those who "shared Tristero's secret as well as its exile" (p. 136). This act would function as an incipient reinheriting of the disinherited, the repatriation of the exiles, and thus fits closely the gnostic paradigm of the Return to the Center.

The apocalyptic nature of this event, also part of the paradigm, is inherent in Oedipa's tentative self-image as "that magical Other" reached by the random dialing of the preterite. This female redeemer—"who would reveal herself out of the roar of relays, monotone litanies of insult, filth, fantasy, love whose brute repetition must someday call into being the trigger for the unnamable act, the recognition, the Word" (p. 136)—will instigate the assembly of the shards of light into their primal unity, bringing to an end the years of desolate and impotent alienation amid an unsatisfactory melange of conflicting passions. There is a strong echo here of the Shekinah, the feminine aspect of God in the Jewish religion. The "exile of the Shekinah" was, according to Gershom Scholem, "assimilated in Jewish circles at a particular stage with the Gnostic idea of the divine spark that is in exile in the terrestrial world, and also with the mystic view . . . of the historical community of Israel" (K, p. 22). Oedipa, herself an alienated wanderer in search of gnosis, fantasizes about incarnating the revelation that will make it possible for her fellow exiles to return to community, that will enable the persecuted preterite to become the chosen people.

The problem remains, however, that the disinherited must indulge in "brute" repetitions that include "insult" and "filth" in order to draw the Word into the fallen cosmos. The dark side of gnostic redemption is intimated here, but appears more literally in the room where the Tristero stamps are to be auctioned and where Oedipa encounters secretive men in "black mohair" with "pale, cruel faces" (p. 137)—figures much like the Tristero agents who slaughtered the party of Diocletian Blobb. The auctioneer spreads his arms "in a gesture that seemed to belong to the priesthood of some remote culture; perhaps to a descending angel" (p. 138).

Edward Mendelson interprets this scene—in an insight absolutely basic to understanding this novel—as "a parody of Pentecost" ("The Sacred," p. 134), since it is lot 49 that is being cried and since Pentecost occurs forty-nine days after Easter. What is at stake in this auction, he asserts, is "the moment before a Pentecost revelation," and this is the reason that "the novel ends with Oedipa waiting, with the 'true' nature of the Trystero never established: a manifestation of the sacred can only be believed in; it can never be proved beyond doubt" (p. 135). My only quarrel with all this is that Mendelson does not pursue the implications of his own term *parody* to their final conclusion. Precisely what sort of sacred manifestation can Oedipa be waiting for that would resemble the caricature of Pentecost in *The Courier's Tragedy*? This "perverted" (p. 134) gift of tongues, as Mendelson calls it, is at least as likely to represent a visitation of the demonic as it is a spiritual blessing. Oedipa's cosmic enlightenment may easily turn out to be the realization of entrapment behind the locked "heavy door" (p. 138) of a malign absolutism.

Another Biblical gloss that supports this possibility is suggested by the auctioneer's name—Passerine—and the likening of his name to that of a "descending angel." The mention of the "Angel of Death" several paragraphs earlier and the inevitable comparison with the descending "Unholy Ghost" of *The Courier's Tragedy* serve to link Passerine to Passover and its visitation of death upon the firstborn of those not privy to certain secret knowledge. Such a myth lends itself naturally to the gnosis of Tristero, with its arcane networks and its mystique of terror.

Oedipa's final vigil in the auction room is one of waiting for this gnosis or else for the knowledge that it does not exist. Ironically, even if the latter is the case, she has been spiritually awakened by the *possibility* of Tristero both to the San Narciso death kingdom and to the vision of transcending it: "For there either was some Tristero beyond the appearance of the legacy America, or there was just America and if there was just America then it seemed the only way she could continue, and manage to be at all relevant to it, was as an alien, unfurrowed, assumed full circle into some paranoia" (p. 137). The paranoid alien, constantly aware of the demiurgic machinations that render her own habitation spiritually desolate, and dreaming beyond this schema of her "true" home—i.e., an uncorrupted America— is the archetypal gnostic victim; and Oedipa is proposing this role as her sole mode of continuation and relevance without Tristero. If, on the other hand, Tristero exists, it seems to offer an equally gnostic alternative of rebellious "exiles" seeking to substitute their version of Control for that of the prevailing powers. One of the things Oedipa must decide is whether the transcendence offered by Tristero's gnosis affirms or negates the human and humane equilibrium she prizes. It is, as we have seen, quite possible that the other "mode of meaning behind the obvious" (p. 137) is a demonic mode inimical to Oedipa's fantasized ideals.

That Pynchon would paint—through Oedipa's eyes—an existential wasteland, and then a normatively ambiguous path of redemption from it, represents a dilemma basic to the gnostic vision of *Lot 49*. This vision contains, reflexively, its own critique in the ironic dialectic that gnostic morality entails; but it is too nearly congruent, at this stage, with Pynchon's own vision for a clear alternative to emerge. If transcendence and its accompanying animation cannot be clearly differentiated from demonic conspiracy, with its apeirontic vectors, we are faced with the normative ambiguities and contradictions that have led a number of intelligent critics to locate Pynchon's "center" in a conscious project of epistemological decentering. But it is at least as plausible—and perhaps truer to the fiction's peculiar urgencies—to argue that these problems of validity, authority, and definitive resolution are the dramatic and cleverly exploited symptoms of a continuing religious quest, not the final record of a secular search that has ended in undecidability.

A crucial indicator of the direction this quest is taking is provided by those motifs in *The Crying of Lot 49* that show an aspect of Pynchon's vision *not* congruent with some variety of gnosticism: the mere possibility of a life-affirming and non-totalizing transcendence, the communications network of spontaneous and unselfish devotion among the preterite, and the suggestion—symbolized by the Pacific—of a locus of redeeming values to be found in the natural order. These survive in stubborn contradistinction to the destructive gnostic pressures permeating the world of the novel and provide the crystal around which Orphic naturalism will form to furnish a powerful and beneficent alternative in Pynchon's *next* novel.

FIVE

Orphic *contra* Gnostic

The Religious Dialectic
of *Gravity's Rainbow*

It seems fair to say that *Gravity's Rainbow* begins where *The Crying of
Lot 49* ends: in a dream of liberation that enfolds a nightmare of more
constricting imprisonment. The "Evacuation" that Pirate Prentice is quite
literally dreaming when the novel opens is suddenly revealed as "not a
disentanglement from, but a progressive *knotting into*" (p. 3). We are
presented here with a now-familiar paradox: an attempt of the preterite
to escape from gnostic menace—symbolized in this instance by the
"screaming" of the Cartel's Rocket—even as the attempt itself is hopelessly compromised by the gnostic assumptions on which it is based. The
path "out" twists back upon itself in insidious permutations of Control,
as power configurations expand to metastructures that stymie the aspiring
fugitive and drive him deeper into the labyrinth of preterition. Thus the
Evacuation proceeds:

> they go in under archways, secret entrances of rotted concrete that only looked
> like loops of an underpass... certain trestles of blackened wood have moved
> slowly by overhead, and the smells begun of coal from days far to the past,
> smells of naphtha winters, of Sundays when no traffic came through, of the
> coral-like and mysteriously vital growth, around the blind curves and out the
> lonely spurs, a sour smell of rolling-stock absence, of maturing rust, devel-
> oping through those emptying days . . . to try to bring events to Absolute
> Zero...and it is poorer the deeper they go...ruinous secret cities of poor, places
> whose *names he has never heard.* (pp. 3–4)

The enmeshment here is in nature denatured, in a hopelessly decadent
existence in which even human beings belong to an encompassing detritus
that no longer participates in cyclical renewal. The density and compre-
hensiveness with which Pynchon presents this gnosticized world's body
are an important aspect of the novel itself as an encyclopedic "knotting
in," but the proliferation of the machinery of gnostic parody and slippage
is equally important. From this latter angle, *Gravity's Rainbow* is a daunt-
ingly intricate web of reciprocities, ironic correspondences, inversions,

and unexpected doublings, one effect of which is to disorient us from our linear, simplistic mappings of experience. The psychologist Pointsman, for instance, is haunted by the mysterious "symmetry" of the two German rockets:

> Outside, out in the Blitz, the sounds of V-1 and V-2, one the reverse of the other.... Pavlov showed how mirror-images Inside could be confused. Ideas of the opposite. But what new pathology lies Outside now? What sickness to events—to History itself—can create symmetrical opposites like these robot weapons?
> Sign and symptoms. Was Spectro right? Could Outside and Inside be part of the same field? (p. 144)

The suggestion here of a profound historical pathology that may finally be indistinguishable from psychopathology, of an ominous doubling mechanism deep in the very scheme of things, works to produce the same sense of cosmic entrapment as the densely realized and apparently ubiquitous toils of the Cartel's Plot. The composite result is a strain of cabalistic gnosticism much more potent and pervasive than the varieties that provided the larger thematic tensions of the earlier fiction. The cosmos of *Gravity's Rainbow* is metaphysically volatile, inspirited in the gnostic sense of tortuous human paths constantly opening into ominous penetralia.

Inspiriting, however, is a double-edged sword; it raises the possibility that a complex of forces which *affirms* the human and the natural can also be invested with a transcendental vitality. In Pynchon's universe the doubling process is a richly creative ferment quite capable of producing a normative antithesis. If the "disentanglement from" turns out to be an oppressive "knotting into," it is conceivable that a benevolent "knotting into" might eventually emerge as a *de facto* disentanglement. By projecting the mirror reversal of the gnostic trap, Pynchon displays an image of the natural matrix—the organic womb of creation construed with religious force and every bit as densely woven as its life-negating counterpart.

He is hardly the first twentieth-century author to return to this prehistoric valorizing, but his peculiar path of return gives his affirmation a distinctive angle. Because he *begins* his literary inquiry with an overpowering sense of gnostic malaise as an apparently inescapable given, he must find the locus of spiritual health in a parodic inversion of this malaise and its generating machinery. Thus, since gnosticism itself parodies the natural order in its pretension of redefining or replacing that order, it is by a parody of a parody that Pynchon eventually locates the normative point of origin. To understand this complex reciprocity is to begin, at least, to understand the funhouse-mirror modality of *Gravity's Rainbow* and the all-too-serious comedy of its multiple interreflections.

Out of this dance of parodic opposites rises the basic conflict of *Gravity's Rainbow*, the religious dialectic that structures the novel. It is marked by mystical and supernatural manifestations on both sides, by the presence of fanatical devotees, and by a drive for nothing less than metaphysical dominance. The stakes are for far more than physical or ethical control; they represent finally the right to define ultimate reality and to decide what the individual's relation to this reality is to be. Pynchon locates at the heart of nature the mystical concept of a living, conscious Earth from which all blessings flow and to which Gravity recalls these dispensations in a benevolent cycle of renewal. The religious response evoked by a full realization of this phenomenon is a variety of Orphism that leans heavily upon the assumptions of Rainer Maria Rilke's poetry in its identification with natural process and its assimilation of life and death into a unifying lyric of praise.

The principal exponent of this religion in *Gravity's Rainbow*—a religion I shall refer to as Orphic naturalism—is the author-persona himself, but he allows several characters experiences of transport in which they are profoundly affected by the perception of a sentient Earth and of ultimate union with it. The ultimate triumph of this persona is a document—*Gravity's Rainbow*—that becomes the "Sacred Text" to which it so frequently alludes. In this capacity—as a sort of scriptural metastructure—the book indeed exposes the inadequate and contradictory "Holy Centers" so incisively explored by Molly Hite; but in the very process it functions itself as the image of a more comprehensive and reconciling Center. The book is, in the last analysis, the Orphic Word that preserves, valorizes, and ultimately redeems the chaotic, transient reality it enshrines.

This religious revalorizing of primordial Earth and natural process is anathema to the gnostic technicians who make up the Cartel. Filled with contempt for the casual flux and the imperfections of nature, refusing submission to natural processes in the name of an absolute and man-imposed control, they work toward establishing a surrogate order, an entirely artificial System that will make nature obsolete and will find its unnatural permanence in the stasis of death. Pynchon works out the conflict between these antithetical religions with such care that Orphic naturalism and the gnostic drive toward synthesis and control are shown to parody each other with an eerily perverse precision at almost every point.

This emergence of a metaphysic that affirms human membership in a living natural order out of reaction to a metaphysic that negates both the human and the natural is anticipated, significantly, by Hans Jonas in *The Phenomenon of Life: Toward a Philosophical Biology*. Significantly, because here once again, though there is no evidence that Pynchon has ever read Jonas, the "philosophical force field" described in my preface is at work to generate conceptual structures common to both. That a scholar who has devoted his career to a study of ancient Gnosticism and its modern variants should eventually be led to seek, in the communion of nature, an ontological basis for an antignostic ethic yields us at least a rough prototype for what we might think of as Pynchon's Progress.

Beginning with the "primitive panpsychism" by which early man animated even "Earth, wind, and water" and sought to explain the seeming contradiction of death as a voyage to a new mode of life, Jonas traces a lengthy process of deanimation that extends from the point at which body and spirit were conceived as a duality to the advent of a materialism that jettisons spirit entirely.[1] He locates the "peak of the dualistic development" in the Gnostic distinction between true life as spirit and "the whole world" as "tomb (prison house, place of exile, etc.) to the soul or spirit, that alien injection in what is otherwise unrelated to life" (p. 14). Finally, the original "panvitalism" is replaced by the parodic "panmechanism" of modern science and philosophy, a "universal ontology of death" that undertakes to explain life as "one of the possible variants of the lifeless" and reduces man to "*L'homme machine*" (pp. 10–11).

After pointing out the contradictions and begged questions in both dualism and materialistic monism, Jonas suggests that we need not be bound by the relativistic, humanity-denying principle of ethics that emanates from the latter, but should seek the ground of such a principle in "an objective assignment by the nature of things (what theology used to call the *ordo creationis*)" (p. 283). This invoking of the "order of creation" parallels Pynchon's consistent valorizing of "Creation" and makes Jonas's concluding speculation a fitting preamble to an examination of the naturalistic value structure that Pynchon attempts to rear against the gnostic devaluation of nature:

> only an ethics which is grounded in the breadth of being, not merely in the singularity or oddness of man, can have significance in the scheme of things. It has it, if man has such significance; and whether he has it we must learn from an interpretation of reality as a whole, at least from an interpretation of life as a whole. But even without any such claim of transhuman significance for human conduct, an ethics no longer founded on divine authority must be founded on a principle discoverable in the nature of things, lest it fall victim to subjectivism or other forms of relativity. However far, therefore, the ontological quest may have carried us outside man, into the general theory of being and of life, it did not really move away from ethics, but searched for its possible foundation. (p. 284)

At its simplest, Pynchon's norm in *Gravity's Rainbow* is life abundant—a spontaneous burgeoning, a thriving, an affirmation of the Earth's natural cycles by which this life is renewed. In order to answer the religious force of gnosticism with a corrective counterforce, Pynchon projects this norm into a transcendental ground a la Voegelin and arrives at the mystical concept of a living Earth whose sentience extends even to its bacteria and its minerals. In a valuable study of the various "paleontologies" underlying *Gravity's Rainbow,* Joel D. Black examines the poetic and philosophical bases of this concept in early nineteenth-century thought, e.g., Emerson's image of Earth as a living "mindbody," Schopenhauer's *Wille,* and Hegel's *Geist.*[2] In our own century, both D. H. Lawrence and Dylan Thomas find their religious center in the Dionysian commonalities of a totally animated cosmos; while Hans Jonas, in turn, undertakes the reanimation of the cosmos by turning the evolutionary assumptions of materialistic monism back upon themselves:

> if it was no longer possible to regard his [man's] mind as discontinuous with prehuman biological history, then by the same token no excuse was left for denying mind, in proportionate degrees, to the closer or remoter ancestral forms, and hence to any level of animality. . . . In the hue and cry over the indignity done to man's metaphysical status in the doctrine of his animal descent, it was overlooked that by the same token some dignity had been restored to the realm of life as a whole. If man was the relative of animals, then animals were the relatives of man and in degrees bearers of that inwardness of which man, the most advanced of their kin, is conscious in himself. . . . the province of "soul," with feeling, striving, suffering, enjoyment, extended again, by the principle of continuous gradation, from man over the kingdom of life. (*Phenomenon,* p. 57)

The sentient Earth for Pynchon is that which alone continues, that which contains the unfathomable mysteries of life processes. It is also that which transcends the individual, whose reverence for this matrix and awareness of its long-term beneficence (despite his short-term fate) constitute the differentiating revelation that pulls him away from blind animality and toward conscious identification with the primal animating powers of procreation and regeneration. It is the most primitive and basic of religious impulses, but in Pynchon as narrator it receives the most subtle differentiation. Having viewed the Earth through scientific lenses, Pynchon is able to return to the contemplation of the "mindbody" with a sophisticated sense of the mysteries and the morality involved.

As the transcendental pole of Pynchon's *metaxy,* animate Earth reflects certain imperatives upon humanity. One is a reverence for the organic mysteries involved in the subtlety and continuity of life. Another is a deep respect for the community of existence, both organic and inorganic, a respect that recognizes the integrity of the various members of that community even as it recognizes the vital kinships between them. Thus, Pirate's banana breakfasts draw even those "allergic or upright hostile to bananas" because they wish to come and revere the miracle of tropical fecundity in freezing wartime England: "the politics of bacteria, the soil's stringing of rings and chains in nets only God can tell the meshes of, have seen the fruit thrive often to lengths of a foot and a half, yes amazing but true" (pp. 5–6).

This passage, which seems at first glance to be a slight arabesque in praise of nature, actually contains the essence of Pynchon's religious reverence. The slightness, in fact, is functional in that it illustrates the tentative gesturing and the subtle diffusions by which Pynchon indicates his approach to the mysteries of Earth as transcendental ground. At its most reductive, "the politics of bacteria" suggests simply such contingencies as species, soil nutrition, heat, light, and moisture. But the term carries with it overtones of practical adjustment and of purpose that suggest some consciousness involved in the process of establishing a particular network of connections. The fruits of this manipulation, the rings and chains of the nutrient molecules, involve a microscopic ramifying so complex that it transcends analysis and partakes of nature's last secrets. The assertion that these meshes are comprehensible only to "God" is not a perfunctory gesture of piety, but is Pynchon's investiture of Earth with transcendental mystery. The implicit contrast is with those Jamfian chemists who manipulate (for quite other "political" ends) their aromatic polymers and thus serve as false priests, desecrating what they cannot hope to unlock.

The motif of the "sacred soil" is established by Pynchon with characteristic flippancy, through a loving description of the detritus that has decayed into this fertile medium. Detritus is, for Pynchon, an index to the spiritual condition of those who have produced it. The rusting steel, peeling paint, and trash-strewn lots of urban decay are symbols of entropy, of society's failure to renew itself through beneficent cycles. In the case of Pirate's greenhouse, however, we have a rich compost formed by the decay of hallucinogenic plants, pig manure, and epicurean vomit. These seemingly ungodly components are actually the opposite of that for Pynchon, who tends to associate them with the "mindless pleasures" of pure being and with the holy innocence of a preindustrial America. Thus the soil directly reflects its culture—or counterculture—one characterized by openness to contingency, harmless trances of communion, and an agrarian closeness to the processes of nature. It is the fertile recycling of Uroboros, as opposed to the steady entropic decline associated with technological bureaucracy.

The banana molecules themselves are of such a "high intricacy" that they share the "conjuror's secret" of "living genetic chains" (p. 10), chains that can preserve a given human face through twenty generations. This combination of unfathomable complexity, benevolent secrecy, miracle, and immortality once again marks the realm of nature's penetralia, the Holy Center of Pynchon's tentative approach. What these complex chains manage, according to Pynchon, is an "assertion-through-structure." The word *assertion* again brushes us with the ghost of cognitive process, of a subjectively active nature as opposed to an objectively passive one, and in the context even suggests "affirmation." The assertion is *through* structure and the assertion *is* the continuity of the living structure, the "no" to entropy and death. The inevitable dissolve into chaos of the individual is countered by an infinitely labyrinthine coding that preserves him in his descendants. This beneficent "knotting into" represents a "disentanglement from" the extinction that otherwise awaits preterite humanity, and thus directly parodies the gnostic labyrinth of death that serves as the novel's inaugural image.

The negatively directed tension of the *metaxy* is seen by Voegelin as a tendency to regress toward "inert, self-opaque 'thinghood' "[3]—in other words, the sort of spiritual entropy encouraged by the death-oriented Cartel. The counterbalance is the drive toward the increasingly refined moral structures reflected by the transcendental ground. To revere and encourage nature's replications and renewals and to attune one's spirit to her processes is—in Pynchon's terms—to participate in that ground. It is precisely through such participation that preterition, in the sense of the universal and inevitable mortality of the individual in nature's scheme, is sanctified into the election of the species and of Life as aggregate.

The sophisticated doubling mechanism of *Gravity's Rainbow* can be seen at work once again here in its normative aspect, bringing to light the positive modalities of spirit that the assumption of an inspirited cosmos generates. The blurring of the distinction between the preterite and the elect in a natural communion parodies the gnostic slippage examined in the earlier fiction as a machinery that traps both groups in a sterile alternation of victimhood and oppression. The parodic reversal of this slippage, on the other hand, makes possible certain crucial moments of Dionysian illumination. These moments are transient of necessity, since the essence of this *metaxy* lies in the simultaneous consciousness of preterite death and elect renewal. What the moment leaves is a desire to create islands of structure and affirmation with the knowledge that they must perish in the entropy integral to nature's scheme. Understanding and acceptance of this dialectic fuel the Pynchonian imperative of reverence for creation.

It is Lyle Bland who has the most explicit and conscious revelation of Earth as "holy center." His extracorporeal voyages reveal to him that Earth is a "living critter" whose history is embodied in coal and oil deposits, and that "Gravity, taken so for granted, is really something eerie, Messianic, extrasensory in Earth's mindbody...having hugged to its holy center the waste of dead species, gathered, packed, transmuted, realigned, and rewoven molecules" (p. 590). This messianic function of gravity is, in fact, gravity's alter-rainbow, the promise of a transformation that will unite all existence in the living substance of Earth. As such, it offers a natural alternative to the supernatural dream of the original Kabbalists, as well as that of their scientific successors, the "coal-tar Kabbalists." The "gathering home" of the fragments is accomplished not by a God beyond fallen nature or by human synthesizers who hold the natural order in contempt, but by sentient Earth.

This same theme, of a living mineral history beneath our conscious history, is at the heart of the Argentine Felipe's meditation on rocks. He "has come to see . . . that history as it's been laid on the world is only a fraction, an outward-and-visible fraction" (p. 612). It is the "untold," the "silence around us," the infinite leisure of mineral consciousness, that brings home to us the pervasive sentience of Earth, its sacredness, and our vital linkage to all its aspects. The "lowland" where the "paths, human and mineral, are most likely to cross" (p. 613) is the place of ultimate unity, the carbonic synthesis of Gravity's holy center. Pynchon's image of a universal melding recalls Dylan Thomas's description of a girl's body returning to Earth—"Robed in the long friends, / The grains beyond age, the dark veins of her mother"[4]—and reminds us of the Dionysian vision that links the two writers.

Tyrone Slothrop's mystical experience is based upon just this sort of absolute identification with natural process. Pynchon places the experience explicitly in the framework of a Rilkean Orphism that furnishes an additional context for the transcendental naturalism of *Gravity's Rainbow*. Slothrop's Orphic harp is, of course, his harmonica of earlier Boston days, rediscovered in a German river. The refraction of particular squares through the water is analogous to the bending of notes by a blues player, exactly the sort of synaesthesia that Dylan Thomas uses in "Fern Hill" when he speaks of "the lilting house" and "the tunes from the chimneys." In both writers, this mixing of sensuous modes dramatizes the Dionysian sense of our existence as a vital melange in which all barriers are dissolved, as a constant heterogeneous ferment that is itself a sort of lyrical flow.

Nietzsche, the supreme analyst of the Dionysian modality, places great emphasis on the precise analogy between music and a hypothetical language of the Will, the direct and necessarily nonverbal expression of the very ground of being. In *The Birth of Tragedy*, following Schopenhauer, Nietzsche asserts that music "*appears* as will" itself "and therefore symbolizes a sphere which is behind and prior to all phenomena." Compared with music, "all phenomena . . . are merely symbols: hence *language*, as the organ and symbol of phenomena, can never by any means disclose the innermost heart of music."[5] The river's playing of "a visual blues" (p. 622) is the embodiment of the dismembered, scattered Orpheus in natural process, the permeation of the living flow by the spirit of music.

It is precisely this Dionysian strain that informs Rilke's *Sonnets to Orpheus*, a sequence so central to Pynchon's imagination that it appears in quotations and allusions throughout the novel. The last of these sonnets (II, 29) furnishes the explicit prelude to Slothrop's moment of mystical unity. "Be conversant with transformation," Rilke urges us, and then continues the imperative:

> Be, in this immeasurable night,
> magic power at your senses' crossroad,
> be the meaning of their strange encounter.
>
> And though Earthliness forget you,
> To the stilled Earth say: I flow,
> To the rushing water speak: I am.[6]

The concluding tercet is actually quoted by Pynchon in connection with Slothrop's recovery of his "harp" (p. 622). "Though Earthliness forget you" is richly ambiguous in that it can refer to what is to come—one's literal absence from earth in death—or to a present alienation from the processes of nature. Counteraction takes the form of asserting one's continual becoming in the face of earthly stasis, and of asserting one's being in the face of earthly flux. In the Orphic experience as both Rilke and Pynchon construe it, being and becoming find their paradoxical union in the constant renewals of a sentient, functioning Earth.

The celebration and mirroring of this union, the moment of clearest consciousness of it, is the marriage of Apollonian lyric and Dionysian music[7]—image and process—in Orphic song: "Song, as you [Orpheus] teach it, is not desire, / not singing for something, yet in the end attained; / song is existence [Dasein]" (I, 3). Song is, in other words, a condition of being that enshrines the poignant processes of desire but transcends them. A crucial pivot of this transcendence is the singer's incorporation of inevitable mortality into his lyric in order to widen the base of his affirmation. Thus Rilke speaks, in connection with the *Sonnets*, of "the resolve that grew up more and more in my spirit to hold life open toward death, and, on the other side, the spiritual needs to situate the transformations of love in this wider whole differently than was possible in the narrower orbit of life (which simply shut out death as the Other)."[8] Rilke's simple formula for this transcendent lyricism is " 'dennoch preisen,' praising in spite, praising nevertheless."[9]

In the opening stanza of Sonnet I, 3, Rilke makes it clear that the perfection of this total praising represents a godlike unification that may be insuperably difficult for divided man:

> A god can do it. But how, tell me, shall
> a man follow him through the narrow lyre?
> His mind is cleavage. At the crossing of two
> heartways stands no temple for Apollo.

The image of an interior crossroads ["der Kreuzung zweier / Herzwege"] is used here to suggest the tension between the impulse to praise and the desire to conquer and assimilate that comes with the blind competitiveness of the Dionysian Will untempered by Apollo, and is thus inimical to the notion of transcendental structure. This tension ultimately points to a Rilkean *metaxy* that is, I suggest, coextensive with Pynchon's *metaxy*. At one pole is an unreflective animality of narrow perspectives and blind egotism; at the other, an Orphic perfection of praising that offers the *direction* of redemption but never the spiritual finality of the Rilkean "Angel" in whom this perfection is realized.

Because the Angel is identified with the transcendental polarity of Orphic naturalism, it is important to examine more precisely the nature of the ideal that it incarnates. Aside from the dramatization of the Angel's presence in Rilke's *Duino Elegies*, our most explicit information on it comes from a letter—now indispensable to discussion of the *Elegies*—that the poet wrote to his Polish translator, Witold von Hulewicz. Rilke distinguishes in this document between a "visible" Earth of beloved but transitory objects—houses, apples, grapevines—in which we have an abiding spiritual investment, and an "invisible" realm, an interiority into which we assimilate these objects in an act of Orphic concentration that is both a praising and a preserving.[10] The Angel, says Rilke, "is that creature in whom the transformation of the visible into the invisible, which we are accomplishing, seems already consummated. . . . that being who vouches for the recognition in the invisible of a higher order of reality" (pp. 375–376). Although our human limitations prevent us from ever achieving this decisive consummation, our task remains a labor of love in the most literal sense: to "*slowly and laboriously transform*" [Rilke's italics] the phenomena of this earth into an inwardness that is also a paean to the given of existence (p. 376).

This "transformation" bears a direct and crucial analogy to that performed by Earth in Lyle Bland's vision. All that has lived upon the surface is gathered inward with infinite patience toward the Center of sentience and fused into a sacred unity. For both Rilke and Pynchon, this transformation generates an imperative that constantly commands a self-transcendent love of the world and an affirmation of total community without barriers of time and space. It also generates a spiritual transcendence of preterition that is based, paradoxically, upon the inevitability of preterition, upon its *fait accompli* status as a mode of natural process.

Charles Hohmann, in what is certainly the longest (over 100 pages) and most scrupulous study of the Rilke-Pynchon connection, reaches some rather different conclusions about the status of Rilkean transformation/transcendence in *Gravity's Rainbow*. Some of these differences would seem, at least, to be resolved in the mechanisms of metaxic balance and gnostic parody; others are the result of a postmodern reading that is finally incompatible with the interpretation set forth here. Denying the existence of a normative transcendental in the novel, Hohmann asserts that

> the "beyond" separates into a dispiriting limbo and an inaccessible *pleroma*. In fact, Pynchon's novel satirizes the longing that impels men to seek the "Angel" for their attempts always fail and leave them exiled in a realm where conditions of existence are worse than they were before. . . . The theme of "transcendence" in *Gravity's Rainbow* is Pynchon's profoundest critical commentary on Rilke's notion of "Verwandlung" [transformation] and the aesthetic tradition it reflects. The novel not only mocks historical misreadings of the *Elegies'* theme of heroic transcendence, but also caricatures its orphic counterpart.[11]

Certainly the *pleroma*—the fullness of time and the perfection of being—is "inaccessible" in that it represents an indefinitely postponed fulfillment; this unattainability is essential to the tension of the *metaxy*. To assert otherwise is to indulge in the self-defeating perfectionism that marks, as we have seen, the gnostic attempt to go "beyond," to transcend the human situation. The novel is replete with mystical cults and with individual eccentrics whose attempts to do just that are indeed treated sardonically by Pynchon. The formidable Blicero, who is *not* so treated, is nonetheless shown participating—as we shall see—in an enterprise of gnostic transcendence that directly parodies Orphic naturalism. But none of this suggests that Pynchon does not valorize the *process* of "transformation" by which humanity is able to achieve a deeper, fuller communion with Earth, or that the moments of mystical insight or identification experienced by Lyle Bland, Slothrop, and others that we shall examine leave them in a "dispiriting limbo." To insist that Pynchon "satirizes the longing" that drives this process is to deny, in a postmodern privileging of indeterminacy, the logos of that well-evidenced norm by which he condemns the betrayers of the earthly and the human.

In the third stanza of Sonnet II, 29, quoted above, the "Kreuzung zweier / Herzwege" that characterizes our inner divisiveness becomes a "Kreuzweg" with all the magical powers that folk legend associates with crossroads. Partaking of these powers after recovering his "harp" and spending hours of naked openness to nature, Slothrop experiences a moment of Orphic transformation that involves absolute unity with Earth: "chiseled in the sandstone he finds waiting the mark of consecration, a cross in a circle. At last, lying one afternoon spread-eagled at his ease in the sun, at the edge of one of the ancient Plague towns he becomes a cross himself, a crossroads, a living intersection" (pp. 624–625). The sperm of the criminal executed at Slothrop Crossroads seeps into Earth and produces a mandrake root, a sexual event that links the *Kreuzweg* experience to another experience of natural unity. Later in the same day Slothrop sees heaven and earth connected by "a very thick rainbow here, a stout

rainbow cock driven down out of pubic clouds into Earth, green wet val-
leyed Earth, and his chest fills and he stands crying, not a thing in his
head, just feeling natural" (p. 626). This vision of what we might call the
copulative universe is similar to that in Dylan Thomas's poem "In the
White Giant's Thigh," with its various images of "the night's eternal curv-
ing act." In both instances the cosmos is unified by the Dionysian sexuality
that pervades it and represents one modality of the animate Earth. In
Pynchon's passage, the regenerative Rainbow arcs in implicit contrast to
the life-denying trajectory of the Rocket, and in more explicit contrast to
the "giant white cock" (p. 693) of the atomic explosion that Slothrop later
views in the wirephoto.

Commenting upon the *Kreuzweg* passage of Sonnet II, 29, Thomas
Schaub asserts: "the difficulty in trying to use these lines as an interpretive
key to Slothrop's experience is that Tyrone's character cannot bear the
weight of Rilke's poetry." Schaub is also reluctant to grant any Rilkean
"salvation" to Slothrop in light of the "forsaking of the very ego which
wanted saving in the first place" and the concomitant scattering of Slothrop's fragments through the Zone.[12] The first charge is best answered by
recalling the way in which Pynchon's satiric machinery functions to produce comic character deformations that ultimately indict the gnostic
Zeitgeist responsible for them rather than the validity of the characters'
quests. Just as Herbert Stencil carries on his bathetic shoulders the larger
significance of V., and is himself lent a mythic import by the deadly serious
import of the book's heroine, so the unheroic Slothrop must represent the
struggle of the all-too-human to retain and even enhance their humanity.
The inevitable analogy with *Ulysses*—in this case, Leopold Bloom—presents itself. This bumbling good-natured figure happens to fit the larger
pattern, humanity's archetypal wandering and return, and it is this mythic
pattern that redeems the figure even as it contributes—ironically—to the
mock-epic perspective in which we view him.

In a sense it is the Rilke-Pynchon mythos that is the "hero" here. Our
perishing and scattering are incorporated into that mythos, which recognizes no indissoluble egos or permanent salvation, but calls for inevitable preterition to become part of the song, whether Greek lament or
harmonica blues. It is not Bloom *per se* who is Ulysses, but Joyce's Bloom,
the "Everyman" recognized by a mythic sensibility as the avatar of an
enduring pattern. The sensibility is an even more powerful and explicit
presence in *Gravity's Rainbow*, as Schaub's own perceptive remarks on
the pervasive "Orphic narrator" (chap. 5) suggest. It is this narrator in
whom the mythic redemption is finally centered, preserved, and made
articulate.

It is inevitable that Charles Hohmann, in his antitranscendental reading
of the novel, would also find Slothrop's mystical moment to be spurious,
an unsympathetic parody of Rilkean *Verwandlung*. His objections overlap
to some extent with those of Schaub; Slothrop is spiritually unsophisti-

cated and is possessed of a trivializing "comicality" not found in Rilke's protagonist.[13] Hohmann also denies Slothrop an "authentic transcendence" on the basis of Pynchon's "ironic follow up": the "recycling" of Slothrop's transformed "seeds" into "the economy of the evil world order," his unfavorable Tarot reading, and the fact that a gallows is erected at the spot of his dissolution (pp. 82–83). Irony there certainly is here, but it lies primarily in the gnostic perversion of authentic religious experience and in the gratuitous disjuncture between a moment of spiritual communion and a lifetime of physical vicissitude. Any "transcendence" or "salvation" purporting to immunity from the latter would be gnostic, not Orphic.

Hohmann mounts what would seem to be more cogent objections when he quotes Pynchon's statement that Slothrop "doesn't even know" (GR, p. 622) what is happening to him, and asserts that "the modalities of Slothrop's transcendence hypostatize a process which remains elusive in the *Sonnets*. Rilke's discursive language veils as much as it reveals about the true nature of 'transformation' " (p. 346). What Hohmann's analysis here does not consider is the crucial role of *music*, with its Dionysian "modalities," in the transformations of both Slothrop and Rilke's Orpheus. As Nietzsche points out, in a passage analyzed earlier, music is ontologically "prior" to language, discursive or otherwise. Thus, its mysterious modes of cognition, the modes that wed human consciousness to primordial reality, also precede the more rational and explicit—i.e., the hypostatizing—modes of language. Slothrop, "just suckin' on his harp" (GR, p. 622), is already engaged in the transforming praise toward which the Orphic Word attempts to lead us.

The force and scope of Pynchon's Orphic naturalism are such that it is able to adapt Christian ceremony to its own normative structure—an assimilation integrally related to the merger of Venus *genetrix* and the Virgin in the symbology that Pynchon adopts from Henry Adams. The aspects of Christianity chosen are—not surprisingly—those which address preterite creation with an invitation to unity and brotherhood in the name of life everlasting; but there remain other, suppressed, aspects that tend to suborn or destroy this unity in the name of a sacred hierarchy, thus reinstituting the preterite/elect dichotomy and signifying yet another form of gnostic slippage.

This immanent ambivalence may explain the Christian/pagan duality that Pynchon has ingeniously built into the novel's chronology, and that Steven Weisenburger has with corresponding ingenuity discovered. "*Gravity's Rainbow*," he points out, "is plotted like a mandala, its quadrants carefully marked by Christian feast days that happened to coincide, in 1944–45, with key historical dates and ancient pagan festivals."[14] Part 3, for instance, "ends on the Feast of the Transfiguration, celebrated on August 6 to mark Christ's final earthly revelation of his divinity—a blaze of illumination followed by a white cloud." But it is on this day, as Weisenburger observes, that Hiroshima is bombed and that Slothrop undergoes his Dionysian transformation into a crossroads. By the same token, the firing of Rocket 00000 takes place on Easter Sunday 1945, which coincides that year with the pagan April Fool's.

For Weisenburger, the incongruity between Christian images of redemptiveness and pagan/historical scenes of revelry or violence suggests a carefully structured indeterminacy on Pynchon's part, a conscious refusal to close the question of history's goal or aimlessness. This may be the case, but the gnostic context we have been developing gives this indeterminacy a focused thematic function. The ghastly "transfiguration" of Hiroshima constitutes the parodic alternative, at the hands of Their technology, to the transfiguring of Christ; and the latter in turn, as a *metaxy*-affirming event, is not subverted but enhanced by Slothrop's Orphic metamorphosis. Similarly, the violation of Easter's spirit and significance by the sacrifice of Gottfried ("God's peace," as Weisenburger reminds us) is the ultimate April foolery, a cosmic trick that does not so much negate the possibility of resurrection as expose the religious basis of gnostic negation.

The novel's most extended and intricate portrayal of what we might call "Orphic Christianity" is the account of the Advent service attended by Roger and Jessica. Arrested by nostalgia, an emotion that has religious force for Pynchon, they visit an obscure church in the Kentish countryside where they find other war-weary, nostalgic people seeking refuge in carols to the ostensible Prince of Peace. The presence of a Jamaican corporal, his magnificent countertenor riding above all the other voices, becomes a symbol of the Empire's (and, by extension, of Control's) inevitable subversion of itself. By singing a fifteenth-century "German macaronic" (p. 129) laced not only with Latin but with subtle calypso rhythms, he recalls a time when the English and the Enemy communed in a common language of worship, and imagines a time when white oppressors and black oppressed commune in a common lyric of celebration. The fueling of "the War" by imperialist rivalry and by imperialist exploitation is ironically undercut, for a miraculous interval, by the War's own "evensong, the War's canonical hour" (p. 130).

The anchorage of this Christian experience in an Orphic polarity is suggested by a catalogue of preterite effluvia that recalls the "gathering-home" witnessed by Lyle Bland on his trip to Earth's mystical Center: "There's the smell of damp wool, of bitter on the breaths of these professionals, of candle smoke and melting wax, of smothered farting, of hair tonic, of the burning oil itself, folding the other odors in a maternal way, more closely belonging to Earth, to deep strata, other times" (p. 129–130). These sacred "other times" open backwards into a pre-Christian nature worship—e.g., Druidism—that sought to invoke a Dionysian unity of all life against the demonic threat of alien life forms:

There must have been evensong here long before the news of Christ. Surely for as long as there have been nights bad as this one—something to raise the possibility of another night that could actually, with love and cockcrows, light the path home, banish the Adversary, destroy the boundaries between our lands, our bodies, our stories, all false, about who we are. (p. 135)

The modern manifestation of this thirst for absolute communion is the desire to cradle the innocent, fragile Christ child "As if it were you who could, somehow, save him" (p. 136). The infant represents—here, at least—a primal harmony that is not only pre-War but prior to the very fragmentation and alienation of Creation that makes war possible, a harmony that calls forth a nurturing reverence in those who long for the way back to this idyll. This symbolism is supported, some pages later, by a pleasant Pynchonian whimsy in which "Christmas bugs," whose ancestors lived deep in the straw of Christ's manger, act as "agents of unification," piercers of "paper and plaster barriers, hard interfaces" (p. 173). It is a comical but profound figure that envelops not only a sanctifying of the "lower" links in the living chain of Creation, but also an attack upon the paper-spewing bureaucracy and plasticizing technology that seek to usurp the priority of Creation's processes. The idyllic, "tranquil world" of the ancestors is presented as "a golden lattice of straw that must have seemed to extend miles up and downward—an edible tenement-world" (pp. 173–174), and thus becomes—as a snugly enclosing, life-sustaining labyrinth—another Orphic parody of the "knotting in" that establishes the initial tonality of gnostic menace.

The climax of the Advent service is the musical exhortation "*praise be to God!*" which rises from the throats of "pre-ulcerous, hoarse, runny-nosed, red-eyed, sore-throated, piss-swollen men" (p. 136). That this "scruffy, obligatory little cry" constitutes our "maximum reach outward" mirrors—in the context of a naturalized Christianity that Pynchon establishes—the Rilkean paradox of *dennoch preisen*, praising in spite of. Out of the calamitous preterition that Creation authorizes swells a hymn magnifying the personified Creator over against the personified adversary, the War that artificially intensifies that preterition.

The insidious spiritual status with which Pynchon endows this adversary produces another of the doublings by which his cosmos becomes an arena of quasi-Manichaean confrontations. If Christianity (and Christmas) can be naturalized, they can also be gnosticized. The War has seen to it that the children integral to the Christmas celebration are conspicuous by their absence—evacuated to safer places—and that the astral announcement of the Advent is parodied by the deadly signifier of a very different advent: "60 miles up the rockets hanging the measureless instant over the black North Sea before the fall, ever faster, to orange heat, Christmas star, in helpless plunge to Earth" (p. 135). In the same vein, the gnostic simulacrum of the Epiphany casts the War as one of the Magi, showing up "under the Star, slyly genuflecting with the other kings" and bearing "gifts of tungsten, cordite, high-octane" (p. 131). The proffering of "precious" war materials to the Prince of Peace is a co-optative ploy of cosmic proportions, analogous to the attempt to usurp the prerogatives of nature. The possibility that the ploy might succeed, that some "greeting or entente will flow between the king and the infant prince," translates into the specter of a fatally compromised sacrality, of gnostic success in infiltrating the very machinery of redemption from gnostic violence.

A parallel example of Christianized naturalism and its malevolent inversion suggests that the vulnerability to compromise and infiltration lies deep in the machinery itself, especially in Christian dependence upon the Word as the apparatus of salvation. Frans van der Groov, a seventeenth-century Dutchman who has dedicated himself to the slaughter of the dodoes on the island of Mauritius, fantasizes a miracle in which these preterite, subverbal creatures are granted the "Gift of Speech" and undergo a mass "Conversion" (p. 110). The spiritual focus of this conversion is a natural communion that sweeps away artificial hierarchies and the invidious exploitation they condone: "And there are tears of happiness in the eyes of the dodoes. They are all brothers now, they and the humans who used to hunt them, brothers in Christ, the little baby they dream now of sitting near, roosting in his stable, feathers at peace, watching over him and his dear face all night long" (p. 111).

Pynchon punctures the fantasy with a brutal interjection: "It is the purest form of European adventuring." The ostensible brotherhood of bird and colonist is founded upon the hypocrisies and legalistic sophistries into which the Word inevitably opens. Misleading promises of "Salvation" in the form of "Everlasting life" and "earthly paradise restored" are used to cloak an invidious economy in which the "sanctified" carcasses and wastes of the dodoes will be used to sustain the settlers in "this world"—a violation rationalized into symbiosis by the argument that "beyond, in Christ's kingdom, our salvations must be, in like measure, inextricable." Even in this fantasized extension of the Word's power, then, that power perverts the normative force of an Orphic communion into a grotesque simulacrum; outside the fantasy, in the reality of Mauritius, the exclusion of the dodoes from the Word's aura constitutes a license for the callous extinction of the species. In both scenarios, as Pynchon points out, "the dodoes die"; and we are left with a highly problematic relation—in terms of Orphic naturalism—between Christ as the "Word . . . made flesh"[15] and the Infant who invites all living creatures to universal concord. It is a tension that is a special case, as we shall see later, of a more embracing dialectic between language and nature.

It is the character of human consciousness *per se*, not just the linguistic mode of that consciousness, that renders a natural unity problematical.

In the novel's most striking apotheosis of the primordial nature that grounds the Orphic norm, psyche is seen as something contaminated from its very origins by an alienating tendency toward gnostic imperialism:

> it was the equinox...green spring equal nights...canyons are opening up, at the bottoms are steaming fumaroles, steaming the tropical life there like greens in a pot, rank, dope-perfume, a hood of smell...human consciousness, that poor cripple, that deformed and doomed thing, is about to be born. This is the World just before men. Too violently pitched alive in constant flow ever to be seen by men directly. They are meant only to look at it dead, in still strata, transputrefied to oil or coal. Alive, it was a threat: it was Titans, was an overpeaking of life so clangorous and mad, such a green corona about Earth's body that some spoiler *had* to be brought in before it blew the Creation apart. So we, the crippled keepers, were sent out to multiply, to have dominion. God's spoilers. Us. Counter-revolutionaries. *It is our mission to promote death.* (p. 720)

Despite the savage ironies of this attack upon human death worship, it would be a serious mistake to assume that Pynchon is embracing some sort of hopeless misanthropy here. The sequel to the quoted passage makes it clear that human beings *are* capable of turning their allegiance to life, of "going over to the Titans" in an affirmation of their membership in nature's communion. Read in this light, the passage and its continuation evoke a metaxic quest strikingly analogous to that imaged by the familiar "Cave" allegory that opens Book VII of Plato's *Republic*. It is an analogy worth exploring because it brings the defects of "human consciousness," the Orphic capacity for transcending these defects, and Earth (or "World") as transcendental ground into a clearer relation to each other and to the Platonic model on which Voegelin structures his notion of an edifying metaxic tension.

"Picture," says Plato for Socrates, "men dwelling in a sort of subterranean cavern with a long entrance open to the light on its entire width. Conceive them as having their legs and necks fettered from childhood, so that they remain in the same spot, able to look forward only, and prevented by the fetters from turning their heads."[16] The basic picture is completed by a fire, built behind the men, that throws the shadows of models of earthly phenomena—including other men—on the cave wall in front of the fettered prisoners. Outside is the sunlit reality of the Platonic Ideal, too full of "dazzle and glitter" (p. 748) for them to apprehend, even if they could turn their heads in its direction. This, of course, is Pynchon's prehuman "World," too "violently pitched alive in constant flow ever to be seen by men directly." It is a realm ruled by "presences" that we are "not supposed to be seeing—wind gods, hilltop gods, sunset gods—that we train ourselves away from to keep from looking further" (GR, 720).

The "shadows" that "deformed" human consciousness, chained in the cave of its death obsession, is limited to comprehending are appropriately subterranean and devitalized—"still strata, transputrefied to oil and coal."

Liberation from these mind-forged manacles, for both Plato and Pynchon, involves a spiritual reorientation, a learning where to "look" in the most profound sense. As Plato puts it: "there might be an art, an art of the speediest and most effective shifting or conversion of the soul, not an art of producing vision in it, but on the assumption that it possesses vision but does not rightly direct it and does not look where it should, an art of bringing this about" (p. 751). Pynchon uses the same metaphor of vision when he suggests that "a few" defectors are "seeing" the Titans even though they are not "supposed to," that they are "looking further" despite being trained not to do so.

It would, of course, be misleading to gloss over the differences between the two metaxic structures we are examining. For Plato, primordial nature *is* the cave we must escape in search of the "Good," whereas for Pynchon it is precisely this nature—properly apprehended—that *constitutes* the Good. The "flesh" that works to obscure transcendental vision for the ancient philosopher becomes the very vehicle of that vision for the modern novelist, who discerns in the enlightened defectors from the cult of death a "striving subcreation" (GR, 720), a reflection of Earth's timeless processes in human sexuality: "how can flesh tumble and flow so," asks the author-persona, "and never be any less beautiful?" This minor mirroring of Creation opens an escape route through the narrow interstices of pervasive nonbeing, or—as Pynchon so poignantly phrases it—"into the rests of the folksong Death (empty stone rooms), out, and through, and down under the net, down down to the uprising." It is "the green uprising" of life to which he refers, a burgeoning symbolically linked here to the resurrection of the primordial Titans and inseparable from the "down down" of the "Earthliness" which threatens to "forget" us.

The mechanisms of the two quests, however, Pynchon's and Plato's, finally suggest a common archetype that embraces even their antithetical valuations. Both represent a constant striving to move, in Plato's words, "from the deeper dark of ignorance into a more luminous world and the greater brightness" (p. 751)—a movement that makes "deformed" human consciousness the medium between an inanimate realm of husks and shadows parodying life, and a polarity that images an impossibly radiant fullness of life. In the case of Pynchon's personae, the "art" of "producing vision" is the art of Orphic praising, but it is an art which—paradoxically—demands artlessness, the spontaneous unlearning of culturally conditioned injunctions *against* seeing Earth wholly and sympathetically.

The reward of this visionary labor, of "looking further" to locate the Titans, is—appropriately—a sighting that overwhelms our limited human capacities:

[We] leave Their [the Cartel's] electric voices behind in the twilight at the
edge of the town and move into the constantly parted cloak of our nightwalk
till

Suddenly, Pan—leaping—its face too beautiful to bear, beautiful Serpent,
its coils in rainbow lashings in the sky—into the sure bones of fright. (pp.
720–721)

The appearance of this apparition as an immediate segue from the search
for the Titans suggests that Pynchon has in mind a Titanic Pan, an interpretation borne out by the mythic genealogies that describe Pan alternately
as the son of Uranus and Ge—the parents of the Titans—or as the son of
Cronus and Rhea, who were themselves Titans. As such, he is the goat-
god whom Greek myth places in the cortege of Dionysus and who signifies
nature's Dionysian commonality—a significance reinforced by his name
(the Greek for "all") and by his philosophical function as a symbol for
"the Universe, the Totality."[17] Steven Weisenburger argues that this reference "pertains less to the Greek mythological figure than to the chief
devil of European witchcraft" described in Grimm's *Teutonic Mythology*.[18] Since the latter figure derives from the former and Pynchon
tends to identify witchcraft with nature-friendly magic (as in the case of
Geli Tripping), it may be that we can have it both ways—a possibility
supported by the derivation of "saturnalia" from the Titan Saturn. At any
rate, Pynchon metamorphoses Pan from faun to "beautiful Serpent," an
image that better resonates with the normative symbology already established in the novel.

Thomas Moore, glossing this passage, recalls Pynchon's allusion to
Uroboros ("the dreaming Serpent which surrounds the World," GR, p.
412), which he classifies as "one of . . . two major mythological/psychic
signs"[19] that Pynchon uses to suggest "the One," the primordial unity
from which we are alienated. Moore also speculates, convincingly, on a
variety of other connections between Pynchon's symbol and mythological
analogues, including "Ayido Hwedo, the beneficent Rainbow Snake of
modern West Africa," and Jung's mandalic symbol of union, the World
Serpent. One of the most useful parallels he traces is D. H. Lawrence's
description, in *Apocalypse*, of the "Sky Snake . . . cast down as Lucifer"
into "the black underworld."[20] Pynchon's revaluation of the Eden myth
is analogous in its denial of a Serpent-inspired Fall by which nature was
supposedly devalued. Similarly, the "rainbow" of Pan's coils comes to
signify a promise of nature's vitalizing permanence antecedent to the
promise of the Serpent's opponent, the Judaeo-Christian God, not to destroy Creation again.

Occurring over nine-tenths of the way through the novel, the vision
of Pan represents the last and perhaps the most decisive of the epiphanies
by which Pynchon establishes his Orphic countertheology. It thus serves

as a convenient pivot on which we can turn to an examination of the gnostic theology that he undertakes to counter—all the more convenient in that the "Pan" epiphany is parodied five pages later by a gnostic apotheosis of the V-2 rocket. Spreading its own form of "panic," the "Rocket" seems to emerge from Earth's most sacred recesses and return to them like some Dionysian specter, a blinding revelation framed by "a controlled burning" and "an uncontrolled explosion" (p. 726).

This quasi-deity, endowed with its own grotesque transcendence, is "not, as we might imagine, bounded below by the line of the Earth it 'rises from' and the earth it 'strikes' No But Then You Never Really Thought It Was Did You Of Course It Begins Infinitely Below The Earth And Goes On Infinitely Back Into The Earth it's only the *peak* that we are allowed to see, the break up through the surface, out of the other silent world." The subterranean matrix and terminus of this apparition is not the rich, dark fecundity that produces the green "steaming fumaroles" of life, but the dead "still strata, transputrefied to oil or coal," that produce the raw materials for unnatural engines of destruction. The parody grows explicit when Pynchon points out that the Rocket, on its way to a "numbered cosmos," leads "past these visible serpent coils that lash up above the surface of Earth in rainbow light, in steel tetany." This simulacrum of Pan is indeed the serpent of forbidden knowledge, of the technological gnosis that brings exile from the Eden of nature's communion. The only promise of its rainbow parabola is that of nature's utter despoliation in painful spasms of exploding metal—"steel tetany"—as it lashes a preterite world.

This mirror-image antithesis is only one among many in which Orphic naturalism is parodically inverted, almost point for point, by the various forms of gnosticism dramatized in *Gravity's Rainbow*. It is this systematic inversion that identifies gnosticism not only as the collection of forces antagonistic to the religious norm, but as a would-be usurper of that norm—as a metaphysical surrogate for it. The Cartel aspires to create an absolutely pervasive system of connections, a definitive and inescapable nexus that would usurp nature's orderings and "correct" nature's randomness with its framework of controlled causality. The shattering of *natural* nexuses, the interdiction of organic renewal, the conscious elaboration of death-oriented processes are not simply the unfortunate by-products of ruthless power hunger. Rather, they are conscious desecrations that are integral to satisfying that hunger, which is ultimately to see Earth nullified and sterilized in the triumph of the artificial and the mechanical—in other words, of the purely man-made. As long as nature transcends man, concealing her ultimate mysteries and sentencing even the Cartel to preterition sure, there must be a constant gnostic assault upon this transcendence, spearheaded by scientists and technologists. The aims are the destruction of nature's *sanctum sanctorum* through omniscience and through mastery over her life processes in a man-made Kingdom of Death.

The Jesuit who serves as a devil's advocate to the Counterforce broaches the awful possibility that They may have succeeded in reaching a "Critical Mass" in their "technical means of control," that their network of connection may be so complex and exhaustive that the concept of "freedom" has "ceased to have meaning" (p. 539). This surrogate system is supposed to transcend the nexuses of nature through its ability to modify them, and to replace nature's fertile randomness with an infallible determinism. What the Jesuit is making clear is the metaphysical scope of the usurpation in which They are engaged.

This gnostic fanaticism explains the chemist Laszlo Jamf's "strangely *personal* hatred, for the covalent bond" (p. 577). This bond suggests not only nature's fundamental organicism but a sharing, a willing commonality that is anathema to cravers of absolute and unshared power. Communion and symbiosis are integral to that Earth-centered value system the gnostics are so anxious to see "transcended," to use Jamf's expression. Not content with transmuting nature's arrangements of carbon and hydrogen, Jamf wishes to move "beyond" them to inorganic bondings such as silicon and nitrogen (Si-N): "Move beyond life, toward the inorganic. Here is no frailty, no mortality—here is Strength, and the Timeless" (p. 580). The refusal to remain in the tension of the Orphic *metaxy*, in the "frailty" and "mortality" of organic process, is a refusal of membership in nature. Kinship and cyclical renewal are renounced in favor of a timeless absolute that is mere projection. As Voegelin points out, the gnostic compulsively rejects reality in favor of "magic operations in the dream world," operations productive of "intellectual and moral corruption" that may "pervade a society with the weird, ghostly atmosphere of a lunatic asylum" (p. 170).[21]

That the inorganic is also death does not disturb the Jamfian company. In their rage for the absolute they imagine a Death that transcends death, and gladly pay the price of organic consciousness for a permanence that is not really immortality because it does not involve the preservation of life. In this view, to identify with Death is to share in its definitive and absolute finality and its inexorable power. Thus, the "virtues" of Death are substituted for those of sentient Earth in an act of gnostic usurpation. Rilke's poignant "Once, only once" (GR, p. 413), intended to suggest the maximization of life by the *inward* appropriation of Earth, is instead used to justify a rapacious *external* appropriation.[22] The path of irreversible process, of entropic nonrenewal, becomes a perverted destiny that parodies Rilke's *eschaton*. It is not the power *of* renewal but the power *over* renewal—the ability to prevent it—that constitutes the badge of the usurping demigods.

Pynchon specifically identifies Calvinism, and in particular the Puritanism of Slothrop's New England forebears, as the precursor of this modern religion of death—an identification echoed by Voegelin's analysis of

Puritanism as a form of gnosticism. Citing Thomas Hobbes, a contemporary of the militant Puritans of seventeenth-century England, Voegelin points out that "he [Hobbes] diagnosed the efforts of the Puritan sectarians to set up the Kingdom of God as an expression of the *libido dominandi* of the revolutionary who wants to bend men to his will. The 'spirit' that he saw inspiring these armed prophets of the new world was not the spirit of God, but human lust for power."[23]

This cynical deconstruction of Puritan "spirituality" is, ironically, justified by the Puritans' own documents. Voegelin quotes from one of these, a 1641 pamphlet entitled *A Glimpse of Sion's Glory:* " 'You see that the Saints have little now in this world; now they are the poorest and meanest of all; but then . . . the world shall be theirs. . . . Not only heaven shall be your kingdom, but this world bodily' " (NSP, pp. 146–147). As Voegelin aptly comments, "All this has nothing to do with Christianity. The scriptural camouflage cannot veil the drawing of God into man. The Saint is a Gnostic who will not leave the transfiguration of the world to the grace of God beyond history but will do the work of God himself, right here and now, in history." This dissipation of a continuing metaxic tension, genuinely open to *agape* and other transcendental ideals, in the illusory pursuit of an immediately realizable perfection produces the same results for the Puritans as it does for the gnosticizing cults we have already examined: spiritual mechanisms in which spirit gives way to mechanism, totalitarian schemes that stifle humanity under the aegis of Control, and a profound alienation from nature in the form of an attempt to suppress and exploit nature's givens. These negations of the higher values stem, ironically, from an all-out assault mounted in the name of these values.

Voegelin credits Richard Hooker, another contemporary opponent of the Puritans, with diagnosing "the nihilistic component of gnosticism in the Puritan belief that their discipline, being 'the absolute command of Almighty God . . . must be received although the world by receiving it should be clean turned upside down; herein lieth the greatest danger of all' " (NSP, pp. 143–144). Ironically, it is to Richard's namesake Thomas Hooker, who fled England in order to *join* the American Puritans, that Pynchon turns for the corroboration of anti-Puritanical concepts of God, nature, and love—concepts not incompatible with Orphic naturalism and its consecration of the flesh.[24] The chosen quotation is placed in the novel as a trope on Tyrone Slothrop's map of romantic conquests, London as a garden of variously hued stars marking points of assignation:

"I know there is wilde love and joy enough in the world," preached Thomas Hooker, "as there are wilde Thyme, and other herbes; but we would have garden love, and garden joy, of Gods owne planting." How Slothrop's garden grows. Teems with virgin's-bower, with forget-me-nots, with rue—and all over the place, purple and yellow as hickeys, a prevalence of love-in-idleness. (GR, p. 22)

Since Slothrop's map is exactly—and mysteriously—coincident with the map of V-2 rocket strikes on London, Hooker's lyric affirmation provides a parodic comment on the "garden" of death sown by the gnostic successors of Slothrop's ancestors and of Hooker himself—a garden ironically prefigured by the Puritan's "one-way" husbandry of earth's bounty. Convinced that God's elect were authorized by the Word to exploit God's creation, they turned the countryside into a "necropolis, gray with marble dust" by their quarrying and despoiled its timberland to make pulp for paper—"toilet paper, banknote stock, newsprint—a medium or ground for shit, money, and the Word" (pp. 27–28). The authorizing Word is parodied here, and its transcendental status subverted, by the hopelessly contaminated character of the "medium" it has authorized and upon which it depends for its propagation. A divine mission that involves a sterilizing assault upon nature stands revealed—within an Orphic framework—as a fruitless gnostic quest. It is a fruitlessness imaged most immediately for the Slothrops by their entropic diminution in a stripped, excavated countryside, as their family trust funds attenuate "in long rallentando, in infinite series just perceptibly, term by term, dying . . . but never quite to the zero" (p. 28).

This negating vacuity is, however, more than the inevitable penalty for desolating nature; it is an aspect of the quasi-transcendental polarity that defines this death-oriented religion. The "necropolis" of a marble-dusted countryside symbolically mirrors a more literal necropolis, the Puritan cemetery in its "long gradient of rot . . . the stones showing round-faced angels with the long noses of dogs, toothy and deep-socketed death's heads" (p. 27). If these demiurgic apparitions are, indeed, the agents of God's will, they reflect a cosmic governance that fits the gnostic paradigm of alienation and hostility—a reflection enhanced by an engraving, on Constant Slothrop's tombstone, in which "the hand of God emerges from a cloud" (p. 26) on its life-canceling mission. Two hundred years later, Constant's descendant Tyrone will note with terror the similarity between the "slender church steeples poised up and down" the New England hillsides and "white rockets about to fire, only seconds of countdown away," and will find in those awaiting God's judgment and those awaiting the V-2 a shared image of apocalyse: "*this is how it does happen—yes the great bright hand reaching out of the cloud...*" (p. 29). It is a religious commonality that dramatizes, in its suggestion of an ominous causal nexus, the antique theological roots of death's most modern technology.

The Puritan valorizing of emptiness becomes explicit in Slothrop's visit to Zurich—"Reformation country, Zwingli's town" (p. 267)—when he senses a "dumb malignity" connecting the great clock of the St. Peterhofstatt with the dim clock towers that presided over the "Ivy League quadrangles" of his "distant youth." He recognizes his desire to surrender to this malignity, to the desolation of "the darkening year," as a desire to embrace the terrifying hour of "vanity, vanity as his Puritan forerunners had known it, bones and heart alert to Nothing." This parodic elevation of the void to the status of spiritual center lies at the heart of "the Puritan Mysteries" into which certain young Harvard men of Slothrop's generation were initiated—men who "took oaths in dead earnest to respect and to act always in the name of *Vanitas*, Emptiness, their ruler...who now according to life-plan such-and-such have come here to Switzerland to work for Allen Dulles and his 'intelligence' network, which operates these days under the title 'Office of Strategic Services' " (pp. 267–268).

It is typical of Pynchon, with his sharp eye for ominous puns, to note that "OSS" was "the late, corrupt, Dark-age Latin word for bone" and to suggest that it is a mantra uttered by the latter-day Puritan "initiates" in times of crisis. The word carries us back to the tomb imagery and generalized death obsession of the *early* Puritans, while the Harvard cult of *Vanitas* reveals the actual ceremonial continuity between the ostentatious religiosity of these founders and the ostensible secularity of their twentieth-century inheritors. The all-too-worldly intricacies of "big business" (p. 267) and espionage, elaborately interwoven in their Zurich plexus, take on an otherworldly aura when they are seen as a gnostic labyrinth centered devotedly upon a consecrated core of emptiness.

The *libido dominandi* that subversively devalues the early Puritan quest for transcendental communion eventually becomes—in the gnostic dialectic of religious-secular slippage—the basis of the Nietzschean revaluation that produces *der Wille zur Macht*, the quasi-transcendental polarity of modern nihilism. Power, a means, is brought into a teleological connection with will, itself a means. The means justifies the end and *becomes* the end in a closed loop of self-enhancement, of pure *Vanitas*. At the loop's center is an ironically potent moral vacancy—the vacuum ensconced and apotheosized, and extending its sway along the tentacles of world-historical conspiracies that ape a metaphysical force field, a transcendental scaffolding for the structures of everyday life.

Whether they belong to the seventeenth or the twentieth century, gnostic enterprises of cosmic domination are valorized by the Word, that vehicle of gnosis in which they find both their inception and their culmination. It is precisely the culmination of gnostic apocalypse, the last judgment of an invisible demiurgic power, that Slothrop fears in the Rocket as Word: "It's nothing he can see or lay hands on—sudden gases, a violence upon the air and no trace afterward...a Word, spoken with no warning into your ear, and then silence forever. . . . the one Word that rips apart the day" (p. 25). The parodic "Let there be light" of the cataclysmic explosion actually amounts to "Let there be night," but the Rocket's function as gnostic Logos is much more complex than this ironic equivalence. Before this function is examined at length, it is important to examine its grounding in the primordial dialectic that Pynchon envisages between language and nature.

The Puritans found in the language of their sacred texts, as Voegelin has noted, a device for delimiting the interpretation of reality so as to make a constricted, self-serving version of reality prevail. John Calvin, in the grip of "pneumapathological" hubris, decides that he can encode in his *Institutes* the *gnosis* whereby a "new truth and a new world" can be begun (NSP, p. 139). Voegelin refers to this commentary, with its hermeneutic tyrannizing and implicit censorship of divine revelation, as "the first deliberately created Gnostic koran." It is a koran applied, as we have seen, to deadly effect by the Dutch Calvinists who colonized Mauritius. Empowered by the interpretive presumptions of a presumed elect, they become the arbiters of existence and extinction, rearranging nature's taxonomy through the extinction of an entire species.

It is an act of cosmic arrogance that pits the Word against the Earth. Another way of understanding this, in Nietzschean terms, is to imagine language as a compartmentalized shadow world of Apollonian representations, as a system of insubstantial units that depend upon their individual autonomy and upon their dissimilarity to each other for the power of signification, and then to imagine this system in a conflict for ascendancy with the Dionysian unity of life itself, the primordial and preverbal oneness that Pynchon valorizes. The ascendancy at stake involves the question of ontological primacy. If the Christian claim "In the beginning was the Word"[25] is admitted, the Word is elevated from its status as shadowy image to ultimate reality and origin, while nature is demoted to a secondary emanation that is subject to the Word's changing will. If the Orphic view prevails, it is the given of nature that is privileged, and words find their highest function in subverting themselves, i.e., in the Orphic lyrics where they serve as dithyrambic reflectors of nature's preverbal unity.

This conflict between Word and Earth, which pervades almost the whole of *Gravity's Rainbow*, is most elaborately epitomized in the episode involving the NTA, the New Turkish Alphabet. The Russian officer Tchitcherine has been assigned, along with other Soviet operatives, to a remote area of The Steppes, with the task of alphabetizing the language—heretofore entirely oral—of the Kirghiz tribesmen who lead their nomadic existence there. Pynchon makes it clear that this enterprise, if successful, will destroy the spontaneous, nature-bound culture of this people, as the Word imposes its mind-forged manacles of abstraction and rigid category on natural, organic development. These manacles inevitably evolve, according to the Weberian processes that so morbidly fascinate Pynchon, into oppressive language bureaucracies—in this case a complex network of wrangling committees, each with its own vested interest in particular letters or scripts.

One of these linguistic bureaucrats, Igor Blobadjian, fleeing a bunch of irate Arabists, is swept up into an experience of gnostic transcendence that takes us to the heart of Pynchon's Word-Earth dialectic. Blobadjian's mystical voyage appears carefully engineered to provide a revealing parody of two episodes already cited as evidence of the novel's Orphic norm: Lyle Bland's passage to communion with "Earth's mindbody" and the "Titans" apotheosis. The voyage begins, fittingly, in an oil refinery, where there is time for "retrospection . . . for refining the recent history that's been pumped up fetid and black from other strata of Earth's mind" (p. 354). This linguistic echo of Bland's experience opens into even more telling parallels, as Blobadjian follows guides who seem themselves to be "coal-tar Kabbalists" down an abandoned oil shaft and into a gnostic simulacrum of the mindbody:

> How alphabetic is the nature of molecules. One grows aware of it down here: one finds Committees on molecular structure which are very similar to those back at the NTA plenary session. "See: how they are taken out from the coarse flow—shaped, cleaned, rectified, just as you once redeemed your letters from the lawless, the mortal streaming of human speech.... These are our letters, our words: they too can be modulated, broken, recoupled, redefined, co-polymerized one to the other in worldwide chains that will surface now and then over long molecular silences, like the seen parts of a tapestry." (p. 355)

It is important to see that the Kabbalistic guide's analogy between molecule-tampering and language-tampering has the effect of stigmatizing the latter. Although there is nothing in language—which is inherently artificial—to correspond to the elemental substances of an unviolated nature, there certainly exist processes of linguistic elaboration that are aimed at enhancing Control and that increase the alienation between nature and human consciousness. The despoliations of the Puritan Word and of Blobadjian's own language bureaucracy are cases in point. In his provocative chapter on the semiotics of *Gravity's Rainbow*, Patrick O'Donnell cites the "Orwellian" vision of manipulation that connects "the textuality of modern culture and its potentially disastrous technocracies."[26] He misses the normative vector of Pynchon's irony, however, by attributing to Lyle Bland the "hermeneutic fantasy" of finding ever-newer combinations of molecules and by failing to consider the *provenance* of the claim—in the Blobadjian episode—that the removal of molecules from the "coarse flow" of Earth's natural processes, and of letters from "the lawless, the mortal streaming of human speech," represents some sort of valid redemption. Both visions emanate from the Kabbalistic spokesmen of the Other Side and represent direct gnostic challenges to Orphic values.

This interpretation is reinforced by the episode's close parodic relation to the "Titans" passage, which sacralizes that primal "constant flow" (GR, p. 720) dismissed by the Kabbalists as "coarse." This flow is itself a lawless streaming that corresponds to "the lawless . . . streaming of human speech," and thus sets up an antithetical correspondence between the "dead strata transputrefied to oil or coal" (p. 720) and the putrefaction of living oral speech by bureaucratic alphabetizers. It is true that the "Titans" epiphany centers upon a primal nature anterior to human consciousness and thus *entirely* preverbal; but Pynchon recognizes a descending (and increasingly gnostic) hierarchy of emanations away from the sort of speech in which an immediate and reverent relationship to Earth is mirrored. All language animals are alienated, but some are more alienated than others.

The massive, intimidating spaces of The Steppes serve as a symbolic landscape, one that supports the conception of an Earth not only prior to language but spiritually incommensurable with it. Somehow sensitive to these geo-psychic vectors, Galina—a member of the NTA task force—becomes a "connoisseuse of silences":

> The great silences of Seven Rivers have not yet been alphabetized, and perhaps never will be. They are apt at any time to come into a room, into a heart, returning to chalk and paper the sensible Soviet alternatives brought out here by the Likbez agents. They are silences NTA cannot fill, cannot liquidate, immense and frightening as the elements in this bear's corner—scaled to a larger Earth, a planet wilder and more distant from the sun.... The winds, the city snows and heat waves of Galina's childhood were never so vast, so pitiless. (pp. 340–341)

As in the "Titans" passage, the elemental processes of nature are apotheosized into a larger-than-life transcendental, a sacred origin that "speaks" in cosmic silences and overwhelms pathetic attempts to circumscribe it by written symbols.

This overwhelming becomes something apocalyptic and threatening when Galina tries to imagine leaving the infinitude of The Steppes for a city analogous to the NTA in its stultifying constriction and artificiality: "some dainty pasteboard model, a city-planner's city, perfectly detailed, so tiny her bootsoles could wipe out neighborhoods at a step" (p. 341). She imagines herself, miniaturized, living in this Lilliputian enclave, "blinking up into the painful daylight, waiting for the annihilation, the blows from the sky." The realization that her "Central Asian giantess self" is the "Nameless Thing she fears" is also the realization that her prolonged communion with the nature apotheosis of The Steppes has resulted in a conversion experience of sorts, a vastly enlarged spirituality that looms as a threat of righteous destruction over projects that seek the enclosure and debasement of nature. And it is precisely this enclosure that is at stake. When Galina finally leaves The Steppes for a real city, late in the novel, Pynchon describes her as returning to "the chain-link fields of the Word" (p. 705).

The Orphic nature of Galina's conversion is underscored by its explicit linkage with Rilke's *Tenth Elegy*. Pynchon quotes (with the presumably inadvertent omission of "*ihnen*") the line "*O, wie spurlos zerträte ein Engel ihnen den Trostmark*—"O, how an angel could trample spoorless their market of comforts"—thus setting up a parallel between Galina as

Earth's avenging angel and the Rilkean avenger who "could" descend to destroy *der Leid-Stadt*, the City of Pain.[27] This "city" is actually designed to avoid pain, or—more precisely—to avoid facing and ultimately assimilating the sorrows that accompany the course of existence. It is full of noisy materialistic distractions, e.g., "coins copulating," that serve—like the alphabetic and scientific bureaucracies of *Gravity's Rainbow*—to insulate its inhabitants from the authentic life of Earth, a life that marries the cosmic melancholy of the Russian plains to the joy of Creation's "green corona" (GR, p. 720). If the angel, in whom this Orphic totalization is complete, ever descended to destroy this obstacle to primal unity, he would leave it *spurlos*—trackless, traceless, the inscriptions of its alienating language and its chemical formulas completely erased.

Tchitcherine, too, has a relation to Rilkean Orphism, but it is a negative one. Winningly human in so many aspects, he nonetheless lacks Galina's capacity to achieve an edifying communion with the Central Asian vastness: "He will not come to love this sky or plain, these people, their animals. . . . never keep any memory of Seven Rivers to shelter with. No music heard, no summer journey taken...no horse seen against the steppe in the last daylight..." (p. 339). This image of the solitary horse apparently has unusual resonance for Pynchon, since he repeats verbatim, late in the novel, the description just quoted (p. 705), and places a horse in the steppelike landscape of the Lüneberg Heath in ironic counterpoint to the firing of the 00000 Rocket (p. 749). It also has unusual resonance for Rilke, from whose *Sonnets to Orpheus* Pynchon borrows it. In Sonnet I, 20, Rilke addresses Orpheus as "master," the teacher of a lyricism that binds all living things, and asks what image he would wish dedicated to him. The choice turns out to be Rilke's "memory of a day in Spring, / its evening, in Russia—, a horse." The horse leaves the village to be "alone for the night on the meadows," and becomes the avatar of Orphic praising:

> How the springs of his steed's blood leapt!
>
> That horse felt the distances, and how
> he sang and heard!—your cycle of myths
> was closed in him.
>   His image—I dedicate.

The whole weight of Rilke's Earth mythos is brought to rest upon this symbol, which thus becomes a critical key to experiencing the naturalistic redemption that this mythos offers. Tchitcherine's failure to retain and utilize this key after his own exposure to Central Asian "distances" represents much more than a casual slip of "memory"; it is the warrant that seals his fate as a gnostic pawn who will never know a transforming communion with Earth's mindbody.

To understand this fatal insufficiency in Tchitcherine is to understand why "his heart was never ready" (p. 359) to experience the Kirghiz Light, an Orphic illumination that utterly transforms its recipients. The episode in which he seeks this mystical accession revealingly dramatizes the dialectic between Word and Earth. Visiting a Kirghiz "singing-duel" (p. 356) with his Tonto-esque companion, Dzaqyp Qulan, Tchitcherine realizes that the spontaneous, improvised nature of the songs will eventually be lost to the mummifying script of some transcriber, thanks to the very NTA that he and others are promulgating. The same deadly antipathy is evident in the words of the song sung by an aged *aqyn*, a wandering singer, about the Kirghiz Light. The place of revelation, he chants, is "a place where words are unknown":

> If the place were not so distant,
> If words were known, and spoken,
> Then the God might be a gold ikon,
> Or a page in a paper book.
> But It comes as the Kirghiz Light—
> There is no other way to know It. (p. 358)

We are faced here with a religious analogue of Heisenberg's indeterminacy principle. Just as the attempt to measure certain subatomic phenomena would in itself alter the measurement sought, so the attempt to textualize the moment of mystical illumination alters the quintessence of that moment. It is dragged—as E. M. Forster says of the equivalent Hindu experience—"under the rules of time" and "becomes history," losing its unique ontological status.[28] As Kant long ago demonstrated, time and space are modes of perception that the human mind imposes upon all sense experience, even if this experience has a possible transcendental origin. That is, the mind immanentizes as it perceives; and the Word, the Text, is one product of this hopelessly delimiting immanentization. If this Word is of gnostic provenance, it ends up consecrating the very process of limitation; if not, it must somehow point beyond the conditions inherent in its framing. This is what the *aqyn* undertakes by communicating in Orphic song rather than holy writ, by emphasizing the inadequacy of human speech and vision, and by discussing the site and the effects of the mystical illumination rather than its specific nature or how to achieve it:

> And my words are reaching your ears
> As the meaningless sounds of a baby.
> For the Kirghiz Light took my eyes,
> Now I sense all Earth like a baby.

The transvaluation invoked here by Pynchon through the *aqyn* is obviously that of Wordsworth's "Immortality" Ode, in which the "clouds of glory" trailed by the newborn infant are badges of a profound sense of cosmic harmony—a sense that rapidly deteriorates as the cognitive processes of adulthood come to control the psyche. Tchitcherine, very much the victim of these processes and of a larger Control, proves hopelessly unsusceptible to the conversion experience offered by the Light. Although he will "see" it and "spend 12 hours then, face-up on the desert, a prehistoric city greater than Babylon lying in stifled mineral sleep a kilometer below his back" (p. 359), he will eventually lose the memory in the horrors of the gnosticized history through which he will live.

Commenting on Tchitcherine's attempt and on the aqyn's denial that the genuine experience of the sacred can ever be textualized, O'Donnell asserts that "the movement through history to written language is thus seen as a loss, but one that is also an awakening from the 'stifled mineral sleep.' "[29] Although O'Donnell is involved here in a deconstructive discourse tangential to my own, the antinomy of loss and gain that he locates in the emergence of the Word bears directly upon the Orphic contradiction cited earlier: language as a fall from Earth's communion and language as a dithyrambic awakening to Earth. It is a dilemma that affects Pynchon himself as the framer, in written words, of the dilemma; and we must eventually return to it in considering what sort of text, or Text, *Gravity's Rainbow* finally represents.

Meanwhile, it is necessary to consider the various gnostic texts—based, in several cases, on ancient Gnostic paradigms—that center upon the Rocket. For those technicians and enthusiasts who cannot see beyond the Rocket, it becomes in itself the quasi-transcendental ground suggested above in the "Pan" parody, the divine event toward which creation moves. Alternatively, it is the sacred Text, a revelation of ultimate reality susceptible to infinite commentary and interpretation.[30] As such it will, predicts Pynchon, give rise to various heresies, complete with heretics:

> Gnostics who have been taken in a rush of wind and fire to chambers of the Rocket throne...Kabbalists who study the Rocket as Torah, letter by letter—rivets, burner cup and brass rose, its text is theirs to permute and combine into new revelations, always unfolding...Manichaeans who see two Rockets, good and evil. (p. 727)

Since both Kabbalism and Manichaeism have crucial links to Gnostic doctrine, we may, in fact, classify all three of these "heresies" as mere specialized branchings of the gnosticism at the heart of the novel, all bound by the immanentization of the *eschaton* and by the notion of absolute technological control.

The notion of the Rocket as Torah is a particularly rich one, since the Torah was conceived by the Kabbalists—according to Scholem—as nothing less than the "Name of God" that was responsible for the creation of the world. It was seen as prefiguring "the law which governs creation as such . . . the cosmos and all nature." Thus, "its order is the order of the Creation" (OKS, pp. 40–41). For its own Kabbalists, then, the Rocket is the Logos, the ultimate rationale and reflection of the connectedness of the cosmos. To interpret it correctly is to understand the purpose of existence, the goal toward which history moves. Like the Torah, it both sets forth that goal and is that goal in its broadest meaning.

"Rocket" is much more than "rocket." It is an alternative to natural process, a surrogate system that replaces cyclical nature with irreversible artifice. As Enzian finally discovers, "the Rocket was an entire system *won*, away from the feminine darkness, held against the entropies of lovable but scatterbrained Mother Nature" (p. 324). Nature is "feminine" and "scatterbrained" because it is progenitive and is permeated by randomness, qualities not only unacceptable but transgressive to those whose religion is the consciously sterile Discipline of Control. The explicit desire to defeat nature's entropies is a desire for the absolutism of gnosis, for a determinism that seeks a divine stasis beyond entropy. While the particular rocket is ultimately defeated by gravity, "the Rocket" symbolizes a constant metaphysical rebellion against this fact.

The Zone-Hereros are another group who have identified the Rocket as both "Destiny" and "Torah." Their sacred mission as "Kabbalists . . . the scholar-magicians of the Zone" (p. 520) is to explicate to exhaustion its "symmetries, its latencies." The ultimate goal of this task is to attain the Holy Center, which is, for Enzian, "the Center without time, the journey without hysteresis, where every departure is a return to the same place, the only place" (p. 319). Schaub cites a passage in Mircea Eliade that would gloss this Center as "the zone of absolute reality," the zone containing such sacred symbols as "trees of life and immortality, Fountain of Youth, etc."[31] Since both the North and the moon have characteristics of this Center for the tribe, the Zone-Hereros believe that firing the Rocket targeted on both will lead them back into this perfect, timeless realm.

What we have in this poignant melange of tribal myth and Rocket technology is a gnostic perversion of the original Herero religion, which was strongly Earth-centered and involved a recognizable *metaxy*. The woman "planted up to her shoulders in the aardvark hole" (GR, p. 315) back in Southwest Africa exemplifies the traditional Herero emphasis upon the ability of Earth's regenerative powers to redeem the preterite. The *Erdschweinhöhle* is a sacred matrix that puts the woman quite literally "in touch with Earth's gift for genesis," enabling her to feel this primordial power flooding "through every gate" of her body (p. 316). Such were the pre-Rocket ceremonies of renewal, and they took place in a *metaxy* defined by the antithesis inherent in the Herero concept of the netherworld-moon: a fallen world in which preterition is the result of a false message from the moon, and a paradisal netherworld where the tree of life grows and makes its power partially and sporadically available to struggling humanity. This lunar netherworld can be entered, however, only after death, with the result that everyday life retains the fertilizing tension of the *metaxy*.

The Rocket, on the other hand, represents an immanentizing of the absolute that is ostensibly attainable. Wedded to the Herero conception of the "absolute reality" of the Center, it becomes the gnostic path to inhabiting this Center perpetually within the terms of this life. The *metaxy* is thus dissipated in favor of a dream of realizable perfection that sells out nature's proven beneficence in favor of technology's promises of power. Disoriented, contentious, desperate, the tribe wanders the Zone as a pathetic example of the disorder and confusion attendant upon the attempt to implement the practices of gnostic magic.

The Herero conjunction of netherworld and moon as Holy Center is parodied by the doctrines of other Rocket cultists in the novel. The Tree of Life, rooted at the *Bodenplatte* where the dead abide, is said to have been brought into existence by "the Great Firing" (p. 753). The ten Sephiroth of the Tree are, according to "Kabbalist spokesman Steve Edelman," associated with the Rocket countdown, which "actually conceals the Tree of Life." The sacred guarantor of Return is thus co-opted by technological mysticism as part of a one-way process designed to thwart the renewal of life, which Captain Blicero disparages as "this cycle of infection and death" (p. 724). He imagines the moon reached by the Rocket as "our new Deathkingdom," a vacuous sphere inhabited by men reduced to little more than "black and white film-images," and dreaming not of warmth and communion but of perpetual separation from "loved ones" in "loneliness" and "sterile grace" (p. 723). It is an utterly perverted ideal, embodying with shocking honesty the gnostic desiderata of antiorganic permanence and of Return rendered unfeasible: "There are ways of getting back, but so complicated, so at the mercy of language, that presence back on Earth is temporary, and never 'real.' "[32]

There is an ominous significance in Enzian's ability to reach an accommodation with the Empty Ones, the faction whose goal of tribal suicide is perhaps the most blatant example of the Death worship that lies beneath Rocket worship: "The Eternal Center can easily be seen as the Final Zero. Names and methods vary, but the movement toward stillness is the same" (p. 319). Obviously, this "stillness" lies at the root of the original Herero perception that gave a common locus of origin to creation and death. Ideally, the Center is like the zero-derivative point of a periodic function, the privileged *Kreuzweg* moment that precedes the renewal of life and motion, the visitation of the *Erdschweinhöhle*. But to seek permanent habitation there is to seek death in the gnostic disguise of life, betraying the sacred role of preterition in the name of an illusory timelessness.

The ironic equation between the Zero and the gnostic Center is further evinced by one of several passages in which Pynchon alludes to the Kabbalistic myth of the *shevirah*, the "breaking of the vessels" outlined earlier (chapter one). These vessels, shattered into sparks of consecrated light and fallen into demonic subjection, are someday to be gathered back into the holy unity from which they are alienated. This is the divine event toward which Lurianic Creation moves. In *Gravity's Rainbow* this myth is at the heart of a typically Pynchonian fantasy in which melanocytes, the dermal cells that produce skin coloring, discuss the possibility of an eventual return to the central nervous system (the CNS), their primordial home. The "older operative" explains to the younger that sooner or later they must all "go Epidermal," migrating to the "Outer Level" where they will stare into the "Outer Radiance": "Millions of *us*, changed to interface, to horn, and no feeling, and silence." Horrified at this possibility, the younger cell pleads the gnostic case:

> —No—how can you say that—you can't feel the *memory?* the tug . . . we're in exile, we do have a home! (Silence from the other.) Back there! Not up at the interface. Back in the CNS.—(Quietly) It's been a prevalent notion. Fallen sparks. Fragments of vessels broken at the Creation. And someday, somehow, before the end, a gathering back to home. A messenger from the Kingdom, arriving at the last moment. But I tell you there is no such message, no such home—only the millions of last moments...no more. Our history is an aggregate of last moments. (pp. 148–149)

The older operative explodes the delusion of a negative entropy that will bring dramatic salvation to the elect, and replaces it with a bleak portrait of entropic apocalypse, a chaotic waste of dead organic matter.

That this stark vision is indeed the Zero is made clear by the succeeding passage, in which Nora Dodson-Truck, a talented medium, is said to have

> turned her face, more than once, to the Outer Radiance and simply seen nothing there. And so each time has taken a little more of the Zero into herself. It comes down to courage, at worst an amount of self-deluding that's vanishingly small: he has to admire it, even if he can't accept her glassy wastes, her appeals to a day not of wrath but of final indifference. (p. 150)

Nora's courage comes precisely from rejecting the soteriological delusions of the cabalistic gnostics, and admitting the Zero of the vacuum as a fact that transcends their peculiar hopes of final transcendence. No Return, no damning wrath of God, no dramatic moment of cosmic reckoning— only the drifting wastes of definitive preterition. It is a vision that portrays, however, despite its courage and honesty, the apocalypse of *existential* gnosticism; and thus reminds us, in its mechanistic reductiveness and its calculated despair, that Pynchon does not locate a desirable alternative to the demiurgic *inspiriting* of nature in a nihilistic *dispiriting*.

In one of the novel's most hauntingly mystical passages, Pynchon gives the gnostic Zero dramatic immediacy and definition by presenting it as a literally vacuous parody of Earth's vital core. He has been describing the tunnels of the Mittelwerke, where the Rocket was assembled, as resembling a mathematical sign: the double integral used to determine the Rocket's *Brennschluss* point, and thus the point on which its fatal load will eventually fall. The sign is gradually revealed, through Pynchon's skillfully engineered accretions—and exercises in poetic license[33]—as an anti-life icon, associated with "the ancient rune that stands for the yew tree, or Death," and with a Nazi architect's "method of finding hidden centers, inertias unknown":

> as if monoliths had been left for him in the twilight, left behind by some corrupted idea of "Civilization," in which eagles cast in concrete stand ten meters high at the corners of the stadiums where the people, a corrupted idea of "the People" are gathering, in which birds do not fly, in which imaginary centers far down inside the solid fatality of stone are thought of not as "heart," "plexus," "consciousness," . . . "Sanctuary," "dream of motion," "cyst of the eternal present," or "Gravity's gray eminence among the councils of the living stone." No, as none of these, but instead a point in space, a point hung precise as the point where burning must end, never launched, never to fall. And what is the specific shape whose center of gravity is the Brennschluss Point? (p. 302)

The answer, of course, is the parabola, the ominous curve described by the Rocket's dialectic with gravity. To locate this iconic death shape, with its critical death point, where Orphism would locate the "heart" of the living stone is to engage in a gnostic surrogation that is also a desecration. This Zero—Ground Zero, perhaps—is an unholy Center defined as not-plexus, not-consciousness, not-eternal present; but these negations are not mere denials of spiritual vectors, not simply a return to existential neutrality. Instead, they are the code of the malign inspiriting that results from the process of extinction (in this case, of negation) *beyond* the Zero, badges of a life-denying presence-in-absence that entails its own theology and religious culture. In this connection, the gigantic concrete eagles that emblematize the Reich come also to represent a stone "fatality" that is not only motionless but inimical to motion, just as the corrupted "Civilization" goes beyond mindless barbarism in systematically subverting the human communion.

The Nazi ideology of the Zero finds its avatar in Blicero, a figure of such portentous evil and insidious capability that his creator Pynchon occasionally seems, like Milton, to be of the Devil's party without knowing it. The reason that Blicero elicits Pynchon's lyricism lies in the peculiarly poetic quality of his gnostic vision. More precisely, he is the embodiment of a demonic Orphism that parodically inverts the Rilkean valuations of the novel's norm. With a virtuoso touch, Pynchon roots this parody directly in Blicero's own affinity for Rilke's poetry. It is ultimately an unfounded affinity, one made possible only by the distortion of the poet's totalizing affirmations into support for the death-oriented values of gnosticism. The *Tenth Elegy*, for instance, used by Pynchon to help valorize Galina's openness to the painful but redeeming vastness of the steppes, is used by Blicero to equate the "Oven"—his own private and distinctly Teutonic *Götterdammerung*—with a Rilkean sense of "Destiny":

> It will come, it will, his Destiny. . . . *Und nicht einmal sein Schritt klingt aus dem tonlosen Los....* Of all Rilke's poetry it's this Tenth Elegy he most loves, can feel the bitter lager of Yearning begin to prickle behind eyes and sinuses at remembering any passage of...the newly-dead youth, embracing his Lament, his last link, leaving now even her marginally human touch forever, climbing all alone, terminally alone, up and up into the mountains of primal Pain, with the wildly alien constellations overhead.... *And not once does his step ring from the soundless Destiny.* (pp. 97–98)

"Pain" for Blicero is not the "primal" pain of disappointments and deaths—one's own and those of loved ones—built into the scheme of nature through preterition sure, but a perversely engineered and artificial pain associated in the short run with sado-masochistic indulgences and in the long run with the culmination of gnostic death worship. Rilke condemns the *Leid-Stadt* as a retreat where escapists subvert Earth's edifying negatives, but Blicero turns it into a retreat where decadents subvert Earth's edifying positives. The latter had found the model for his own "city" twenty years before in Southwest Africa; it remained only to transfer the sadistic rituals of Foppl's villa, as described in *V.*, to a V-2 launching site in Holland and to enthrall Gottfried and Katje as fairy-tale "children" waiting with him for the Oven.

His meditation on the attitude of the latter leads him into yet another gnostic misprision of Rilke. Suspecting that Katje does not take his perverted death games seriously, that she only "plays at playing" (p. 97), Blicero mentally accuses her of betraying the imperative from Sonnet II, 12, "*Wolle die Wandlung. O sei für die Flamme begeistert*":

> "Want the Change," Rilke said, "O be inspired by the Flame!" To laurel, to nightingale, to wind...*wanting* it, to be taken, to embrace, to fall toward the flame growing to fill all the senses and...not to love because it is no longer possible to act...but to be helplessly in a condition of love.... (p. 97)

The Rilkean provenance of these metamorphoses, with their seductive naturalism and their air of mystical affirmation, suggests at first glance some authentically Orphic strain in Blicero's make-up; but this seeming authenticity is merely the hallmark of how closely gnostic surrogation follows the outline of Orphic processes. The "Flame" itself is glossed, a few paragraphs later, as the Nazi war-conflagration that is destroying hundreds of thousands of "royal moths"—young Germans who probably do *not* "want the Change," but are "only being used" (p. 98). It is also, for Blicero, the flame of the transforming Oven and—by extension—of the Rocket.

In this latter regard, the sonnet offers a number of ironic echoes. The "transformed Daphne," asserts Rilke, "wants you to change yourself into wind"—a natural phenomenon with which Pynchon constantly associates the Rocket's turbulent passage, and which in turn provides a shocking metaphor for the macabre "transformation" of the Rocket's victims into an invisible rush of particles. Similarly, the poem's admonition for those who seek safety in stasis applies easily to those who seek refuge from the V-2: "Beware, from afar a hardest comes warning the hard. / Woe—, an absent hammer lifts!" And if we understand the notion of "mastering" in its gnostic sense, rather than in its Rilkean sense of inward assimilation, we can find the Rocket's parabola and the parabola's cusp (a focus of mystical meditations by Pynchon) in Rilke's description of "that project-ing spirit, which masters the earthly" and which "loves in the swing of the figure nothing so much as the point of inflection" (in German, literally, "*den wendenden Punkt*," the turning point).

These equations must, of course, remain quite tentative, since Pynchon does not introduce the whole of the sonnet into his text; but they serve to demonstrate the more-than-gratuitous correspondence between an Orphic mysticism that incorporates death into a larger life and a gnostic mysticism that incorporates life into a larger death. Blicero has taken to heart, from his twisted perspective, the admonition of Sonnet II, 29: "Know transformation through and through." His "planetary" mission is to aid in transforming Earth into the Kingdom of Death and—on a personal level—to sever all ties with humanity and nature. He is the apotheosis of gnostic alchemy, seeking nothing less than a surrogate order that will dominate natural cycles through artifice and stasis.

Descriptions of Blicero's personal transformations vary, but all suggest that he is on his way to achieving some infrahuman demonic status beyond the remotest extremes of natural existence—toward becoming some sort of Qlippoth in a gnostic hierarchy. His fate is explicitly connected with this hierarchy by Enzian, who speculates that Blicero has become a "fab-ulous monster":

"If he is alive," he may have changed by now past our recognition. We could have driven under him in the sky today and never seen. Whatever happened at the end, he has transcended. Even if he's only dead. He's gone beyond *his* pain, *his* sin—driven deep into Their province, into control, syn-thesis and control. (pp. 660–661)

These terms—*synthesis* and *control*—are exactly those used by the ghost of Walter Rathenau, a member of the Astral I. G., to describe the gnostic principles that actually drive history, as opposed to surface illusions of cause and effect. As an adherent to the Cartel, Blicero joins in encouraging the proliferation of "structures favoring Death"—Death which impersonates life in its growth and ambiguity (p. 167). To understand the secrets in "the hearts of certain molecules" is to gain the power to synthesize an alternative to natural process and to control the unfolding of events, thus fulfilling gnostic dreams of stasis and omnipotence. It is this gnosis that has enabled Blicero to lose his last vestiges of moral responsibility in the transcendental labyrinths of control.

The result of this divestiture is an aura of absolute and disembodied evil, of Qlippoth spirituality, that causes the band of homosexual prisoners—the "175's" from the Dora camp—to choose Blicero as the head of an "invisible SS" that will carry beyond earthly bounds the principles of Nazi oppression: "He is the Zone's worst specter. He is malignant, he pervades the lengthening summer nights. Like a cankered root he is changing, growing toward winter, growing whiter, toward the idleness and the famine. . . . His power is absolute" (p. 666). Transformation means then, for Blicero, freedom from the limitations of physicality and of place that usually restrict the exercise of power. Gnosis brings ubiquity, a permeation of the structure of events by an evil presence that has successfully completed its Faustian compact.

Death's parody of life, technology's parody of nature, is systematic here. The obvious connotations of "malignant" include the irony that cancer is a fatal excess of life, a killing disguised as regeneration. The "growing" of Blicero as "cankered root" is pernicious anemia, a metastasizing sterility that will substitute perpetual "famine" for harvests dependent upon Orphic return from a fertile, nourishing Underworld. In Thanatz's descriptions of Blicero retreating toward the Lüneberg Heath, we find atavistic transformations that are grotesque simulacra of the Orphic *Kreuzweg* experience. Screaming at the sky in an "ungodly coloratura," his eyes "White blank ovals," Blicero has "wired his nerves back into the pre-Christian earth we fled across, into the Urstoff of the primitive German, God's poorest and most panicked creature" (p. 465). His "renewal" by the primordial powers of Earth is actually a degeneration reminiscent of Conrad's Kurtz, a reversion to subhuman savagery incapable of spiritual orderings.

It is precisely spiritual order, in fact, that is at stake here. As Voegelin points out, the gnostic *eschaton* involves an illusion of definitive organization, of perfected pattern, while the attempt to realize it entails a descent into disorder and mindless violence.[34] The preserving tension of the *metaxy* is destroyed, opening the way for simultaneous movements toward hollow apocalyptic fantasy in one direction and toward animal chaos in the other. Both movements involve the dissolution of humanity as a higher moral construct. Blicero is not embraced and renewed by Earth as Gaea-Tellus. Rather he is "wired"—a technological trope—into the Dionysian "Urstoff" that is the source of primordial panic. The specifically Teutonic nature of Blicero's atavism reminds us that the word berserk originally referred to Norse warriors who put on a bear skin in order to revert to the frenzied fury of the bear.

This animalistic degeneration continues past the persona of the primitive Teuton. By the time he reaches the Heath, he has "grown on, into another animal...a werewolf...but with no humanity left in its eyes" (p. 486). And again: "the wrinkled wolf-eyes had gone even beyond these domestic moments of telepathy, on into its animal north, to a persistence on the hard edge of death I can't imagine, tough cells with the smallest possible flicker inside, running on nothing but ice, or less" (p. 486). This transformation explicitly perverts those functions of Orphism that involve nature—communion and Apollonian harmonization. The whole thrust of the Kreuzweg experience is the enhancement of humanity, the enlargement of the spirit through the internalizing of nature. Blicero abdicates his humanity, using our affinity with nature for a reductio that will destroy all vestiges of higher consciousness. The music of Rilke's Orpheus raised the beasts from savage cacophony—"Bellow and cry and roar"—to spiritual harmony.[35] Blicero's is the converse journey, the search for an infra-human exit from a harmony intolerable because it involves the fait accompli of nature's dominance.

This negative transcendence is closely related to that sought by the Dionysiacs of ancient Greece, as Marcel Detienne describes them. Driven to annihilate "the barriers erected by the politico-religious system between gods, beasts, and men . . . the devotees of Dionysus . . . become savage themselves and behave like ferocious beasts. They escape the human condition by way of bestiality, taking the lower route among the animals, while Orphism proposes the same escape on the divine side."[36] While we must be wary of parallels between Greek Orphism and the sort reflected by Pynchon's norm, it is nonetheless clear that we are dealing, in the case of Blicero, with an inverted—and perverted—Orpheus who descends ad infinitum, betraying Apollonian balance and moderation in a quest for savage godhead.

That this is also a gnostic quest is made clear by the configuration of veins in Blicero's "wolf-eyes." They form a map that is, according to Blicero himself, " 'the map of my Ur-Heimat . . . the Kingdom of Lord Blicero. A white land' " (p. 486). "Ur-Heimat" inevitably recalls the Original Home of Lurianic Kabbalism, the Holy Center to which the fallen sparks will return in their escape from impotent exile to a reunion with Omnipotence. Blicero's substitution of "mythical regions" for the limited and limiting reality about him is a classical exercise in what Voegelin calls gnostic "magic." His "own space" is an imaginary space, gained through a wild and irresponsible usurpation that destroys the *metaxy* and brings suffering and disorder upon those dragged along with him as the denied reality takes its inexorable toll. Significantly, this Bliceronian Kingdom is divided into islands that are firing sites for the Rocket, the holiest icon of technological gnosticism.

Blicero's descent into a phantasmal netherworld parallels his projected ascent—discussed earlier—to the "Deathkingdom" of the Moon, and together these transcendental journeys parody the corresponding Herero journeys of renewal. It is Gottfried's ascent in the 00000, however, that provides the paradigmatic gnostic ascent. Pynchon links this ascent with the aspect of mystical Kabbalism that centers upon the "ascent to the Merkabah," the throne-chariot of God (p. 750). According to G. H. Box, those occupying this chariot " 'are supposed to ascend to the heavens, where in the dazzling light surrounding them they behold the innermost secrets of all persons and things otherwise impenetrable and invisible.' "[37] The mystic undertaking this journey was called a "rider"—a term of ominous significance in *Gravity's Rainbow*—and was subjected, according to Charles Poncé, to all sorts of horrendous dangers at the hands of "demons & evil spirits which would attempt at every turn to destroy him."[38]

Pynchon's description of these dangers as they apply to the mystic who has chosen "the active way" is rather similar to that of Poncé, and one detail mentioned by the latter has unusual resonance in the novel's closing pages: "Throughout the entire experience he was threatened with death. At one point he is caused to stand erect in space without his feet."[39] In his description of the Moon as Deathkingdom, Blicero warns Gottfried that "Gravity rules all the way out to the cold sphere, *there is always the danger of falling*" (p. 723). Even the Qlippoth, the accomplished demonic powers, are suspected by Pynchon to have "just the wee vulnerability here to a sensation of falling, the kind of very steep and out-of-scale fall we find in dreams, a falling more through space than among objects" (p. 748).

The gnostic path to omniscience and Control is treacherous precisely because it attempts the transcendence of powerful earthbound realities (and of the Earth that binds them) through a tenuous network of abstruse magical formulas, symbolized by Blicero's launching incantation as it moves from "Steuerung Klar?" through "Durchschalten" to the mystically inspired "Hauptstufe" (pp. 757–758). This sequence corresponds to Poncé's assertion that the Merkabah rider, in order to continue his passage, "had to have prepared beforehand talismans, seals & magical incantations."[40] Even the Imipolex shroud protecting Gottfried's body has talismanic importance, since its secret formula represents the apex of the synthesizer's art, a surrogate for human flesh. The shocking extent of this gnostic usurpation is made clear in the section "Some Characteristics of Imipolex G," where we find that the "Erection of the Plastic" determines the shape and sensations of the "creature" encased in it (pp. 699–700).

As I indicated in an earlier discussion of this passage (see above, pp. 19–20), the human being beneath the shroud is reduced to the status of "the Subimipolexity"—a mantra typical of technological gnosticism.

The Merkabah ascent that involves insidious dangers and the constant exercise of arcane knowledge to combat them is the one distinguished by Pynchon as the active way of "the working mystic" (p. 749). The aggressive, determined progress through various stages of initiation would seem to mark it as the mode of Blicero, the gnostic adept who is the agent of his own grotesque metamorphoses. The "other way," according to Pynchon's analysis of an Aggadic tradition, "is dark and female, passive, self-abandoning. Isaac under the blade" (p. 750). Blicero's Isaac is, of course, Gottfried, whose Merkabah vision is to be the blinding detonation of the Rocket that carries him, the "ultrawhite" *eschaton* of technological gnosticism. Additionally, his sacrifice would appear to be one of those esoteric rites by which Blicero himself approaches, as a "working mystic," his own culminating vision of the surrogate Kingdom. A parodic Abraham undertakes the sacrifice of a parodic Isaac, and the Rocket-God declines to intervene.

The socio-political implications of this gnostic perversion are made clear by René Girard's comments on the traditional role of religious sacrifice: "The victim is. . . . a substitute for all the members of the community, offered up by the members themselves. The sacrifice serves to protect the entire community from *its own* violence. . . . The purpose of the sacrifice is to restore harmony to the community, to reinforce the social fabric."[41] The Rocket, whose purpose is either gnostic violence or gnostic transcendence, has nothing to do with the commonweal; quite the contrary. It is an instrument for suppressing or destroying the preterite masses and the means by which a technological elite can dream of escaping a living Earth. From either angle, Gottfried's violent epiphany is to be a death in the greater cause of Death.

Gottfried has been a crucial part of Blicero's assault on the natural order through his participation in the increasingly bizarre and unnatural sexual fantasies enacted by the latter. Blicero's perversion is a systematic and aggressive subversion of the male-female polarity integral to Return, and is symbolic of the "once only" sterility that attaches to the gnostic enterprise. In his review of Norman Mailer's *Ancient Evenings*—a novel replete with Bliceronian aberrations—Harold Bloom cites Richard Poirier to the effect that "it is almost as though in the Kabbalah of Norman Mailer, buggery constitutes the trope of the breaking of the vessels, as a negative creation that is a prime Gnostic image."[42]

Buggery, however, is only the starting point of Blicero's violations. By dressing as a woman with artificial genitalia fashioned from various synthetics and by interdicting the natural attraction between Gottfried and Katje, Blicero is undertaking to found a competing sexual order, one that is entirely the product of human imagination rather than the natural instincts and that serves Death—the Oven—rather than Life. The ultimate perversion in this wildly escalating fantasy is to sacrifice the Beloved, garbed in feminine stockings and shrouded in Imipolex, to the very principle of perversion. The firing of the 00000 symbolizes an artificial apocalypse, engineered to celebrate the religion of gnostic artifice.

Greta Erdmann furnishes us with yet another example of ritual murder in the name of this religion. She lures Jewish children to their death in the mud pool at Bad Karma, apparently possessed by the vision that Thanatz sees in the eyes of Blicero but associates with her: "a world below the surface of Earth or mud—it crawls like mud, but cries like Earth, with layer-pressed generations of gravities and losses thereto—losses, failures, last moments followed by voids stringing back, a series of hermetic caves caught in the suffocated layers, those forever lost" (p. 672). Bereft of organic connections and of vital transformations, this "knotted-in" Death-kingdom is another parodic inversion of the living Earth whose core Lyle Bland visited on one of his mystical voyages. The "voids stringing back" constitute a sterile negative of the complex chains of the banana molecule, Pynchon's early established touchstone for natural beneficence.

Greta presides over this realm of unredeemed preterition as a demonically perverted goddess. She describes herself to one of her potential victims as "the Shekhinah, queen, daughter, bride, and mother of God," promising the "fragment of smashed vessel" the long-awaited Lurianic reunion with primordial "Light" (p. 478). The Shekhinah—discussed above, in chapter four, in connection with Oedipa Maas's dream of redeeming the preterite—is one of those Kabbalistic notions quite compatible with Pynchon's own gospel of Earth, since the term refers literally to the "in-dwelling . . . of God in the world" and is identified with "the notion of feminine potencies in God."[43]

On occasion, however, according to Scholem, the Shekhinah is "demonically cut off from the Tree of Life" and becomes " 'the Tree of Death' . . . the vehicle of the power of punishment and stern judgment" (OKS, p. 107). Greta can obviously be viewed in this role, but her demonic function can be seen even more precisely in Scholem's description of Lilith, the evil Queen of the Night. Like Greta, she is a dedicated murderess of young children, a false Shekhinah, and the partner of a Satanic figure:

Wholly new in the Kabbalistic concept of Lilith is her appearance as the permanent partner of Samael, queen of the realm of the forces of evil. . . . In that world (the world of the *kelippot*) she fulfills a function parallel to that of the *Shekhinah* ("Divine Presence") in the world of sanctity: just as the *Shekhinah* is the mother of the House of Israel, so Lilith is the mother of the unholy folk who constituted the "mixed multitude" . . . and ruled over all that is impure. (K, p. 358)

Samael is actually mentioned in Pynchon's reading of Blicero's Tarot as one of the Qlippoth responsible for the emergence of a "new kind of demon . . . the Rocket's guardian demons" (p. 748). When we put this reference together with Scholem's citation of " 'Samael the wicked, the head of all the devils' " (K, p. 386), and Pynchon's description of Blicero as " 'Dominus' " (p. 322)—and with Greta's cooperation in Blicero's Im-ipolex orgy—we discover a Kabbalistic nexus of considerable scope and of crucial importance to the novel's religious antithesis.

Insofar as gnosticism triumphs, then, the network of Control is woven so tightly that even the unfolding of history proceeds according to its dictates. The corollary of this determinism is that those who seek return to a pregnostic innocence and freedom, the Way Back, must somehow undo the meshes of the Plot that has obscured this path. At this point, however, a twofold contradiction arises. The Way In to the heart of the gnostic labyrinth is comprehensible only to those who are themselves willing to become adept in the Kabbalistic speculation that fashioned the labyrinth, and the Way Back to an idyllic state is itself a version of the Lurianic return to the Gnostic Center.

Enzian is caught in this paradox as he speculates that the "Real Text," which can lead the Hereros back to the Holy Center, may transcend even the Rocket. It may lie encoded in the ruins of bomb sites, where each shock wave has been "plotted in advance to bring precisely tonight's wreck into being thus decoding the Text, thus coding, recoding, rede-coding the Holy Text" (pp. 520–521). Obviously, the tracing of gnostic plots through all possible permutations and convolutions involves a re-gressus ad infinitum that requires in turn infinite paranoia and infinite bureaucracy. Enzian even imagines a Kabbalistic "planetary mission" (p. 521) for which technological gnosticism is merely a cover. Thus, one sets (or becomes) a meta-Kabbalist to catch a Kabbalist, and plots with gnostic subterfuge to divert tribal resources into a constantly metastasizing "Search" (p. 525) for the Real Text and its meaning. Meanwhile, the Holy Center is comprised by the means used to approach it and by its association with a stasis and perfection beyond nature.

The resolution of this paradox is a coup de grâce of reflexivity by which Gravity's Rainbow itself becomes the Real Text. Encyclopedic, religious, focused on the ultimate issues of ethics and metaphysics, the novel func-tions as a Torah of Orphic naturalism, revealing the nature of gnostic evil at the same time that it reveals the Way Back to communion with Earth. The complex stratagems by which gnosticism has damaged or obliterated this communion are made clear through a demonstration of its method-ology and its paradigms, while the unraveling of its tortuous, unending regressus is exposed as a formula for a life of paranoid sterility.

This knowledge of gnosticism and its dangers helps us to separate from manipulated history certain moments and vistas that bear directly upon a return to communion. In the section entitled "Streets," Pynchon evokes transient experiences of gentleness, natural beauty, and fraternal rapport, all viewed through the poignance of their preterition. One of these is a "dyed afternoon (coaltar-impossible orange-brown, clear all the way through)" (p. 693). If the coloring of this unique afternoon is beyond the resources of I. G. Farben and the Cartel, the afternoon itself, as well as the other experiences, transcends the gnostic grid and represents a triumph "of humanity, of Earth" over the attempt to render these obsolete through artificial surrogates. This transcendence leads, for Pynchon, to the crucial corollary concerning Return that was quoted earlier (chapter one) to link his sense of metaphysical yearning to that of Henry Adams: "At least one moment of passage, one it will hurt to lose, ought to be found for every street now indifferently gray with commerce, with war, with repression . . . finding it, learning to cherish what was lost, mightn't we find some way back?" (p. 693).

Nostalgia is one of the dominant emotions of *Gravity's Rainbow*, and it is obviously connected with the impulse of Return. It is a blessed inertia, a drag against the one-way time of the gnostics. The conscious cultivation of nostalgia and of the deeply human values enshrined in its transcendent moments is a variety of the renewal-within-preterition at the heart of Pynchon's norm. These rescued moments, which resemble Wordsworth's "spots of time" in their redemptive powers, are themselves a part of the Real Text, enshrined in the novel as normative affirmations that counterbalance and heighten the exposure of gnostic designs.

The positing of *Gravity's Rainbow* as the Real Text involves us, of course, in the paradoxical notion of an Orphic Word. If preverbal Earth represents in some sense a transcendental unity, the mere existence of an immanentizing Word—however normative—violates that unity. The paradox is, in its most literal sense, unresolvable, and is the principal source of the stress that cracks the novel into fragments of narrative—a break-up that escalates dramatically in the book's final pages. Unable to fashion a narrative coherence that does not mirror the immanent, artificial unity of a gnostic Text—a simulacrum that falsifies reality—Pynchon is forced to unfold his own perception of reality in sporadic, irregular sequences that are antitextual both in the antipathy of their content to gnostic writ and in their resistance to formal considerations of symmetry, consistency, and continuity. The numerous abrupt segues, for instance, from serious exposition to comic musical parody, fulfill this subversive function. Thus, Enzian's meditation on his difficulties as the leader of the faction-ridden Schwarzkommandos suddenly fades into a fantasy of microscopic "Fungus Pygmies" engaged in a song and dance "to some well-known swing riff" (p. 523). Pynchon's high-spirited banality here conceals a systematic disruption of the deadly high seriousness that usually attends the coagulation and enshrinement of the Real Text.

But the fragmentation of narrative in Pynchon's Text also has a positive function. It both symbolizes a shattering that is loss and incarnates a poignant lyricism that preserves what is lost from oblivion. As the novel and its world fall to pieces more and more rapidly, the pieces continue to sing like those of the dismembered Orpheus, insisting on that larger continuity of Earth that redeems and enshrines the preterite shards. This lyric dissolution is mirrored in microcosm in Gottfried's last moments, which are presented as discrete memories viewed through a stereopticon. The periodic "CATCH" that separates them is not only the snapping into place of the next slide, but a desperate injunction not to let go of the red setter, the slate-blue pigeons, the last words of Blicero—all of the cherished images that have somehow sustained him.[44] The concluding injunction to Gottfried—"Always remember" (p. 759)—constitutes an axiom that has religious force in Pynchon's enterprise.

The Orphic song of Creation's fragments also represents an antitextual Text in another sense, mentioned above in connection with the dialectic of language and primordial nature. The use of a text to praise an aboriginal, preverbal unity represents an attempt to emphasize the capacity of words as self-transcending signs in order to offset their inherent tendency to immanentize the totality of experience—a tendency that reaches its apogee in the gnostic Text. If words can point to an idealized origin that not only predates but transcends the use of words, they can become the means of return to a redeeming sense of this origin—to a communion in which their users and auditors are awakened from the "mineral sleep" of Tchitcherine's buried city and from the anaesthesia of gnostic verbiage to a mystical sense of Earth as living stone. This transcendental function is enhanced when the words become part of Orphic song. As I indicated earlier, the Rilkean mythos adopted by Pynchon relies upon the analogy between music and a nonverbal language of primordial being. To sing, in the fullest and most committed sense, is to experience some sort of unity with this being and to overcome the alienation and divisive competition that unadorned speech tends to foster.

The conflict between Orphic song as Word and gnostic Rocket as Word structures the novel's climax, as the final rocket descends to destroy the novel's audience. We are seated—appropriately enough—in the Orpheus Theatre, a favorite haunt of those Slothropian "harbodica" players who love to torment manager Richard M. Zhlubb with their musical nonconformity. Music, it seems, cannot be managed. "Song," asserts Pynchon, is a "magic cape" for its singers: "the terrible politics of the Grail can never touch them" (p. 701). The communal song that concludes the novel is such a cape. It cannot, obviously, ward off the Rocket; but it can, and does, affirm the norms of Orphic naturalism that provide our only intimations of transcendence:

> There is a Hand to turn the time,
> Though thy Glass today be run,
> Till the Light that hath brought the Towers low

Find the last poor Pret'rite one . . .
Till the Riders sleep by ev'ry road,
All through our crippl'd Zone,
With a face on ev'ry mountainside,
And a Soul in ev'ry stone. . . . (p. 760)

The Puritan conventions of the lyric subvert themselves, thanks to William
Slothrop's feeling for Earth. It is nature's "Hand" that inverts the hour-
glass, ensuring human continuity in the face of individual extinction. The
"Towers" are in the most obvious instance "brought . . . low" by the
"Light" of the Rocket; but Pynchon's interpretation of Blicero's Tarot reading (pp. 746–749) makes it clear that the Tower is identified with the
Rocket, the apotheosis of gnostic technology. Thus, the Light can also be
identified with those forces of nature and human resistance that destroy
a gnostic "System" unable to "tolerate heresy" (p. 747). The mention of
sleeping "Riders"—identified with gnostic apparitions in the sky as well
as with the Merkabah ascent—would tend to confirm this interpretation.
Even the definitive ending suggested by "Till"—in this case the end of
human life—paradoxically coincides with an Orphic apotheosis, an Earth
on which the very mountainsides and stones are assimilated to a mystical
living unity.

It is here that the novel returns decisively upon itself. The "Soul in
ev'ry stone" inevitably recalls us to Felipe's vision of living history—of
what I described earlier as "the place of ultimate unity, the carbonic synthesis of Gravity's holy center"—as well as to Lyle Bland's vision of a
"Messianic" Gravity gathering the fragments home to "Earth's mindbody."
In the final analysis it is *Gravity's Rainbow* itself as Orphic song, as a
comprehensive lyric of commemoration, that performs this gathering. The
novel *is* Gravity, drawing and compressing the wild, disparate shards of
Wartime existence into a living unity. And in the promise that this synthesis offers of preservation and continuing currency for the world it
treats—a world now otherwise lost—we also have the novel as rainbow,
arising out of the animated "mineral" past and arcing to connect it with
the living tissue of the present.

Still and all, a screaming comes across the sky and the Rocket continues
to fall. Whatever rainbow of memory the novel offers is subject to the
ubiquitous shroud of nuclear winter, and Orphic song is not a shield
against radiation. In this sense, Pynchon sustains his gnostic vision to the
end, offering glimpses of a lost communion, even hints that a "Way Back"
might exist, at the same time that he depicts the relentless spread of Control, with its wake of apocalyptic violence. Examined on its own terms,
as what I called earlier "a gnosis that is ultimately antignostic," Orphic
naturalism offers a potent theoretical norm, a valid metaphysical alternative to the dehumanizing systems it opposes. But in the historical process as construed by Pynchon, its transcendental steadily recedes before

the antitranscendental of existential gnosticism and the negative transcendental of the cabalistic variety. From this angle of *praxis*, Harold Bloom is correct when he makes the assertion—quoted in my preface—that "Pynchon's is a Gnosis without transcendence." But it *is* a gnosis haunted by the *possibility* thereof—both positively and negatively—and by a characteristically modernist nostalgia for a quality of human consciousness that a logos beyond human agency seems once to have empowered.

Notes

PREFACE

1. Moore, *The Style of Connectedness: "Gravity's Rainbow" and Thomas Pynchon* (Columbia: University of Missouri Press, 1987); Hume, *Pynchon's Mythography: An Approach to "Gravity's Rainbow"* (Carbondale: Southern Illinois University Press, 1987). For a more detailed commentary on the "reconstructionist" approaches of Moore and Hume, see my review article "The Figure in the Carpet Bombing: Pynchon's Patterns of Chaos," in *Review* 10, ed. James O. Hoge and James L. W. West III (Charlottesville: University Press of Virginia, 1988), pp. 155–169.

2. Eliot, "Ulysses, Order, and Myth," *Dial* LXXV (November 1923): 483.

3. See, for example, Sara M. Solberg, "On Comparing Apples and Oranges: James Joyce and Thomas Pynchon," *Comparative Literature Studies* 26 (March 1979): 33–40.

4. Fekete, "Value Agenda," in *Life after Postmodernism: Essays in Value and Culture,* ed. John Fekete (New York: St. Martin's Press, 1987), pp. i–xix.

5. T. S. Eliot, *The Waste Land,* in *Collected Poems* (London: Faber and Faber, 1963), ll. 425, 430. James Joyce, *Ulysses,* ed. Hans Walter Gabler (New York: Random House, 1986), p. 170. All further citations of Eliot's poetry and of *Ulysses* are to the editions cited here.

6. Arthur Kroker and David Cook, *The Postmodern Scene: Excremental Culture and Hyper-Aesthetics* (New York: St. Martin's Press, 1986), p. 27.

7. Kroker and Cook, p. 8.

8. Bloom, "Introduction," in *Thomas Pynchon,* ed. Harold Bloom, Modern Critical Views (New Haven: Chelsea House, 1986), p. 3.

9. Hohmann, *Thomas Pynchon's "Gravity's Rainbow": A Study of Its Conceptual Structure and of Rilke's Influence,* American University Studies, Series IV, Vol. 48 (New York: Peter Lang, 1986). Hereafter cited as TPGR. The relevant section is entitled "The Gnostic Cosmos" (pp. 172–195).

10. Eddins, "Orphic *contra* Gnostic: Religious Conflict in *Gravity's Rainbow,*" *Modern Language Quarterly* 45 (June 1984): 163–190.

1.INTRODUCTION

1. Pynchon, *Gravity's Rainbow* (New York: The Viking Press, 1973), p. 239. Hereafter cited as GR. Pynchon's ellipses in this novel are indicated in quotations by single-spaced periods (...), my own by double-spaced periods (. . .).

2. Hite, *Ideas of Order in the Novels of Thomas Pynchon* (Columbus: Ohio State University Press, 1983), p. 66.

3. Schaub, *Pynchon: The Voice of Ambiguity* (Urbana: University of Illinois Press, 1981), p. 4.

4. Cooper, *Signs and Symptoms: Thomas Pynchon and the Contemporary World* (Berkeley: University of California Press), p. 222.

5. Seed, *The Fictional Labyrinths of Thomas Pynchon* (Iowa City: University of Iowa Press, 1988), p. 219.

6. McHale, *Postmodernist Fiction* (New York: Methuen, 1987), p. 11.

7. Joyce, *Ulysses,* pp. 63, 94.

8. Henry Adams, *Novels; Mont Saint Michel; The Education* (New York: The Library of America, 1983), pp. 1138–1139. All further citations of Adams

are to this edition. *The Education of Henry Adams* is cited hereafter as EHA, and *Mont Saint Michel and Chartres* as MSMC.

9. Lyon, *Symbol and Idea in Henry Adams* (Lincoln: University of Nebraska, 1970), p. 288.

10. Jules Siegal, "Who Is Thomas Pynchon . . . and Why Did He Take Off with my Wife?" *Playboy*, March 1977, p. 122.

11. Pynchon, "Is It O.K. to Be a Luddite?" *New York Times Book Review*, 28 October 1984, p. 41.

12. Nietzsche, *Ecce Homo*, in *Basic Writings of Nietzsche*, trans. and ed. Walter Kaufmann (New York: Modern Library, 1968), p. 780.

13. Nietzsche, *The Will to Power*, trans. and ed. Walter Kaufmann and R. J. Hollingdale (New York: Random House, 1968), p. 3.

14. René Girard, *Violence and the Sacred* (Baltimore: The Johns Hopkins Press, 1977), pp. 24–25.

15. This is the image that opens Book I of *The Will to Power*. The translation is by Hans Jonas, *The Gnostic Religion: The Message of the Alien God and the Beginnings of Christianity* (Boston: Beacon Press, 1963), p. 322. Hereafter cited as TGR.

16. Scholem, *Kabbalah* (New York: Quadrangle/The New York Times Book Company, 1974), p. 5. Hereafter cited as K.

17. Scholem, *On the Kabbalah and Its Symbolism*, trans. Ralph Manheim (New York: Schocken Books, 1965), pp. 112–114. Hereafter cited as OKS.

18. Jonas quotes Spengler as declaring that the two ages are " 'contemporaneous' in the sense of being identical phases in the life cycle of their respective cultures" (TGR, p. 326).

19. Voegelin, *Anamnesis* (South Bend, Ind.: University of Notre Dame Press, 1978), p. 106. Hereafter cited as A.

20. Webb, *Eric Voegelin: Philosopher of History* (Seattle: University of Washington Press, 1981), p. 287. Hereafter cited as EV.

21. Stevens, "Sunday Morning," in *The Collected Poems of Wallace Stevens* (New York: Alfred A. Knopf, 1957), p. 69.

22. Levin, "Art and the Sociological Ego: Value from a Psychoanalytical Perspective," in *Life after Postmodernism*, ed. Fekete, p. 24.

23. Smith, "Value without Truth-Value," in *Life after Postmodernism*, ed. Fekete, p. 1.

24. Nietzsche, *Beyond Good and Evil*, in *Basic Writings of Nietzsche*, trans. and ed. Kaufmann, p. 201.

25. The phrase is actually Arthur Kroker's formulation of Lyotard's insight, in *The Postmodern Scene*, p. 159. For Lyotard's own discussion (and an incisive discrimination between modernism and postmodernism) see his *The Postmodern Condition: A Report on Knowledge*, trans. Geoff Bennington and Brian Massumi, Theory and History of Literature, Vol. 10 (Minneapolis: University of Minnesota Press, 1984), pp. 79–82.

26. Derrida, *Writing and Difference*, trans. Alan Bass (Chicago: University of Chicago Press, 1979), p. 292.

27. Spanos, "*boundary 2* and the Polity of Interest: Humanism, the 'Center Elsewhere,' and Power," *boundary 2* 12–13 (Spring/Fall 1984): 181.

28. Foucault, *The Order of Things: An Archaeology of the Human Sciences* (New York: Vintage Books, 1973), pp. 385–386.

29. Todorov, "All against Humanity," rev. of *Textual Power: Literary Theory and the Teaching of English*, by Robert Scholes, *Times Literary Supplement*, 4 October 1985, p. 1094.

30. Wilde, *Middle Grounds*, Penn Studies in Contemporary American Fiction (Philadelphia: University of Pennsylvania Press, 1987), p. 6.

31. Docherty, *Reading (Absent) Character* (Oxford: Clarendon Press, 1983), pp. 152–153.

32. Redfield, "Pynchon's Postmodern Sublime," *PMLA* 104 (1989): 159.

33. Docherty, *Reading (Absent) Character*, p. 6.

34. Voegelin, "Immortality: Experience and Symbol," *Harvard Theological Review* 60, No. 3 (1967): 269. Quoted by Webb, p. 240.

35. Chapter 6, section II, of *Anamnesis* is entitled "Psychopathology," and contains a detailed discussion of the sense in which the "phenomena of existential closure toward the ground of reality" (p. 98) constitute a variety of "mental disease . . . a disturbance of noetically ordered existence" (p. 101). Voegelin cites the "modern Western history of unrest . . . from the Hobbesian 'fear of death' to Heidegger's *Angst*" as a shift "from joyful participation in a theophany . . . to the hostile alienation from a reality that hides rather than reveals itself." He also cites Schelling's use of the term *pneumapathology* as a formula for the "progressivism" of an earlier time (p. 102).

36. Wordsworth, *The Prelude*, ed. E. De Selincourt (London: Oxford University Press, 1933), Book Eleventh, 1. 206.

37. Foucault, "Revolutionary Action—'Until Now,' " in *Language, Counter-Memory, Practice*, ed. and trans. Donald F. Bouchard and Sherry Simon (Ithaca: Cornell University Press, 1977), pp. 221–222.

38. Seidel, "The Satiric Plots of *Gravity's Rainbow*," in *Pynchon: A Collection of Critical Essays*, ed. Edward Mendelson (Englewood Cliffs, N.J.: Prentice-Hall, 1978), p. 198.

39. Where I see Pynchon's development as a steady progress toward a liberating vision, Edward Mendelson sees it as a sort of pendulum: "The transformation of binary choice, from the vitalizing choice of *Lot 49* to the restrictive mechanism of *Gravity's Rainbow*, continues Pynchon's procedure of inverting his central metaphors from one book to the next. In *V.*, thermodynamic entropy increases, to the detriment of the world; while in *Lot 49* it is information entropy that increases, to the enrichment of those who live in the world" ("Gravity's Encyclopedia," in *Mindful Pleasures: Essays on Thomas Pynchon*, ed. George Levine and David Leverenz [Boston: Little, Brown, 1976], p. 188). The main factor determining this critical divergence, as my final chapter makes clear, is whether or not one believes that Pynchon is privileging the Orphic experience in *Gravity's Rainbow*.

2.PROBING THE NIHIL

1. *Slow Learner* (Boston: Little, Brown, 1984), p. 4. All further citations of Pynchon's short stories, except for "Mortality and Mercy in Vienna," are to this collection.

2. Fowler, *A Reader's Guide to "Gravity's Rainbow"* (Ann Arbor: Ardis, 1980), p. 33. Fowler's study of the Eliot-Pynchon nexus in the section "Pynchon as Gothicist" (pp. 28–43) contains some valuable insights into the gnostic perceptions that link these two authors, e.g., "both Eliot and Pynchon . . . take the same situation for the heart of their work: humanity imprisoned within a cage designed for an experiment upon it" (p. 31). When Fowler suggests that "Eliot's supernatural is benign" (p. 30), he seems to be referring to the later, explicitly Christian phase of the poet's work.

3. *A Farewell to Arms* (New York: Scribner's, 1929), p. 327.

4. "Contributors" Notes, *Epoch* 9, No. 4 (Spring 1959). All citations of "Mortality and Mercy in Vienna" are to this issue (pp. 195–213).

5. *Slow Learner*, p. 4.

6. *Heart of Darkness,* ed. Robert Kimbrough (New York: Norton, 1963), p. 18.

7. Virginia Moore, *The Unicorn: William Butler Yeats's Search for Reality* (New York: Macmillan, 1954), p. 135.

8. Slade, *Thomas Pynchon* (New York: Warner Paperback Library, 1974), p. 21. Hereafter abbreviated TP.

9. *The Aeneid of Virgil,* trans. Allen Mandelbaum (New York: Bantam Books, 1972), Bk. VI, 11. 391–393.

10. Conrad himself, of course, hints at such an inversion in Marlow's observation that London, too, " 'has been one of the dark places of the earth' " (p. 5), and in his constant equation between the remote heart of darkness and the immediate darkness of the heart.

11. Cf. Joseph Slade's observation that the Ojibwa motif "involves an assumed moral superiority of 'primitive' cultures over the decadent, 'civilized' type. Superseding the Ojibwas in later stories will be Maltese and Africans, cultures which have been laid waste by colonialism, but which still retain some spark of vitality" (TP, p. 24).

12. Pynchon, *The Crying of Lot 49* (New York: Bantam Books, 1967), p. 47. Hereafter cited as CL49.

13. Pynchon, *V.* (New York: Modern Library, 1966), p. 325.

14. Seed, *Labyrinths,* p. 52.

15. Miller, *Tropic of Cancer* (London: Calder and Boyars, 1977), p. 1.

16. *The Complete Poetry and Selected Prose of John Keats,* ed. Harold Edgar Briggs (New York: Modern Library, 1951).

17. Fowler, "Story into Chapter: Thomas Pynchon's Transformation of 'Under the Rose,' " *The Journal of Narrative Technique* 14, No. 1 (1984): 34.

18. Peter Cooper elaborates on this connection under the heading "Political Possibilities: The Counterforce" (*Signs and Symptoms,* pp. 92–93).

3.DEPRAVED NEW WORLD

1. Tanner, *Mindful Pleasures: Essays on Thomas Pynchon,* ed. G. Levine and D. Leverenz (Boston: Little, Brown and Co., 1976), pp. 49–67.

2. Pynchon's two most important sources of material on traditional embodiments of the eternal feminine are Robert Graves, *The White Goddess,* and Sir James Frazier, *The Golden Bough.* These debts, and others, are discussed by Slade (TP); Catherine Stimpson, "Pre-Apocalyptic Atavism: Thomas Pynchon's Early Fiction," in *Mindful Pleasures,* ed. Levine and Leverenz, pp. 31–47; and Douglas Mackey, *The Rainbow Quest of Thomas Pynchon* (San Bernardino, Calif.: Borgo Press, 1980).

3. Meixner, "The All-Purpose Quest," *Kenyon Review* 25 (Autumn 1963): 731.

4. *Henry Adams and His Friends: A Collection of His Unpublished Letters,* ed. Harold Dean Cater (Boston: Houghton Mifflin, 1947), pp. 558–559.

5. Rowe, *Henry Adams and Henry James: The Emergence of a Modern Consciousness* (Ithaca: Cornell University Press, 1976), pp. 74–75.

6. Lyon, *Symbol and Idea,* p. 132.

7. See, for example, *Anamnesis,* pp. 112–113, where Voegelin quotes Mircea Eliade on a modern *degradation de symboles,* the historical co-optation and subversion of "noetic symbols" by various metaphysical credos for what finally amount to antispiritual ends.

8. Cooper, *Signs and Symptoms,* p. 160. Cooper marshals a number of telling arguments in favor of accepting Stencil's account "provisionally" (p. 159).

9. Camus, *The Rebel* (New York: Vintage, 1956). The penultimate section,

"Moderation and Excess" (pp. 294–301), contains an indictment of modern gnosticism particularly apropos of the historical perspective opened up by V. "The profound conflict of this century," Camus asserts, is "between history and nature." German ideology "consummates twenty centuries of abortive struggle against nature, first in the name of a historic god and then of a deified history" (p. 299).

10. According to Jung, this wise man appears in male dreams as "the Self, the innermost nucleus of the psyche" when "an individual has wrestled seriously enough with the anima . . . problem so that he . . . is no longer partially identified with it. . . . With his [the wise old man's] help the ego avoids destruction and is able to overcome—and even redeem—a highly dangerous aspect of his anima" (C. G. Jung, *Man and His Symbols* [New York: Doubleday, 1964], p. 1961). Mehemet's eventual fate suggests, ironically, that this overcoming may not be final.

11. Neumann, *The Great Mother: An Analysis of the Archetype*, trans. Ralph Manheim (Princeton: Princeton University Press, 1972), p. 166.

12. *Slow Learner*, p. 107.

13. Rowe, *Henry Adams and Henry James*, p. 75.

14. See especially Chapter VI of *The New Science of Politics* (Chicago: University of Chicago Press, 1952), where Voegelin singles out National Socialism as an example of "Gnostic politics . . . self defeating in the sense that measures which are intended to establish peace increase the disturbances that will lead to war" (p. 171). The "suicidal nature" inherent in the Nazis' "activist success" is evidenced, he asserts, "by the atrocious internal corruption of the regime while it lasted as well as by the ruins of the German cities" (p. 177)—a modality of decadence and apocalypse closely tied to the career of V. as activist.

15. Kroker, "Panic Value: Bacon, Colville, Baudrillard, and the Aesthetics of Deprivation," in *Life after Postmodernism*, ed. Fekete, p. 182.

16. Camus cites, for instance, Baudelaire—"The real saint . . . is he who flogs and kills people for their own good" (*The Rebel*, p. 52)—and André Breton's assertion that "the simplest surrealist act consisted in going out into the street, revolver in hand, and shooting at random into the crowd" (p. 93).

17. See Chapter I, "All That Is the Case," in Plater, *The Grim Phoenix: Reconstructing Thomas Pynchon* (Bloomington: Indiana University Press, 1978).

18. Yeats, "Sailing to Byzantium," in *Collected Poems* (New York: Macmillan, 1959).

19. Luke 18:16, King James Version.

20. Zacharias, *The Satanic Cult*, trans. Christine Trollope (London: Allen and Unwin, 1980), p. 31.

21. Zacharias, p. 109.

22. Lhamon, "Pentecost, Promiscuity, and Pynchon's *V.*: From the Scaffold to the Impulsive," in *Mindful Pleasures*, ed. Levine and Leverenz, pp. 80–81.

23. Molly Hite points out this possibility in *Ideas of Order*, p. 58, but slips in asserting that "Victoria Wrenn seduced the elder Stencil in the year preceding Herbert Stencil's birth." The Florentine episode takes place in "April of 1899" (*V.*, p. 156), and Stencil *fils* was born in 1901. Obviously, we would have to project an elephantine gestation on V.'s part in order to avoid violating the unforgiving mathematics of biology.

24. Hite (p. 162) notes the source of this "pearl" metaphor in EHA.

4.CLOSURES AND DISCLOSURES

1. Mendelson, "The Sacred, the Profane, and *The Crying of Lot 49*," in *Pynchon: A Collection of Critical Essays*, ed. Mendelson, p. 122. Mendelson

borrows this term from Mircea Eliade, who defines it in *The Sacred and the Profane* as "the *act of manifestation* of the sacred" (quoted by Mendelson, p. 122).

2. Schaub, "Open Letter in Response to Edward Mendelson's 'The Sacred, the Profane, and *The Crying of Lot 49*'," *boundary 2* 5 (Fall 1976): 96.

3. Wilde, *Middle Grounds*, p. 99.

4. Tanner, "V. and V-2," in *Pynchon: A Collection of Critical Essays*, ed. Mendelson, p. 43.

5. Yeats, "The Second Coming," in *Collected Poems*.

6. Whether through error or subtle design, Pynchon has altered the actual name of this group, which was the "Society for Promoting Christian Knowledge." Pynchon's probable source was Maxwell's book *Matter and Motion* (London: Committee of General Literature and Education, Society for Promoting Christian Knowledge, 1876) or the Dover reprint (1965) of this text in the two-volume *Scientific Papers of James Clerk Maxwell*. I am indebted to Steven Weisenburger for this observation.

7. "A Clean, Well-Lighted Place," in *The Short Stories of Ernest Hemingway* (New York: Charles Scribner's Sons, n.d.), p. 383.

5. ORPHIC CONTRA GNOSTIC

1. Jonas, *The Phenomenon of Life: Toward a Philosophical Biology* (Chicago: University of Chicago Press, 1982), p. 7.

2. Joel D. Black, "Probing a Post-Romantic Paleontology: Thomas Pynchon's *Gravity's Rainbow*," *boundary 2* 8 (Winter 1980): 229–254.

3. Webb, *Eric Voegelin*, p. 140.

4. Dylan Thomas, "A Refusal to Mourn the Death, by Fire, of a Child in London," in *The Collected Poems of Dylan Thomas* (New York: New Directions, 1957). All further citations of Thomas are to this edition.

5. *Basic Writings of Nietzsche*, trans. and ed. Kaufmann, p. 55.

6. I have used what I presume is Pynchon's own translation of the second tercet (GR, p. 622), but the first tercet and all other quotations of the *Sonnets to Orpheus* in this book are taken from the translation by M. D. Herter Norton (New York: Norton, 1942), cited in Pynchon's acknowledgments to *Gravity's Rainbow*.

7. Compare Nietzsche on the Greek lyrist: "The Dionysian musician is, without any images, himself pure primordial pain and its primordial re-echoing. The lyric genius is conscious of a world of images and symbols—growing out of his state of self-abnegation and oneness" (*The Birth of Tragedy*, in *Basic Writings*, p. 50).

8. Letter to Nanny von Escher, 22 December 1923, in *Letters of Rainer Maria Rilke: 1910–1926*, trans. Jane Bannard Greene and M. D. Herter Norton (New York: Norton, 1969), p. 330.

9. The phrase "dennoch preisen" occurs in II, 23, of Rilke's *Sonnets to Orpheus*. The gloss is from the introduction to the translation by J. B. Leishman (2nd ed. [London: Hogarth Press, 1957], p. 29).

10. Rilke, letter to Witold von Hulewicz, 13 November 1925, in *Letters*, pp. 372–377.

11. Hohmann, *Thomas Pynchon's "Gravity's Rainbow,"* pp. 352–353.

12. Schaub, *Voice of Ambiguity*, pp. 72–73.

13. Hohmann, *Thomas Pynchon's "Gravity's Rainbow,"* p. 345. *Contra* Hohmann (and Schaub), Lance Ozier envisages an Orphic Slothrop who enters "a realm of mystical fullness" ("The Calculus of Transformation: More Mathe-

matical Imagery in *Gravity's Rainbow*," *Twentieth Century Literature* 21, No. 2 [1975]: 206). Similarly, David Cowart sees a sympathetic echo of a "sparagmos," the ritual dismemberment and scattering of a vegetation god (*Thomas Pynchon: The Art of Allusion* [Carbondale: Southern Illinois University Press, 1980], p. 47).

14. Weisenburger, *A "Gravity's Rainbow" Companion: Sources and Contexts for Pynchon's Novel* (Athens: University of Georgia Press, 1988), pp. 9–10.

15. St. John 1:14, King James Version.

16. *The Collected Dialogues of Plato*, ed. Edith Hamilton and Huntington Cairns, trans. Lane Cooper et al., Bollingen Series 72 (Princeton: Princeton University Press, 1961), p. 747.

17. Pierre Grimal, *The Dictionary of Classical Mythology*, trans. A. R. Maxwell-Hyslop (Oxford: Basil Blackwell, 1986), p. 341.

18. Weisenburger, *A "Gravity's Rainbow" Companion*, p. 299. For a survey of the Pan figure in literature, including a consideration of the figure's demonic metamorphoses, see Patricia Merivale, *Pan the Goat-God* (Cambridge: Harvard University Press, 1969).

19. Moore, *The Style of Connectedness*, p. 262.

20. Moore, p. 263.

21. Voegelin, *The New Science of Politics* (Chicago: University of Chicago Press, 1952), p. 170. Hereafter abbreviated NSP.

22. The misappropriated phrase is from the ninth of Rilke's *Duino Elegies*, the life-affirming context of which gives the line a thrust entirely compatible wth Orphic naturalism. The poem celebrates not exploitation but an assimilation that is a form of return: "Earth, isn't this what you want to resurrect / in us invisibly?" (*Duino Elegies and the Sonnets to Orpheus*, trans. A. Poulin, Jr. [Boston: Houghton Mifflin, 1977], ll. 68–69).

23. Voegelin, *Science, Politics, and Gnosticism* (Chicago: Henry Regnery, 1968), p. 103.

24. David Seed has pointed out that this apparent celebration of worldly love is immediately subverted in its original context—a 1637 sequence of sermons entitled *The Soules Implantation into the Natural Olive*—by the comment "for such hypocriticall love and joy we will not meddle her." Pynchon, as Seed observes, "cuts out the dismissive comment at the end of the passage and renders Hooker's whole distinction ironic by quoting it within such a profane context" ("Thomas Hooker in Pynchon's *Gravity's Rainbow*," *Notes on American Literature* 8 [1984]: item 15).

25. St. John 1:1, King James Version.

26. O'Donnell, *Passionate Doubts: Designs of Interpretation in Contemporary American Fiction* (Iowa City: University of Iowa Press, 1986), p. 84.

27. *Gravity's Rainbow*, p. 341. The emended version is from Poulin's translation of the "Tenth Elegy," l. 20. John Stark suggests that this elegy's themes pervade *Gravity's Rainbow* to the extent that the novel can be read as "an expanded version of the poem" (*Pynchon's Fictions: Thomas Pynchon and the Literature of Information* [Athens: Ohio University Press, 1980], p. 151). Hohmann discusses the elegy at some length in *Thomas Pynchon's "Gravity's Rainbow"* (pp. 353–356), citing what he believes to be various misreadings of its relation to the novel.

28. Forster, *A Passage to India*, p. 288.

29. O'Donnell, *Passionate Doubts*, p. 85.

30. Joseph Slade recognizes this religious dimension in his assertion that the Rocket "resacralizes the world," though we differ on the nature of this conse-

cration (Slade, "Religion, Psychology, Sex, and Love in *Gravity's Rainbow*," in *Approaches to "Gravity's Rainbow*," ed. Charles Clerc [Columbus: Ohio State University Press, 1983], p. 166).

31. Schaub, *Voice of Ambiguity*, p. 85.

32. Hohmann perceptively locates in this "moon colonist" passage a significant echo of Rilke's "Fifth Elegy" (*Thomas Pynchon's "Gravity's Rainbow*," pp. 300–302).

33. Steven Weisenburger has discovered, from examining photographs of the Mittelwerke tunnels in Pynchon's sources, that "the double-S configuration is . . . Pynchon's fiction, a sigmoid fraud that becomes suggestive in its link to related images" (*A "Gravity's Rainbow" Companion*, p. 158). Pynchon also takes liberties with these images, as Weisenburger goes on to point out: "According to Graves (White Goddess 194–95, 245–46), the yew (or *Taxus*) was represented by the rune "I. . . . The rune 'SS' signified the blackthorn (*Bellicum*), a tree symbolizing 'strife' " (p. 159).

34. See note 14, chap. 3.

35. Rilke, *Sonnets to Orpheus*, (I, 1).

36. Detienne, *Dionysos Slain*, trans. Mireille Muellner and Leonard Muellner (Baltimore: Johns Hopkins Press, 1979), p. 88.

37. *The Apocalypse of Abraham and the Ascension of Isaac*, ed. G. H. Box and R. H. Charles (London: Macmillan, 1918), pp. xxix–xxx. It appears probable that this is Pynchon's source for the "Merkabah" passage.

38. Poncé, *Kabbalah: An Introduction and Illumination for the World Today* (San Francisco: Straight Arrow Books, 1973), p. 57.

39. Poncé, *Kabbalah*, p. 57.

40. Poncé, *Kabbalah*, p. 57.

41., Girard, *Violence and the Sacred*, p. 8.

42. Bloom, "Norman in Egypt," *The New York Review of Books*, 28 April 1983, p. 4.

43. Scholem, OKS, pp. 104–105.

44. David Cowart suggests that these "CATCH" interruptions represent "the film catching in the projector, prior to its sputtering and freezing and going out" (*Thomas Pynchon: The Art of Allusion*, p. 59). Such a dramatization of incoherence would obviously lend itself better to a postmodern reading like that of Hohmann, who indeed cites Cowart (*Thomas Pynchon's "Gravity's Rainbow*," p. 213).

Bibliography

PRIMARY SOURCES

Pynchon, Thomas. "Mortality and Mercy in Vienna." *Epoch* 9, No. 4 (1959): 195–213.
————. *V.* New York: Modern Library, 1966.
————. *The Crying of Lot 49*. New York: Bantam, 1967.
————. *Gravity's Rainbow*. New York: Viking, 1973.
————. *Slow Learner*. Boston: Little, Brown and Co., 1984.
————. "Is It O.K. to Be a Luddite?" *New York Times Book Review*, 28 October 1984.

SECONDARY SOURCES

Adams, Henry. *Novels; Mont Saint Michel; The Education*. New York: The Library of America, 1983.
Bass, Thomas A. "*Gravity's Rainbow* as Orphic Text." *Pynchon Notes* 13 (October 1983): 25–46.
Black, Joel D. "Probing a Post-romantic Paleontology: Thomas Pynchon's *Gravity's Rainbow*." *boundary 2* 8 (Winter 1980): 229–254.
Bloom, Harold. "Norman in Egypt." *New York Review of Books*, 28 April 1983, pp. 3–6.
————. "Introduction." In *Thomas Pynchon*, ed. Harold Bloom. Modern Critical Views. New Haven: Chelsea House, 1986, pp. 1–9.
Box, G. H., and Charles, R. H., eds. *The Apocalypse of Abraham and the Ascension of Isaac*. London: Macmillan, 1918.
Camus, Albert. *The Rebel*. New York: Vintage, 1956.
Cater, Harold Dean, ed. *Henry Adams and His Friends: A Collection of His Unpublished Letters*. Boston: Houghton Mifflin, 1947.
Conrad, Joseph. *Heart of Darkness*. Edited by Robert Kimbrough. New York: Norton, 1963.
"Contributors" Notes. *Epoch* 9, No. 4 (Spring 1959): 195–213.
Cooper, Peter. *Signs and Symptoms: Thomas Pynchon and the Contemporary World*. Berkeley: University of California Press, 1983.
Cowart, David. *Thomas Pynchon: The Art of Allusion*. Carbondale: Southern Illinois University Press, 1980.
Derrida, Jacques. *Writing and Difference*. Translated by Alan Bass. Chicago: University of Chicago Press, 1979.
Detienne, Marcel. *Dionysos Slain*. Translated by Mireille and Leonard Muellner. Baltimore: Johns Hopkins Press, 1979.
Docherty, Thomas. *Reading (Absent) Character*. Oxford: Clarendon Press, 1983.
Eddins, Dwight. "Orphic *contra* Gnostic: Religious Conflict in *Gravity's Rainbow*." *Modern Language Quarterly* 45 (June 1984): 163–190.
————. "The Figure in the Carpet Bombing: Pynchon's Patterns of Chaos." In *Review* 10, ed. James O. Hoge and James L. W. West III, pp. 155–169. Charlottesville: University Press of Virginia, 1988.
Eliade, Mircea. *Rites and Symbols of Initiation: Mysteries of Birth and Rebirth*. Translated by Willard R. Trask. New York: Harper and Row, 1965.
————. *The Myth of the Eternal Return; or Cosmos and History*. Translated by Willard R. Trask. Bollingen Series 46. Princeton: Princeton University Press, 1971.

Eliot, T. S. "Ulysses, Order, and Myth." *Dial* LXXV (November 1923): 480–483.
———. *Collected Poems*. London: Faber and Faber, 1963.
Fekete, John. "Value Agenda." In *Life after Postmodernism: Essays in Value and Culture*, ed. John Fekete. New York: St. Martin's Press, 1987, pp. i–xix.
Forster, E. M. *A Passage to India*. New York: Harvest Books, 1952.
Foucault, Michel. *The Order of Things: An Archaeology of the Human Sciences*. New York: Vintage Books, 1973.
———. "Revolutionary Action—'Until Now.'" In *Language, Counter-Memory, Practice*, ed. and trans. Donald F. Bouchard and Sherry Simon. Ithaca: Cornell University Press, 1977, pp. 218–233.
Fowler, Douglas. *A Reader's Guide to "Gravity's Rainbow."* Ann Arbor: Ardis Press, 1980.
———. "Story into Chapter: Thomas Pynchon's Transformation of 'Under the Rose.'" *The Journal of Narrative Technique* 14, No. 1 (1984): 33–43.
Girard, René. *Violence and the Sacred*. Baltimore: The Johns Hopkins Press, 1977.
Grimal, Pierre. *The Dictionary of Classical Mythology*. Translated by A. R. Maxwell-Hyslop. Oxford: Basil Blackwell, 1986.
Hamilton, Edith, and Cairns, Huntington, eds. Lane Cooper et al., trans. *The Collected Dialogues of Plato*. Bollingen Series 72. Princeton: Princeton University Press, 1961.
Hayles, N. Katherine. *The Cosmic Web: Scientific Field Models and Literary Strategies in the Twentieth Century*. Ithaca: Cornell University Press, 1984.
Hemingway, Ernest. "A Clean, Well-Lighted Place." In *The Short Stories of Ernest Hemingway*. New York: Scribner's, n.d.
———. *A Farewell to Arms*. New York: Scribner's, 1929.
Hite, Molly. *Ideas of Order in the Novels of Thomas Pynchon*. Columbus: Ohio State University Press, 1983.
Hohmann, Charles. *Thomas Pynchon's "Gravity's Rainbow": A Study of Its Conceptual Structure and of Rilke's Influence*. American University Studies, Series IV, Vol. 48. New York: Peter Lang, 1986.
Hume, Kathryn. *Pynchon's Mythography: An Approach to "Gravity's Rainbow."* Carbondale: Southern Illinois University Press, 1987.
Hume, Kathryn, and Thomas J. Knight. "Orpheus and the Orphic Voice in *Gravity's Rainbow.*" *Philological Quarterly* 64 (1985): 299–315.
Jonas, Hans. *The Gnostic Religion: The Message of the Alien God and the Beginnings of Christianity*. Boston: Beacon Press, 1963.
———. *The Phenomenon of Life: Toward a Philosophical Biology*. Chicago: University of Chicago Press, 1982.
Joyce, James. *Ulysses*. Edited by Hans Walter Gabler. New York: Random House, 1986.
Jung, C. G. *Man and His Symbols*. New York: Doubleday, 1964.
Keats, John. *The Complete Poetry and Selected Prose of John Keats*. Edited by Harold Edgar Briggs. New York: Modern Library, 1951.
Kroker, Arthur. "Panic Value: Bacon, Colville, Baudrillard, and the Aesthetics of Deprivation." In *Life after Postmodernism: Essays in Value and Culture*. New York: St. Martin's Press, 1987, pp. 181–193.
———, and Cook, David. *The Postmodern Scene: Excremental Culture and Hyper-Aesthetics*. New York: St. Martin's Press, 1986.
Levin, Charles. "Art and the Sociological Ego: Value from a Psychoanalytical Perspective." In *Life after Postmodernism: Essays in Value and Culture*, ed. John Fekete. New York: St. Martin's Press, 1987, pp. 22–63.
Levine, George. "Risking the Moment: Anarchy and Possibility in Pynchon's Fiction." In *Mindful Pleasures: Essays on Thomas Pynchon*, ed. George Levine and David Leverenz. Boston: Little, Brown, 1976, pp. 113–136.

Lhamon, W. H., Jr. "Pentecost, Promiscuity, and Pynchon's *V.*: From the Scaffold to the Impulsive." In *Mindful Pleasures: Essays on Thomas Pynchon*, ed. George Levine and David Leverenz. Boston: Little, Brown, 1976, pp. 69–86.

Lyon, Melvin. *Symbol and Idea in Henry Adams*. Lincoln: University of Nebraska Press, 1970.

Lyotard, Jean-Francois. *The Postmodern Condition: A Report on Knowledge*. Translated by Geoff Bennington and Brian Massumi. Theory and History of Literature, Vol. 10. Minneapolis: University of Minnesota Press, 1984.

McHale, Brian. "Modernist Reading, Post-Modern Text: The Case of *Gravity's Rainbow*." *Poetics Today* 1 (1979): 85–110.

———. *Postmodernist Fiction*. New York: Methuen, 1987.

Mackey, Douglas. *The Rainbow Quest of Thomas Pynchon*. San Bernardino, Calif.: Borgo Press, 1980.

Mackey, Louis. "Paranoia, Pynchon, and Preterition." *Sub-stance*, No. 30 (1981), pp. 16–30.

Meixner, John. "The All-Purpose Quest." *Kenyon Review* 25 (Autumn 1963): 729–735.

Mendelson, Edward. "Gravity's Encyclopedia." In *Mindful Pleasures: Essays on Thomas Pynchon*, ed. George Levine and David Leverenz. Boston: Little, Brown, 1976, pp. 161–195.

———. "The Sacred, the Profane, and *The Crying of Lot 49*." In *Pynchon: A Collection of Critical Essays*, ed. Edward Mendelson. Englewood Cliffs, N.J.: Prentice Hall, 1978, pp. 112–146.

Merivale, Patricia. *Pan the Goat-God*. Cambridge: Harvard University Press, 1969.

Miller, Henry. *Tropic of Cancer*. London: Calder and Boyars, 1977.

Moore, Thomas. *The Style of Connectedness: "Gravity's Rainbow" and Thomas Pynchon*. Columbia: University of Missouri Press, 1987.

Moore, Virginia. *The Unicorn: William Butler Yeats's Search for Reality*. New York: Macmillan, 1954.

Nietzsche, Friedrich. *The Birth of Tragedy*. In *Basic Writings of Nietzsche*, trans. and ed. Walter Kaufmann. New York: Modern Library, 1968, pp. 1–144.

———. *Beyond Good and Evil*. In *Basic Writings of Nietzsche*, trans. and ed. Walter Kaufmann. New York: Modern Library, 1968, pp. 191–435.

———. *Ecce Homo*. In *Basic Writings of Nietzsche*, trans. and ed. Walter Kaufmann. New York: Modern Library, 1968, pp. 655–791.

———. *The Will to Power*. Edited and translated by Walter Kaufmann and R. J. Hollingdale. New York: Random House, 1968.

O'Donnell, Patrick. *Passionate Doubts: Designs of Interpretation in Contemporary American Fiction*. Iowa City: University of Iowa Press, 1986.

Ozier, Lance. "The Calculus of Transformation: More Mathematical Imagery in *Gravity's Rainbow*." *Twentieth Century Literature* 21, No. 2 (1975): 193–210.

Plater, William. *The Grim Phoenix: Reconstructing Thomas Pynchon*. Bloomington: Indiana University Press, 1978.

Poirier, Richard. "The Importance of Thomas Pynchon." *Twentieth Century Literature* 21, No. 2 (1975): 151–162.

Poncé, Charles. *Kabbalah: An Introduction and Illumination for the World Today*. San Francisco: Straight Arrow Books, 1973.

Redfield, Marc W. "Pynchon's Postmodern Sublime." *PMLA* 104 (1989): 152–162.

Rilke, Rainer Maria. *Duino Elegies and the Sonnets to Orpheus*. Translated by A. Poulin, Jr. Boston: Houghton Mifflin, 1977.

———. *Letters of Rainer Maria Rilke: 1910–1926*. Translated by Jane Bannard Greene and M. D. Herter Norton. New York: Norton, 1969.

———. *Sonnets to Orpheus*. Translated by J. B. Leishman. 2nd ed. London: Hogarth Press, 1957.

———. *Sonnets to Orpheus*. Translated by M. D. Herter Norton. New York: Norton, 1942.

Rowe, John Carlos. *Henry Adams and Henry James: The Emergence of a Modern Consciousness*. Ithaca: Cornell University Press, 1976.

Russell, Charles. "Pynchon's Language: Signs, Systems, and Subversion." In *Approaches to "Gravity's Rainbow,"* ed. Charles Clerc. Columbus: Ohio State University Press, 1983, pp. 251–272.

Sanders, Scott. "Pynchon's Paranoid History." In *Mindful Pleasures: Essays on Thomas Pynchon*, ed. George Levine and David Leverenz. Boston: Little, Brown, 1976, pp. 139–159.

Schaub, Thomas. "Open Letter in Response to Edward Mendelson's 'The Sacred, the Profane, and *The Crying of Lot 49*.'" *boundary 2* 5 (Fall 1976): 93–101.

———. *Pynchon: The Voice of Ambiguity*. Urbana: University of Illinois Press, 1981.

Scholem, Gershom. *Kabbalah*. New York: Quadrangle/The New York Times Book Company, 1974.

———. *On the Kabbalah and Its Symbolism*. Translated by Ralph Manheim. New York: Schocken Books, 1965.

Seed, David. "Thomas Hooker in Pynchon's *Gravity's Rainbow*." *Notes on American Literature* 8 (1984), item 15.

———. *The Fictional Labyrinths of Thomas Pynchon*. Iowa City: University of Iowa Press, 1988.

Seidel, Michael. "The Satiric Plots of *Gravity's Rainbow*." In *Pynchon: A Collection of Critical Essays*, ed. Edward Mendelson. Englewood Cliffs: N.J.: Prentice-Hall, 1978, pp. 193–212.

Siegal, Jules. "Who Is Thomas Pynchon . . . and Why Did He Take Off with My Wife?" *Playboy*, March 1977, pp. 97, 122, 168–170, 172, 174.

Slade, Joseph. *Thomas Pynchon*. New York: Warner Paperback Library, 1974.

———. "Religion, Psychology, Sex, and Love in *Gravity's Rainbow*." In *Approaches to "Gravity's Rainbow,"* ed. Charles Clerc. Columbus: Ohio State University Press, 1983, pp. 153–198.

Smith, Barbara Herrnstein. "Value without Truth-Value." In *Life after Postmodernism: Essays in Value and Culture*, ed. John Fekete. New York: St. Martin's Press, 1987, pp. 1–21.

Smith, Marcus, and Tölölyan, Khachig. "The New Jeremiad: *Gravity's Rainbow*." In *Critical Essays on Thomas Pynchon*, ed. Richard Pearce. Boston: G. K. Hall, 1981, pp. 169–186.

Solberg, Sara M. "On Comparing Apples and Oranges: James Joyce and Thomas Pynchon." *Comparative Literature Studies* 26 (March 1979): 33–40.

Spanos, William. "*boundary 2* and the Polity of Interest: Humanism, the 'Center Elsewhere,' and Power." *boundary 2* 12–13 (Spring/Fall 1984): 173–214.

Stark, John. *Pynchon's Fictions: Thomas Pynchon and the Literature of Information*. Athens: Ohio University Press, 1980.

Stevens, Wallace. *The Collected Poems of Wallace Stevens*. New York: Alfred A. Knopf, 1957.

Stimpson, Catherine. "Pre-Apocalyptic Atavism: Thomas Pynchon's Early Fiction." In *Mindful Pleasures: Essays on Thomas Pynchon*, ed. George Levine and David Leverenz. Boston: Little, Brown, 1976, pp. 31–47.

Tanner, Tony. "Caries and Cabals." In *Mindful Pleasures: Essays on Thomas Pynchon*, ed. George Levine and David Leverenz. Boston: Little, Brown, 1976, pp. 49–67.

―――. "V. and V-2." In *Pynchon: A Collection of Critical Essays,* ed. Edward Mendelson. Englewood Cliffs, N.J.: Prentice-Hall, 1978, pp. 16–55.

Thomas, Dylan. *The Collected Poems of Dylan Thomas.* New York: New Directions, 1957.

Todorov, Tzvetan. "All against Humanity." Rev. of *Textual Power: Literary Theory and the Teaching of English,* by Robert Scholes. *Times Literary Supplement,* 4 October 1985, pp. 1093–1094.

Tölölyan, Khachig. "War as Background in *Gravity's Rainbow.*" In *Approaches to "Gravity's Rainbow,"* ed. Charles Clerc. Columbus: Ohio State University Press, 1983, pp. 31–68.

Virgil. *The Aeneid of Virgil.* Translated by Allen Mandelbaum. New York: Bantam, 1972.

Voegelin, Eric. *Anamnesis.* South Bend, Ind.: University Of Notre Dame Press, 1978.

―――. "Immortality: Experience and Symbol." *Harvard Theological Review* 60, No. 3 (1967): 235–279.

―――. *Science, Politics, and Gnosticism.* Chicago: Henry Regnery, 1968.

―――. *The New Science of Politics.* Chicago: University of Chicago Press, 1952.

Von Neumann, Erich. *The Great Mother: An Analysis of the Archetype.* Translated by Ralph Manheim. Princeton: Princeton University Press, 1972.

Webb, Eugene. *Eric Voegelin: Philosopher of History.* Seattle: University of Washington Press, 1981.

Weisenburger, Steven. "The End of History? Thomas Pynchon and the Uses of the Past." *Twentieth Century Literature* 25 (1979): 54–72.

―――. *A "Gravity's Rainbow" Companion: Sources and Contexts for Pynchon's Novel.* Athens: University of Georgia Press, 1988.

Wilde, Alan. *Middle Grounds.* Penn Studies in Contemporary American Fiction. Philadelphia: University of Pennsylvania Press, 1987.

Wolfley, Lawrence C. "Repression's Rainbow: The Presence of Norman O. Brown in Pynchon's Big Novel." *PMLA* 92 (1977): 873–889.

Wordsworth, William. *The Prelude.* Edited by Ernest De Selincourt. London: Oxford University Press, 1933.

Yeats, W. B. *Collected Poems.* New York: Macmillan, 1959.

Zacharias, Gerhard. *The Satanic Cult.* Translated by Christine Trollope. Boston: Allen and Unwin, 1980.

Index

DWIGHT EDDINS is Professor of English at the University of Alabama.